WOMEN, FAMILIES
▼   ▼   ▼   ▼   ▼

McGraw-Hill Ryerson Series in Canadian Sociology

UNDERSTANDING DATA
B.H. Erickson and T.A. Nosanchuk

THE SURVIVAL OF ETHNIC GROUPS
Jeffrey G. Reitz

THE URBAN KALEIDOSCOPE: CANADIAN PERSPECTIVES
Leslie W. Kennedy

RELIGION: CLASSIC SOCIOLOGICAL APPROACHES
Roger O'Toole

THE DISREPUTABLE PLEASURES, Third Edition
John Hagan

THE CANADIAN CLASS STRUCTURE, Third Edition
Dennis Forcese

IDEOLOGICAL PERSPECTIVES ON CANADA, Third Edition
M. Patricia Marchak

DEVIANCE: TOLERABLE DIFFERENCES
Robert Stebbins

THE ETHNIC FACTOR: IDENTITY IN DIVERSITY
Leo Driedger

WOMEN, FAMILIES, AND WORK, Third Edition
S.J. Wilson

WOMEN, FAMILIES, AND WORK
▼ ▼ ▼ ▼ ▼ ▼ ▼ ▼ ▼

THIRD EDITION

S. J. WILSON

McGRAW-HILL RYERSON LIMITED
Toronto Montreal New York Auckland Bogotá Caracas Hamburg
Lisbon London Madrid Mexico Milan New Delhi Paris
San Juan São Paulo Singapore Sydney Tokyo

WOMEN, FAMILIES, AND WORK
▼ ▼ ▼ ▼ ▼ ▼ ▼ ▼ ▼

THIRD EDITION

Copyright © McGraw-Hill Ryerson Limited, 1991, 1986, 1981. All rights reserved. No part of this publication may be reproduced or transmitted in any form or by any means, or stored in a data base or retrieval system, without the prior written permission of McGraw-Hill Ryerson Limited.

ISBN: 0-07-549763-8

2 3 4 5 6 7 8 9 10 W 0 9 8 7 6 5 4 3 2 1

Printed and bound in Canada

Care has been taken to trace ownership of copyright material contained in this text. The publishers will gladly take any information that will enable them to rectify any reference or credit in subsequent editions.

Sponsoring Editor: Catherine O'Toole
Supervising Editor and Copy Editor: Margaret Henderson
Cover Design: Brian Bean
Text Design: Hania Fil
Technical Artist: Carole Giguere
Typesetting and Page Make-Up: Robin Brass Studio
Printing & Binding: Webcom
Text Set In: Adobe ITC Palatino

Canadian Cataloguing in Publication Data

Wilson, S.J. (Susannah Jane)
   Women, families, and work

(McGraw-Hill Ryerson series in Canadian sociology)
3rd ed.
Earlier eds. published under title: Women, the family and the economy.
Includes bibliographical references and indexes
ISBN 0-07-549763-8

1. Women – Canada – Social conditions. 2. Women – Employment – Canada. I. Title. II. Title: Women, the family and the economy. III. Series.

HQ1453.W55 1991   305.4'0971   C90-095683-6

CONTENTS

Preface vii
Chapter 1 SETTING THE STAGE 1
    The Women's Movement and Women's Studies 2
    The Feminist Critique of Sociology 5
    The Underpinnings of Feminist Theory 6
    Feminist Theory and Feminist Practice 8
    Conclusion 12
Chapter 2 THE IDEOLOGY OF MOTHERHOOD 13
    Pre-Industrial Family Life 13
    The Early Industrial Period 15
    Separate Spheres and the Cult of Domesticity 17
    The Early Twentieth Century 21
    "Working Moms": Changing Family Life Since the 1950s 23
    Conclusion 27
Chapter 3 FEMINISM AND THE DILEMMAS OF FAMILY LIFE 29
    The Feminist Critique of Motherhood 29
    Juggling Motherhood and Employment 34
    The Dark Side of Economic Dependence 39
    Conclusion 44
Chapter 4 HOUSEWORK 47
    The Evolution of Domestic Labour 48
    Housework and Motherwork Today 51
    Women's Double Day 54
    The Value of Housework 57
    Conclusion 60
Chapter 5 HISTORICAL TRENDS IN WOMEN'S PAID EMPLOYMENT 63
    Historical Analysis: Problems and Prospects 63
    Women's Paid Work in the Nineteenth Century 67
    The Early Twentieth Century 70
    Conditions of Work 72
    Rosie the Rivetter 80
    Collective Action 82

	The Early Postwar Years 83
	Conclusion 85
Chapter 6	CURRENT PATTERNS OF LABOUR-FORCE PARTICIPATION 86
	Labour-Force Trends 86
	The Reproduction of Labour-Force Segregation 96
	Policy Implications 103
	Conclusion 108
Chapter 7	THE WOMEN'S MOVEMENT AND WOMEN'S POLITICAL PARTICIPATION 110
	The Women's Movement in the Nineteenth Century 110
	Women in Electoral Politics 113
	The Contemporary Women's Movement 118
	Antifeminism 123
	Conclusion 125
Chapter 8	CIRCLES OF SOCIAL CONTROL 126
	Normative Restriction 126
	Patterns of Interaction 128
	Sexual Coercion, Violence, and The Threat of Violence 131
	Conclusion 134

References 137

Name Index 155

Subject Index 159

PREFACE

In the nine years since the first edition of this book was published the circumstances of Canadian women's lives have changed considerably. Women increasingly exercise choice regarding decisions to marry, parent, and seek employment. Their decisions are supported by legislation and by changing social attitudes. Nevertheless, the organization of women's work at home, and in the labour force, has not kept pace with changing economic and demographic circumstances. The labour force remains highly segregated, women earn less than men, and employed mothers are overburdened by their ongoing domestic responsibilities. The relationship between women's paid and unpaid work provides the framework for this book. My intention has been to frame current patterns in historical perspective and explain changing ideas about women as responses to particular demographic and economic shifts.

This edition has retained the structure of the first two editions, although the content has changed substantially. Chapters 2 and 3, which have been entirely rewritten, focus on the ideology of motherhood, its historical roots, and the implications of its inherent contradictions; Chapter 4 is about housework, and Chapters 5 and 6 about paid employment. Entrenched patterns of labour-force segregation and continued social ambivalence about the responsibility for child care and domestic work make it difficult for women to establish economic independence. Women have adopted different strategies in their struggle to overcome the structural and attitudinal barriers they confront. These initiatives, from finding a voice in formal politics to community activism, are described in Chapter 7. Chapter 8 locates patterns of interaction in the context of the structural inequities outlined in the first six chapters. The lack of power women have in determining the economic conditions of their lives is reflected and reinforced in interpersonal interaction.

In a book of this nature the greatest debt is owed to others writing in the field; scholars who have tested assumptions against the rich variety of women's lives. The more I read, or listen to, or talk with these women, the more encouraged I am about the difficult process of change.

I appreciate the support I have received from McGraw-Hill Ryerson. Susan Erickson, Danelle D'Alvise, Catherine O'Toole, Margaret Henderson, and Norma Christenson have, at different stages, been patient and encouraging. I particularly appreciate the feedback of two anonymous reviewers who read an earlier draft of the manuscript. The final version benefited from their thoughtful critique.

Thank-you also to Susan Neeb for sending me reams of clippings, and to Sue Bradley and Martha Watson for helping me track down an elusive piece of information. Paul Wilson and Cheryl Zimmerman read early drafts too sketchy to give to anyone but good friends. Paul, Leslie, and Jay affably accepted my preoccupation. I thank them for their support and (not insignificantly) their practical help.

Sue Wilson
November 1990.

1 SETTING THE STAGE

This book focuses on changes in Canadian women's work and family lives, and the ideological forces that have encouraged and resisted these changes. Over the last several decades, demographic and economic shifts have radically altered the lives of Canadian women. More women live independently, and more women are employed, whether or not they are self-supporting. Yet the labour force remains highly segregated so that most women work in a limited range of jobs for which they receive less pay relative to equally qualified and experienced men. The wage gap means that women, particularly those with family responsibilities, are less well off than their male counterparts.

Now most married women, including mothers of young children, are gainfully employed. Yet the organization of domestic work has not changed in response to increased labour-force participation. While fathers today are more active parents than in the past, they typically do not share the responsibility equally, and most husbands resist doing housework. Consequently, the burden of the "double day" falls on employed married women, leaving them emotionally and physically drained.

Because the demands of paid employment and family life are so incompatible, it is difficult to balance the two. Some women cope by reducing family responsibilities, others by reducing work responsibilities. Young, independent, childless women, who have made a strong commitment to the labour force, have made inroads in what were once male-dominated professional and management jobs. But it is inevitably at some cost to their personal lives. Marital instability, inflation, and male employment instability mean that few married women can afford to be full-time housewives. Currently, about one-third of Canadian women are full-time housewives; but few make this a long-term commitment. Most re-enter the labour force after a short period of childrearing. Women whose employment is intermittent or who work part-time are economically disadvantaged by lack of job security, employment benefits, and pension coverage. Within marriage, these may be reasonable trade-offs; outside of marriage, the economic consequences are severe.

In the past it was assumed that women were "naturally" suited to domestic and maternal roles and men to their roles as breadwinners. This division of labour had strong ideological support. Even as more women entered the labour force, the belief in "separate spheres" remained largely unchallenged. Women's employment was defined as temporary and secondary to family responsibilities. The social expectation that women will marry and assume the major responsibility for domestic work persists, despite major changes in work and family.

In the 1960s, the increased labour-force participation of married women, the instability of marriage, and the growing awareness of economic inequality among women as well as between women and men so contradicted the ideology of "separate spheres" that the disjunction could no longer be ignored. Women throughout the world became increasingly vocal in their demands for legal equality, a representative political voice, and sexual and reproductive control. Although these had been longstanding issues, the social and economic climate of the 1960s brought them to a head. The women's movement refers to the combined efforts of countless women working to combat sexism in the media, in interpersonal relationships, at work, on university campuses, in political parties, and in community groups. "The women's movement has a shifting, amoeba-like character; it is and has always been, politically, ideologically, and strategically diverse. It has not, and has never been, represented by a single organizational entity; it has no head office, no single leaders, no membership cards to sign. Indeed much of the widespread support for women's liberation has had no organizational identification at all." (Adamson, et al., 1988: 7)

This chapter provides a framework for the discussion of sexual inequality in Canadian society. The first section outlines the academic roots of the women's movement and offers critiques of explanations of gender difference based on biology or socialization. The next section describes specific criticisms made of sexist assumptions and practices in sociology. The final section outlines three currents of feminist theory.

THE WOMEN'S MOVEMENT AND WOMEN'S STUDIES

The universities were important sites of change during the 1960s. Student radicals in Europe and North America were active in civil rights and anti-war movements. Within the universities students questioned the relevance of the education they were receiving and protested against the institutions' lack of autonomy. In campuses across Canada students demanded a voice in determining university policies. (Kostash, 1980) Women, active in campus-based movements, were made increasingly aware that their concerns as women were not being addressed—neither in the content of their education nor in the student movement itself. The pervasiveness of sexism, and the growing awareness of sexual inequality as a separate issue, sparked an independent *Women's* Liberation movement on college campuses. By giving voice to their frustrations and concerns, women students and faculty began a process that has changed the way social science is thought and taught.

Women's studies programs were introduced in part as a response to women students' demands for education more appropriate to their specific needs. Courses about women provided a forum for exchange and stimulated research about the nature of sexual differentiation and the origins of sexual inequality. Many social scientists were frustrated in their attempts to analyze sexual inequality or to understand the social relations between women and men using existing social science models. Sharing a critical assessment of mainstream social science, these women found more in common with like-minded people in other disciplines than within the traditional disciplinary boundaries. Consequently, much feminist research has both an interdisciplinary and an international flavour. What began as a search for understanding the origins of sexual inequality, continued as a critique of mainstream theory, and resulted in a reconceptualization in feminist terms. (While the term *feminist* has many connotations, we can begin by defining it simply as a point of view that "does not treat men as the norm and women as deviations from the norm." [Eichler, 1977a: 410])

As feminist anthropologists, biologists, and psychologists explored the issue of sex difference, they challenged what had once been held to be universal truths about women's nature. Many characteristics once thought innate were discovered to be the result of the exigencies of daily living reinforced by social conditioning. But biological determinism was not so easily dismissed. In the past two decades, sociobiology has given new life to the idea that differences between men and women are rooted in innate biological differences. (Wilson, 1975) While most socio-biologists speak in terms of propensities and predispositions, they nonetheless claim that many behavioural differences between men and women are genetically based, arguing that evolution has supported the biological basis of human behaviour, including dominance behaviour in men. Psychological studies of traits long associated with masculinity and femininity do not support this determinist position. Psychologists have done literally thousands of studies of gender differences in cognitive ability, dependence, aggression and so on. Reviews of this body of research (Maccoby and Jacklin, 1974; Fischer and Cheyne, 1977; Tarvis and Wade, 1984) find few behaviours or traits that universally distinguish males and females. Some differences, including verbal, spatial, and mathematical abilities, do not appear until mid-childhood or adolescence, so they cannot be assumed to be innate. Moreover, that some studies find sex differences in psychological traits does not imply a *predisposition* based on sex. The same behaviour may be perceived differently if attributed to men rather than women, or if observed in this or another cultural setting. Contrary to popular stereotypes, men and women are not as different as social treatment implies.

If gender differences are not biologically determined, why do we find such clear indications of gender inequality in adults? Despite much evidence to the contrary, most people continue to hold rather firm beliefs about gender differences. However subtly, people react to boys and girls, men and women differently and, in the process, encourage different behavioural responses. Small behavioural and attitudinal differences are created in infancy and childhood, are reinforced through adolescence, and become pronounced in adults. Socialization is in many ways based on nuance and subtlety, and children are perceptive readers of their social environment. They observe the gender-relatedness of tasks and come to define these as natural. For example, children develop opinions of which jobs are more appropriately done by men and women; some of these opinions are based on quite erroneous stereotypes. Interviews with young Canadian schoolchildren (Ellis and Sayer, 1986) revealed some classic misunderstandings. One boy thought women could not become ministers because their voices were too soft to be heard at the back of the church. Another child explained that women could not become fire rangers because if the fire got too close they would have trouble running in high heels!

While it would be folly to deny the importance of socialization in shaping adult behaviour and expectations, it is also important to understand that socialization is only a partial explanation. Childhood experiences influence but do not determine life scripts. People change their behaviour and their ideas in response to the conditions of their lives. After reviewing studies of sex and gender differences, Epstein (1988: 15) concluded:

> The overwhelming evidence created by the past decade supports the theory that gender differentiation ... is best explained as a social construction rooted in hierarchy, not in biology or in internalization, either through early experiences, as described by psychoanalysis, or through socialization, as described by psychologists and sociologists.

In sociology the legacy of functionalism gave the concepts of male and female roles and socialization a central place. But traditional socialization proved an inadequate explanation of sexual inequality. True, many employers blatantly discriminated against women, openly assuming that women would leave the labour force as soon as they married or became pregnant. Granted, the mass media from children's books to mass advertising portrayed women as passive, tentative, and nurturant. But the problems of sexual inequality were more deeply rooted than wrongheaded ideas about women's nature. One couldn't explain the structural inequalities in the labour force, the lack of control women had over reproduction, or the abject poverty some groups of women faced in terms of socialization and sex roles. Feminists argued that an emphasis on roles, like the emphasis on a division of labour, diverts attention away from the interactive effects of race and class and away from questions of power. It makes no more sense to talk in such determinist terms about gender than it does to talk about class or race roles.

The notion of "role" focuses attention more on individuals than on social structure, and implies that "the female role" and "the male role" are complementary (i.e. separate or different but equal). The terms are depoliticizing; they strip experience from its historical and political context and neglect questions of power and conflict. (Stacey and Thorne, 1985: 307)

THE FEMINIST CRITIQUE OF SOCIOLOGY

Feminist sociologists, political scientists, economists, and historians have all argued that mainstream social science underrepresented, ignored, or distorted the experiences of women. In the worst cases, the poor representation of women served to justify differential treatment and sexual inequality. The women's movement and the increased number of women students and faculty combined to draw attention to sexism in theory and practice. These challenges have done much to curtail many of the most blatant examples of sexism, although the job is far from complete.

The choice of topics studied by sociologists has reflected a concern for the public sphere in which men are most active. "Social theorists, like societal members, tend to define a society and discuss its social organization in terms of what men do, and where men are located in that society." (Chodorow, 1978: 12) Whether the comparison is explicit or implicit, male experience is the norm. Oakley (1974: 24–28) describes the set of beliefs and ideas responsible for various manifestations of sexism as "the ideology of gender." One way sociologists perpetuate the ideology of gender is by dichotomizing human experience as male/female, work/nonwork, and so on. In this way, attention is focused *on* some issues and *away from* others. As Oakley describes it: "A way of seeing is a way of not seeing."

Early reviews of various substantive areas of sociology (for example, the sociologies of education, work, deviance, mass communications, and urban sociology) found that women were by and large ignored or studied in a sexist way. (Millman and Kanter, 1975; Eichler, 1984, 1988) In a study of introductory textbooks, references to women were few, and those were primarily limited to their place in the "egalitarian" family. (Kirschner, 1973) Questions of the sexual division of labour (itself a misnomer, for it implies a complementarity that does not exist) were confined to the institution of the family, and male experience was the point of departure. For example, childbirth, motherhood, and housework were not studied; but when increased female labour-force participation was analyzed, it was from the point of view of its effect on other family members. Women were not studied as political actors, employees, and so on. "Even when male sociologists have accurately described the situation of women, such as their segregation in the work force, they have generally not sought explanations for such conditions not defined them as problematic." (Hooyman and Johnson, 1977: 450)

Because women were of marginal theoretical importance, they were far less apt to be included in empirical studies. Since male experience was the norm, studies of men generalized to the population, while studies of women generalized only to women. Although there has been a steady increase in the number of articles about women in the major sociological journals, most (about 70 per cent)—as recently as 1986—ignore gender, and the number of studies using male-only samples remains high. (Ward and Grant, 1985; Rong, Grant and Ward, 1989) The vast majority of studies about women are of the "add-and-stir" variety. In other words, they are simply replications of previous work introducing sex as a variable. Very few journal articles challenged existing models, and these did not influence subsequent articles on the same topic—published in the same journal! (Ward and Grant, 1985)

The structure of the discipline of sociology, its content, and its methodology are related issues. Most practitioners are men; they study social life from their vantage point, using samples that are most available to them and interpretations with which they can identify. In universities, male faculty outnumber female, and women are concentrated in the lowest ranks and dominate the numbers of part-time teachers. In 1985 only 17 per cent of full-time university faculty in Canada were women: a mere 6 per cent gain from 1960, when 11 per cent of full-time faculty were women. (Hollands, 1988: 6) In 1985 their average salary was $10 000 less than the average male salary. (*Ibid.:* 7) Indeed, the proportion of women faculty in Canadian universities in 1980–81 was the same as it was in 1921! (Mackie, 1986) Nevertheless, women faculty are as productive as men faculty when compared on the established yardstick of mainstream journal publication. (*Ibid.*)

The numerical and political imbalance in university departments has meant that the experiences of women and their awareness of the world have not been voiced, or if voiced, not legitimated. Morgan (1981) used the term "academic machismo" to describe the predominantly masculine culture that pervades university life in both its formal and informal aspects. It is reflected in the combative repartee of conference presentations, or exchanges in scholarly journals, or in sexist jokes in the faculty club. This bastion of masculinity was no more receptive than other institutions to feminist critiques. Few men showed any interest in women's studies: they "rarely attended gender sessions at professional meetings, showed little awareness of research on the topic ... and rarely cited work about women." (Ward and Grant, 1985: 143)

THE UNDERPINNINGS OF FEMINIST THEORY

Consciousness-raising groups of the 1960s brought women together to talk about their experiences. These groups created an environment that reinforced the relevance of personal experience and underscored the inconsistency between that experience and the theoretical models used by social scientists to characterize it. In the 1970s, special editions of various sociological journals were devoted to exploring what a sociology free of these biases might be like.[1] Many questioned the failure of traditional sociological models to use the experiences of women as a basis of analysis. To impress this point, some editors departed from the expected formal style to write in a familiar way about their own experiences. Pauline Bart began her lengthy editorial: "I should explain the reasons for the personal, informal and emotional quality of this editorial. In the women's movement we believe that the personal and the political cannot be separated." (Bart, 1971: 734) In one way or another, it was argued, personal experiences are data. To argue that research questions be rooted in personal experience, and that these be the basis of theory development is a significant departure from the objectivity assumptions of positivist social science. Yet decades of research based on the premise of objectivity produced a body of knowledge fraught with bias.

Hester Eisenstein (1984: 35–41) has argued that consciousness-raising groups played an important role in the development of feminist theory. "A first assumption of consciousness raising was that what women had to say about the details of their daily lives, about their personal experiences and histories, mattered, it had significance, and above all it had validity." (*Ibid.*: 37) These shared experiences came to be understood not as private or individual concerns, but as public, *social* issues. Reproductive choice, rape, and family violence thus became focal issues around which the women's movement organized. Women's experience became the point of departure in feminist theorizing. As Smith (1985: 4) has argued: "The first and fundamental step is to begin where women are in the society, with the everyday worlds of our experience, and to be prepared to reconceptualise the accepted concepts, frameworks and theories."

Since these criticisms were first voiced, the study of women in sociology has mushroomed. Over fifty new journals document the course of development providing a "thoughtful record of intellectual theory in action." (Bernard, 1989: 25) While feminism may have had less impact on the discipline as a whole than many would like to see (Stacey and Thorne, 1985; Acker, 1989), feminism has had an undeniable influence. As feminists grappled with questions of sexual oppression and explored the nature of sex and gender differences, their emphasis shifted from a study of women based on existing models to a position that fundamentally challenged these models—and challenged the foundation of scientific knowledge. A substantial body of feminist theoretical and empirical literature developed, built on the premise of relevance to the needs and experiences

---

[1] These include *Transaction* (1970); *Journal of Marriage and the Family* (1971); *American Journal of Sociology* (1973); *Sociological Inquiry* (1975); and the *Canadian Review of Sociology and Anthropology* (1975).

of women. This research has had a proactive component. Many academic feminists were active in the women's movement and were motivated to do research that would ultimately benefit women. Theoretical development in this field is very much an iterative process. Women's experiences in the labour movement, in the fight against sexual assault, in feminist politics, and in the peace movement—indeed in all aspects of women's lives—have become the basis of theoretical generalizations. These in turn are tested against further experience and used as the basis of strategy development.

FEMINIST THEORY AND FEMINIST PRACTICE

Today the women's movement reflects a range of concerns and priorities and different strategies for achieving these. When we talk of feminist theory today we are referring to a mosaic. There are, however, several currents or frameworks that characterize the principle voices of feminism in Canada today. (Adamson et al., 1988; Jaggar and Rothenberg, 1984) These are: liberal feminism, radical feminism, and socialist feminism.[2] Each has roots in nineteenth-century feminism, and each is influenced by parallel movements in Europe and the United States. The most readily recognized point of view is liberal feminism, with its emphasis on equality of opportunity through legislative reform. By giving priority to improving the position of women within existing political and economic structures and by identifying barriers to equality, liberal feminists seek to increase opportunities for women through legislative changes and educational reform. Middle-class professional women, who form the backbone of liberal feminism, were drawn together in the mid-1960s to initiate a Royal Commission on the Status of Women. Its intention was to "ensure for women equal opportunities with men in all aspects of Canadian society." (RCSW, 1970: vii) Its 167 recommendations set the agenda for liberal feminists for the decade to follow.

The first English translations of the early writings of Marx became available in North America in 1961 (Kostash, 1980: xix), and these inspired an analysis greatly at odds with the principles of individualism and liberal democracy. "Earlier feminists used the language of 'rights' and 'equality,' but in the 1960s 'oppression' and 'liberation' became the key words for the political activists of the new left." (Jaggar, 1983: 5) Women in the New Left agreed with Juliet Mitchell (1973: 99) that "we should ask the feminist questions, but try to come up with some Marxist answers."

---

[2] Stanley and Wise (1983: 38) object to typologies such as these because they create the false impression that there *are* clear theoretical distinctions among feminists. Their point is that feminist theory is so diverse as to preclude categorization.

> In the early days of the women's liberation movement, heady with their new-found understandings of oppression and liberation, feminists set out to explore the terrain of male domination and female subordination. They took with them what maps were available and as they travelled, they confirmed, redrew and charted anew. Of the existing theoretical maps, marxism was among the most promising. It had a well-developed theory of class oppression, it acknowledged women's oppression and argued that a radical social transformation was necessary for women's liberation. One of the major debates which has engaged feminist theorists is the extent to which marxism in fact provides a useful guide. Some feminists reject marxism altogether but most contemporary feminist theory has been profoundly influenced by it. (Luxton, 1985: i)

Radical feminists and socialist feminists reacted in different ways to what they saw as the limitations of liberalism *and* Marxism. Both were fundamentally concerned with the issue of sexual oppression, but socialist feminism defines sexual oppression as confounded by issues of race and class. For radical feminists, sexual oppression is at once the most fundamental and the most universal oppression. Radical feminism was born in women's caucuses of New Left groups like Students for a Democratic Society and the Student Union for Peace Action. But Marxism, which guided the thinking of the New Left, failed to address the issue of male privilege (either on a theoretical level or in the day-to-day interactions within the New Left.)[3] First-hand experience made clear that sexual oppression was more deeply rooted than Marxism suggested.

Radical feminists borrowed the concept of patriarchy, or "rule of the fathers," from anthropology. The term is usually used in its broadest sense to refer to all systems of male dominance (Jaggar, 1983: 103), although radical feminism's particular focus has been sexual and reproductive control. Radical feminists were particularly critical of heterosexist assumptions that defined women primarily in terms of relationships with men. "Alternate sexual expression, living arrangements, interpersonal relationships and contractual agreements are ignored or penalized. This heterosexism is born out in law, government, social policy, social services, school curricula, even in casual conversation." (Lenskyj, 1987: 4)

One of the most vehemently argued radical-feminist contentions is found in Firestone's *The Dialectic of Sex* (1970). According to Firestone, biology, specifically reproduction, is the origin of sexual dualism. Women's childbearing function has made women dependent on men for physical survival, and this has given men power over women. Sexual inequality, then, is embedded in the biological family, the basic reproductive unit of

---

[3] A blatant and frequently quoted example of such sexism was Stokely Carmichael's remark (made in 1964 at a meeting of the Student Nonviolent Coordinating Committee) that "the only position for women in the SNCC is prone." (Quoted in J. Freeman, 1975. *Women: A Feminist Perspective*, p. 450. Palo Alto: Mayfield Publishing Co.)

mother/father/infant. According to Firestone, the cycle of oppression can be broken if women seize control of reproduction, take advantage of the available technology to ensure that childbirth is voluntary, and separate from the institution of the family. In the words of another radical feminist: "Since marriage constitutes slavery for women, it is clear that the women's movement must concentrate on attacking this institution. Freedom for women cannot be won without the abolition of marriage." (Cronan, 1984: 333)

The immediate goals of radical feminism were to gain for women control of sexual expression and reproduction. To this end, radical feminists led initiatives for access to birth control and abortion. They have been the most vocal critics of pornography, and they have been instrumental in providing shelters and services for victims of male violence. As the issues of rape, wife battering, and pornography were taken up by liberal feminists, the radical feminist emphasis on sexual oppression has been replaced in the 1980s by the goal of social transformation based on women's greater humanism, pacificism, and nurturance. (Segal, 1987; Adamson, et al., 1988; Alcoff, 1988) The change in emphasis is highlighted by the new label "cultural feminism."[4] When assumptions about the biological basis of human behaviour, or inherent male/female differences in human nature, were challenged by liberal feminism, it seemed important to underline the *insignificance* of sex differences. Cultural (or radical) feminists (Daly, 1978, Rich, 1976) reverse this assumption, saying that we should value rather than dismiss or deny our biological differences.

Many women were introduced to radical feminism by their involvement with the peace movement; peace continues to be an important focus in radical feminism. Violence, the ultimate expression of male power, is (according to cultural [or radical] feminism) as socially conditioned as female nurturing. It is expressed and tolerated privately, in individual acts of violence against women (rape, incest, wife abuse), and publicly, in street violence and militarism. Both private and public violence are, in the view of radical feminists, consequences of the way masculinity is culturally defined. (Atlantis, Vol 12, No. 1 and No. 2; Peace Issues) The issue of cultural definitions of masculinity and femininity is taken up in Chapter 8.

Marxism and radical feminism represent what Kelly (1984: 55) calls the "doubled vision" of feminist theory. "We are pulled in one direction by a Marxist-feminist analysis of the socioeconomic basis of women's oppression, and in another by a radical feminist focus on male control of women's bodies as a key to patriarchy." (*Ibid.*: 55) Mitchell's analysis (1973) was one of the first attempts to reconcile these two points of view.

---

[4] Angela Miles (1984) has used the term "integrative feminism" to describe this viewpoint. Integrative feminism is based on a recognition and affirmation of women's distinctiveness and their special role in reproduction. It envisions a world transformed by female values.

Recognizing the importance of both class and male privilege in maintaining women's oppression, Mitchell's solution was to differentiate four key structures relevant to the condition of women: production, reproduction, sexuality, and the socialization of children. These, Mitchell argued, develop unevenly in relation to each other over time. Women's oppression predates capitalism and continues where socialist revolutions have occurred. Like Engels, Mitchell assumed that an active role in production is a necessary precondition for women's liberation. Unlike Engels, she is aware that despite the importance of demands for equality in the labour force, these demands will not guarantee equality within the family. "The family as it exists at present is, in fact, incompatible with either women's liberation or the equality of the sexes." (Mitchell, 1973: 150) Mitchell agreed with Firestone about the need to separate sexuality from reproduction, and the need to separate both of these from the socialization of children. What Mitchell was objecting to, (and an objection that we will return to throughout this book), is not families *per se*, but the "monolithic fusion" of production, reproduction, sexuality, and the socialization of children. The liberation of women, as Mitchell saw it, depends on the transformation of all four structures.

Socialist feminism is sometimes called dual-systems theory because it identifies the contradictions of women's lives as issues of both class and sex domination. Where liberal feminism focuses on changing institutions to better meet the needs of women, socialist feminists see the need to radically alter institutions that (as presently construed) perpetuate class and gender inequality. Where radical feminism focuses on the universality of patriarchy and a consequent unity among women, socialist feminists focus on ways sexual oppression intersects with race and class *differentially* affecting women. Production (the social organization of work), reproduction (childbearing and gender socialization), and sexuality have a dynamic impact on women's lives. "The mother-child relation, and the motherwork involved in raising a child, are at the heart of this process. The way the work is organized, the way it is defined, the degree of autonomy women have in the process all have changed historically." (Fox, 1988: 176) These processes are shaped by material and economic conditions and are reinforced by ideology. In some cases (e.g. union activism), men's and women's interests coincide; in other cases (who takes responsibility for housework), they are in contradiction.

It would be misleading to exaggerate the consequences of theoretical differences between liberal, radical, and socialist feminists. "There is no rigid separation of issues and tactics of feminist practice into different theoretical categories. On the contrary members of different currents often agree about many basic demands for women and frequently organize together." (Adamson et al., 1988: 169) So while radical feminists have focused on sexuality and violence against women, and socialist feminists have been most active in the trade-union movement, both violence against women and the rights of employed women are of vital concern to liberal feminists. Both radical feminists and liberal feminists are concerned with the unequal balance of power between husbands and wives, although they explain its basis differently. Radical feminism is most strongly identified with the women's movement of the 1970s. Today, liberal feminism, through its extensive organizational network, is the most readily recognized voice. But, if Adamson et al., (1988: 262) are correct in their analysis, socialist feminism offers "a coherent basis on which to build an effective strategy for the future."

CONCLUSION

The chapters that follow describe and analyze demographic and economic shifts in the family and working lives of Canadian women. The intention is threefold: to understand current patterns in historical context, to show how ideas about women and women's place have changed in response to these shifts, and to create a framework for understanding both the resistance to change and feminism. In brief, this book asks what Zillah Eisenstein (1984: 206) referred to as the important feminist question: "What does sexual equality mean and how does one try to create truly egalitarian relationships while recognizing the biological difference constituted by women's ability to bear children?" [5]

The book is organized as follows: chapters 2 and 3 focus on family issues; chapters 4, 5, and 6 on women's work; chapter 7 on political participation and the women's movement; and chapter 8 on social control. Because the patterns we see now are historically grounded, it is important to look at family life and work patterns in historical perspective. Chapter 2 provides a historical context for understanding the roots of the ideology of motherhood. Despite sweeping economic and demographic shifts, ideas about women's family and work responsibilities have changed little. Chapter 3 describes ways feminists have tried to come to grips with this contradiction and the economic costs to particular groups of women when it is ignored.

---

[5] It attests to the impact of the women's movement that my daughter, who is ten, sees the answer to this question in simple terms. I quote without editing: "Women should be treated as equally as men, except for one thing. Women have a choice to have a child. If they [women] choose to, men should support them in every way possible."

2 THE IDEOLOGY OF MOTHERHOOD

Our understanding of what constitutes a family has changed over time. References to the "traditional" family imply a particular configuration of a married, heterosexual couple and their children. But fewer families fit this description than did in the past. Now, more people live independently or communally; an increasing number of unmarried people live together, including same-sexed couples; more couples are childless; and more children are raised by lone parents.[1] (*Women in Canada*, 1990) Family structures have changed, yet most Canadians (approximately 90 per cent) marry and most women (approximately 85 per cent) have at least one child. This chapter focuses on ways families have changed over time and the implications of these changes for the institution of motherhood.

While motherhood is often described as women's traditional role, it was not until the latter part of the nineteenth century that motherhood was a full-time responsibility for most women. The demise of the household economy, the growth of factories and offices, and the increased availability of mass-produced goods for home consumption, which paralleled industrialization, changed family economic responsibilities. Men's entry to the paid labour force meant that families came to depend economically on their wages. It also meant that domestic work was more exclusively women's responsibility; a responsibility for which they were thought to be "naturally" suited. This chapter shows how ideas about women's maternity and domesticity evolved as Canada became more industrialized. In the twentieth century, despite longer life expectancy, smaller families, increased labour-force participation, and the instability of marriage, the ideology of motherhood has been remarkably resistant to change.

PRE-INDUSTRIAL FAMILY LIFE

Although the recent work of social and feminist historians has greatly added to our understanding of family life in the colonies that were to be-

---

[1] The Canadian Census defines a family as "either a husband-wife couple with or without never-married children of any age living at home, or a lone parent and his/her never married child(ren)." (*Women in Canada*: 1990: 7) This includes unmarried heterosexual couples, but not same-sexed couples or communal groups.

come Canada, the picture is far from complete. With the exception of Van Kirk's work (1986), we know little of the life of native women before European immigration. However, because the first European women settlers were an educated group, we have more information about their lives in seventeenth and eighteenth century New France. For the most part, these women were either members of religious communities, who came to establish monasteries, or *filles de roi*, who were sent as prospective brides in order to encourage permanent settlement. Both groups were relatively wealthy and well educated. The structure of the fur trade economy, the importance of the military, and the fact that there were so few women in the colony further enhanced their status. (Noel, 1986) Many were actively involved in managing the family farm or business, and some were active in direct military combat.

The privileged status of these *femmes favorisee* changed with the British conquest of Quebec. British settlers, from Great Britain or from the American colonies, brought with them traditions that were far more restrictive to women. Under British law, which applied to all English-speaking parts of British North America, husbands were legally obliged to provide for their wives, but they also controlled their wives' property and income. Men also had legal authority over their children. Women could not vote or hold public office. Yet despite its patriarchal structure, pre-industrial family life depended on the labour of both men and women, and women's work was valued.

At the beginning of the nineteenth century, Canada was a sparsely populated colony whose economy was based on farming, fishing, lumbering, and fur trading. While the cities of Montreal, Quebec, Kingston, Toronto, and Hamilton were developing as centres of trade and commerce, most people lived in small rural communities or on independent farms. The lives of women in pre-industrial Canada were affected by where and when they settled; but for most, day-to-day living was arduous by our standards. Family life reflected ways families coped with the exigencies of frontier living. Most people married (and remarried if widowed) because marriage and children were keys to economic survival for both men and women. Life expectancy was short, marriage occurred late, and fertility was high, so few women lived much beyond their child-rearing years. Childbirth was dangerous for both women and children, and there were high rates of maternal, infant, and child mortality.

All family members, including children, worked to make farm life economically viable. The economic interdependence of family members made family commitment and family obligation strong, although the ever-present possibility of death meant that family life was far from stable. Parenting in pre-industrial Canada meant preparing children for adult life. In most cases this literally meant following in parents' footsteps. Children worked alongside their parents from an early age. Girls learned domestic skills by working with their mothers; boys worked with their fathers.

Although fathers were not involved in the care of infants, they taught their sons to farm, and in this sense they were active parents. Older children worked on their own or another farm, or (if boys) apprenticed into a trade. With the exception of convent education, which had existed in Quebec since the seventeenth century, schooling was sporadic and children's attendance irregular.

The nature of women's domestic responsibilities depended on where families settled and their economic resources. Many households included boarders, servants, or labourers; farm wives managed these large households. Women were responsible for the medical, spiritual, and educational welfare of the family and community. (Errington, 1988: 57) Women passed these skills along to their daughters, who learned to sew, cook, prepare medicines, and make countless other household products. Typically, women had prime responsibility for two aspects of household labour that men rarely shared (Cowan, 1987: 166): First, mothers cared for infants and young children with the help of older daughters. As soon as sons were old enough to be useful helpers, they became their father's responsibility. Second, women also cared for domestic animals, grew and preserved food, and made the family's clothes. But many families combined farming with lumbering, fishing, and so on. That meant women often had sole responsibility for running the farm while men earned seasonal income elsewhere. Some women who were married to fur traders, mariners, or fishermen accompanied their husbands and shared his work. (Prentice *et al.*, 1988: 77)

THE EARLY INDUSTRIAL PERIOD

Canada's vast size and sparse population meant that the transition from a rural agricultural to a cash-based economy was unevenly felt across the country. As the economy became more diversified, more families came to depend on wage labour to supplement farming. With the growth of capital and advances in manufacturing, the demand for labour increased and more work became concentrated in urban centres. At the same time, the population increased from 2.4 million in 1851 to 5.4 million in 1901, and it further increased to 8.8 million by 1921. (Statistics Canada, 1990) This growth in population occurred because migrants and an increasing number of immigrants were attracted to western Canada by land grants and to urban areas in the east by the possibility of employment. The women and men who moved north or west in search of economic opportunity faced the same isolation and hardship experienced by settlers in eastern Canada a century before. The nature of farm life in the east changed with industrial development. Farms became increasingly specialized, and more goods were produced for sale rather than home consumption. More household products were purchased rather than made at home. By 1901,

35 per cent of the Canadian population was urban and one quarter of the urban dwellers lived in what were then Canada's four largest cities: Quebec, Montreal, Ottawa, and Toronto. European immigration continued to swell the population until World War I, and the majority settled in urban areas. Most immigrants were poor to begin with and the economic swings of these early years of industrialization did little to improve their economic prospects. Overcrowding and poverty became recognized social problems.

Young women whose labour was no longer necessary at home also migrated to the cities in search of work. Men outnumbered women in frontier areas and women outnumbered men in cities—a situation that continued well into the twentieth century. Urban sex-ratio imbalances are reflected in marriage statistics in the late nineteenth century. The mean age of first marriage for women increased from 23 in 1851 to 26 in 1891, and many did not marry at all. In 1871 in Montreal, one woman in three was unmarried at age 40. (Danylewycz, 1987) In Hamilton in the same year, there were only 82 men for every 100 women between ages 25 and 29. (Katz and Davey, 1978: S100) While some may have remained single by choice (Light and Prentice, 1980: 38), others delayed marriage in order to limit family size. (Prentice et al., 1988: 164) However, the low wages paid to women made it difficult to be self-supporting. With few opportunities for independent living, marriage and motherhood were attractive alternatives to remaining in the parental home or doing domestic work for another family. Since the employment of married women was strongly discouraged, some married women may have claimed to be single in order to work. We cannot know how many remained unmarried because their wages were needed at home. (Kelly, 1984: 134) The majority of women who entered the paid labour force in the first decades of the twentieth century were young and single; although in cities where the garment industry was a major employer, there were high rates of employment for married women. Although the employment of children was more important than maternal employment as a supplementary source of family income until the twentieth century, many married working-class women worked intermittently.

> The view of the family as a collective economic unit and the expectation that family members would forego or modify their own career choices in the service of their families were carryovers from rural societies that served as a major form of adaptation in working-class life. (Harevan, 1984: 150–151)

Family networks were important in securing employment and housing for rural migrants. Family members often worked together: older relatives eased the way for younger entrants and were able to both supervise and protect them.

Women worked primarily as domestics and factory workers, and, as opportunities increased, in the service sector and in retail sales. Increases in women's labour-force participation were met with mixed reactions. Trade unionists worried about increased competition from women; reformers worried about the implications of the exposure of women to factory conditions; and male co-workers worried about women's future roles as wives and mothers. Women, too, expected to marry, so most saw their work as a temporary interlude. Whatever their occupation, women typically left the labour force when they married.

During the latter half of the nineteenth century as the trade union movement matured, the idea of a family wage took hold. Male workers demanded the right to earn enough to support their family, to free children to attend school, and to free women to attend to household tasks and childrearing. Yet it was decades before it was literally possible for families to survive on the wages of one family member, or for working-class women to begin to emulate the popular image of the middle-class housewife. Implicitly, the demand for a family wage recognized the importance of women's unpaid work at home. It did not, however, acknowledge that many women also needed a "living wage." The idea of a family wage for male workers "assumed that all women would, sooner or later become wives, and thus it was legitimate to argue for the exclusion of women from the labour force." (May, 1987: 113) Ironically, poverty studies in the United States in the early years of the twentieth century found that most destitute families were female headed. "The response to this seeming inequality was to propose charitable aid for women and children, not higher wages." (May, 1987: 115)

SEPARATE SPHERES AND THE CULT OF DOMESTICITY

It could be argued that married women's economic dependence peaked during the first decades of the twentieth century. Before this, women had made concrete economic contributions to their family's welfare. Nineteenth-century women cared for infant children, nursed the sick, and laboured to feed and clothe their families. Their labour was physically taxing and time-consuming work, and it had a direct impact on the family's standard of living. As wage earning became a way of life, the economic responsibilities of husbands and wives changed, although the change was gradual and had its greatest impact on urban middle-class families. Because wage labour took most men away from home during the day, home management and childrearing increasingly became a woman's responsibility—at least for the middle class. Laslett (1977: 106) describes the absence of men from home during the working day as the single most important event in the history of the modern family. For urban middle-class families, financially dependant on a male breadwinner, and able to find and afford substitutes for domestically produced goods, the public world of work and the private domestic world became increasingly separated.

The idea of dual spheres was built on the presumption that men as husbands and fathers would perform wage-earning work and women as wives and mothers would be responsible for domestic maintenance. In fact, the separation was more illusion than reality for all but urban middle- and upper-class families. (Bose, 1987) Working-class family life was economically much more tenuous. Working-class families may have accepted the presumption that women's place was in the home, but they were not in a position to organize their lives accordingly. The "cult of domesticity" ignored the economic contributions of married women and the economic needs of women who were not dependents. While the idea of dual spheres may have given support to the efforts of male workers to secure a "family wage," it stood in the way of employed women's efforts to improve their working conditions or wages.

The decline in home production and the availability of manufactured substitutes freed middle-class women from some of the more taxing and time-consuming domestic jobs. Motherhood and family life began to assume increased personal and social significance. In the early nineteenth century, popular literature "began to emphasize the maternal role and portray it as somewhat other-worldly and sublime." (Light and Prentice, 1980: 134) As early as the 1820s in the United States, childrearing manuals and magazine articles advised women about their maternal responsibilities and clarified the importance of mothering, not only to the mother and her child, but also to the nation. (Margolis, 1984: 28) Women, it was believed, were temperamentally different from men and naturally suited to their roles as wives and mothers, ideas given credibility by the church and by contemporary science. (Welter, 1966) Femininity was characterized by domesticity; masculinity by labour-market success. The home was to be a "haven" from the world of work. In this way, family life conformed rather neatly to the needs of capital expansion, rejuvenating current employees, and grooming the next generation. In a sense, motherhood became the glue that held the family together in the face of the rapid changes brought about by industrialization.

As moulders of the next generation, women were encouraged to take their responsibilities as mothers seriously. Because industrialization required an educated labour force, children stayed in school longer, and mothers were important agents in ensuring educational progress. For this reason, mothers, too, needed some formal training. While the education of women generally was frowned upon, there was support for training in child care, domestic science, and home economics. In the early years of the twentieth century, courses in domestic science were introduced in most school systems. The motives were twofold: domestic science would better prepare women for their future roles as wives and mothers, and, in the shorter term, girls trained in domestic science could be encouraged to work as domestics before they married.

The responsibilities of child care increased as the distinct needs of children were identified. In the nineteenth century, mothers were primarily responsible for moral guidance; in the twentieth century the emphasis shifted to the emotional arena. Because technology also made child care less physically demanding, mothers had more time to focus on what would later be called socialization. (As baby bottles and commercially prepared baby food became available, mothers were freed from another time-consuming aspect of infant care. Until the 1930s, preparing an infant's food required many hours of work, which is why commercially prepared baby food gained immediate acceptance. Sales increased 3000 per cent between 1936 and 1946. [Klein, 1984: 59]) The new discipline of psychology reinforced the belief that fairly consistent interaction between young children and their mothers was necessary for psychological well-being. Canadian women in the 1920s were inundated with advice by everyone, from child-care experts and the federal Division of Child Welfare, to newspaper and magazine columns and medical professionals. (Strong-Boag, 1982) "Advice from every quarter was informed by an unshakable confidence in the universality of the maternal role, the centrality of the mother-child bond, and the indispensability of external advice to the optimum functioning of the modern family." (*Ibid.*: 162–163) "'Woman exists for the sake of the womb' declared a popular [Canadian] health manual of the 1890s." (Prentice *et al.*, 1988: 146)

We might wonder how women reconciled the presumption that they were "naturally" suited to motherhood yet needed the advice of men! The belief that women needed such advice and the fact that the advice was not always consistent, left women open to accepting responsibility for the success or failure of their children. It was clear where responsibility rested if children did not mature as healthy, well-adjusted adolescents and adults.

One of the reasons for such strongly voiced pronatalist sentiments was declining fertility among the middle class. Although part of a long-term trend, fertility declines were seen as portents of Canada's future in the face of high immigration and the urban problems of poverty and overcrowding. In fact, fertility had begun to decline in the mid-1800s. At the beginning of the nineteenth century many women bore as many as seven or eight children. A century later, the "average" Canadian family had three or four children, although there were class differences. Fertility declined first among the urban middle class. It took longer for the effects of increased mechanization of farming, compulsory education, and child-labour legislation to change fertility patterns among farm families and among the urban working class who depended on the economic contributions of their children. It was during this lag between the fertility of middle- and working-class women that the concern for declining fertility peaked. A key issue was the assumption that Canada's future depended on the vitality of its future labour force. Women's responsibility (in this case to America's future) was pointedly expressed by none less than President Theodore Roosevelt. "The woman who flinches from childbirth stands on a par with the soldier who drops his rifle and runs in battle." (quoted in McLaren, 1985: 84) Advanced education and labour-force participation for women were feared because they might give women too much independence and make them disinclined toward marriage or maternity. In retrospect these concerns (at the time expressed in terms of "race suicide") seem misguided at best. Nevertheless, fears about the effects of declining fertility were widely voiced in both Canada and the United States.

Women were encouraged to be mothers by more than rhetoric. An 1892 amendment to the Criminal Code of Canada prohibited the sale, display, or advertisement of birth-control devices. This remained in effect until 1969! Nonetheless, the fact that the birth rate continued to decline while the marriage rate remained stable indicates that a significant number of women were actively controlling their own fertility. Doctors advised women to use "natural" methods of birth control, including the rhythm method. Unfortunately, until the 1920s ovulation was "completely misunderstood and the so-called 'safe period' was mistakenly calculated to fall at mid-month." (McLaren, 1985: 88) Since prolonged breast-feeding, rhythm, and coitus interruptus were fallible, women intent on avoiding childbirth used abortion as a back-up. As McLaren (1985) documents, there were many advertised abortifacients (potions) available at the time. Abortionists advertised in personal and medical columns of Canadian newspapers (*Ibid.*), although doctors publicly condemned the practice unless the mother's life was threatened. Of course, abortion itself was life-threatening. Based on records of maternal deaths in British Columbia, McLaren and McLaren (1990) conclude that an undetermined but significant number of maternal deaths in the first half of the twentieth century were the result of abortion—indicating the fairly widespread use of abortion as a means of fertility control.

The period between 1880 and 1920 was a time of rapid urban and industrial growth. But the price of industrial expansion was becoming increasingly evident in urban unemployment, poverty, crime, and infant and maternal mortality. The churches and, later, other reform groups sought to protect working-class families from the evils and temptations of urban life. Many women were motivated to action by their concern that Canada's future depended on family stability; and they believed that they as mothers were essential to preserving this stability. These middle-class women established a host of organizations, including the National Council of Women of Canada (NCWC), to improve the lot of working-class women and children. Through their organizational networks, they were responsible for a great many educational and welfare programs. These women, who we now call *maternal feminists*, felt morally responsible to extend their mothering to society. Lady Aberdeen, NCWC's first president, spelled out the nature of women's social responsibility at the founding convention:

> She must learn that if the poor around her doors are not cared for, the orphans housed, the erring not reclaimed because she was too much engrossed in her own home to lend a helping hand, the results of her self-absorption may be in the future to provide pitfalls for her own children whom she so desires to cherish." (Quoted in Roberts, 1979: 30)

The NCWC was particularly concerned about the high rates of infant and maternal mortality in Canada compared with other industrializing countries. Although the Victorian Order of Nurses is a legacy of their concern, by and large, their reforms did little to reduce infant and maternal mortality, which were symptoms, not causes, of more deep-seated problems. Nevertheless, the reforms initiated during this period (prevention of child labour, protection of women in the workplace, the provision of health care) established the foundations of the modern welfare state. (Pupo, 1988: 213)

Without questioning the sanctity of marriage or their responsibilities as mothers, the women's reform movement of the late nineteenth and early twentieth centuries wanted to protect the rights of women and children. Because they did not have the option of paid employment, women had little possibility of supporting themselves if separated from or abused by their husband or widowed. It was within this context that women argued for the right to work, be educated, vote, and participate in public life. The right to vote became the key to social reform. Many suffragettes did not question existing beliefs about male and female differences or maternal and paternal responsibilities. They saw the vote as necessary to *protect* maternity and to extend women's realm in areas of social reform. In short, the activities of the "first wave" feminists expanded but did not challenge the ideology of motherhood.

THE EARLY TWENTIETH CENTURY

In the early years of the twentieth century there were signs that motherhood was not, and could not be, a lifelong preoccupation for women. A significant number of women did not marry or become mothers. Although the numbers remained small, more women were seeking careers. Improvements in medical technology and obstetrical care, lower fertility, and increased longevity all meant that a smaller proportion of a mother's life was taken up with child care. Modern appliances, infant formula, and prepared baby food made domestic work less physically demanding, but at the same time, reduced its visibility—and ultimately its perceived value. Women were pushed toward motherhood by socially accepted beliefs about the family as women's sphere. At the same time, their control over motherhood was eroding as the education and welfare of children became more publicly scrutinized. In short, the contradictions that were to become glaring in the 1960s were beginning to be evident in the 1920s—and had their roots in demographic and economic processes that reached back into the nineteenth century.

Most employed women in the first decades of the twentieth century were young and single. While far from the norm, there was a gradual increase in the employment of married women who responded to economic expansion and the demand for clerical workers and sales people on one hand and economic need on the other. An increasing number of women found jobs in the professions. Granted most of these jobs were in teaching, nursing, and social work, but there were exceptions. Labour shortages during World War I, while less serious than those during World War II, did create opportunities for women in occupations previously considered unsuitable. (Ramkhalawansingh, 1974) Motherhood was clearly understood to be incompatible with paid employment. "Even during the depression when economic necessity forced more married women than ever before to take jobs, the experts' relentless insistence on the centrality of the mother role did not abate." (Margolis, 1984: 44) The Depression restricted women's employment opportunities relative to men's since it was generally assumed that employed women took jobs away from men. Nevertheless, the proportion of employed married women reached a new high during the Depression years. The decade-long economic downturn discouraged marriage and childbearing. Fertility and average family size continued to decline; spacing of children increased. Large families were less common and only children or childlessness increased.

The belief that women's place was in the home remained unchallenged even as more women entered the paid labour force during the economic recovery following the Depression. The demand for female labour increased during World War II, but this was understood to be a temporary solution to employment shortages. In part because of increases in the marriage rate during this period, a substantial proportion of employed women were married. Women's proven competence challenged assumptions about women's "natural" capabilities, but did not yet fuel demands for the *right* to paid employment. At the war's end, women and men accepted that returning servicemen had priority. Women's exit from the labour force was orchestrated by government policies and reinforced by social attitudes. (These are discussed in greater detail in Chapter 5.) The nurseries that had been set up to allow mothers to work were closed. Income tax legislation was amended to reduce the amount of money wives could earn and still be claimed as dependents. In one short year following World War II, the labour-force participation rate for Canadian women dropped seven per cent.

"WORKING MOMS": CHANGING FAMILY LIFE SINCE THE 1950s

In the comparative affluence of the early postwar period there was a strong desire to see family life return to "normal." Encouraged by rising real incomes and low unemployment, couples could realistically expect to raise large families in the growing suburban communities. The media played an important role in reinforcing family values, particularly motherhood. As Betty Friedan (1963: 38) argued in her critique of women's magazines, "fulfillment as a woman had only one definition for American women after 1949—the housewife mother." In Rosen's (1973) book about movie heroines, the chapter dealing with this period is called "Losing Ground." Certainly, the emphasis on family and motherhood is an understandable reaction to the disruption of the previous decades. In Rosen's opinion (*Ibid.*: 246), "The emotional strain of wartime separation and denial accounted for both sexes eagerly embracing traditional social roles." The desire to return to domesticity also reflected ambivalence about the changes in women's lives. "It seems likely that the ideological message touting domesticity was as shrill as it was because for the first time masses of women had real options." (Breines, 1985: 601)

Popular writing reflected a concern for the consequences of maternal employment and the inadequacies of nonmaternal care. "The experts' directives were simple: women were to enter and withdraw from the job market in accordance with the family life cycle; part-time work was preferable to full-time employment; and under no circumstances should the demands of a career interfere with a woman's primary responsibilities for her children." (Margolis, 1984: 78) On the other hand, much of the popular literature was contradictory and some "explicitly misogynist" (Breines, 1985: 603), blaming mothers for a litany of social ills. It is an understatement to say that mothers in the 1950s experienced contradictions. Motherhood was defined as their biological destiny, but women had no control over the conditions of childbirth. They were expected to be everpresent, but not overprotective. They could seek employment, but not at the expense of neglecting their homes or families.

When viewed against long-term patterns of marriage, childbearing, and maternal employment, parents of the 1950s were a unique generation. Families were large and children spaced close together in a pattern very different from previous or subsequent generations. The economic prosperity that followed World War II encouraged marriage, children, and strong family commitment. Women who didn't embrace either marriage or motherhood were thought to be unnatural. In 1957, four out of five Americans described never-married people as neurotic, selfish, and immoral. (Shostak, 1987: 366) Childlessness and one-child families, both common in the Depression, were rare in the fifties. The rise in fertility, now referred to as the baby boom, was dramatic and its effects felt in all social institutions as this generation entered schools, the labour force, and the housing market. But this was a short-term reversal of a long-term trend. Fertility declines in 1970s were so clear we now call this the "baby bust."

Through the 1960s and into the 1970s, more young women were attending universities and colleges, yet the attitudes of male professors and course content reinforced traditional roles for women. Sociology taught that a sexual division of labour was a necessary feature of family life because it established a mutual dependency between family members. Until well into the 1970s, women's sociological home was the study of marriage and family. Yet in this area particularly, traditional thinking seems to have interfered with accurate social analysis. In a content analysis of marriage and family texts used in the 1960s, Ehrlich (1971) found that the texts supported a traditional division of labour in the family as "biologically logical and practical," "efficient," and "responsible," a "primary source of harmony in a marital relationship," "directly beneficial to the survival and order of society," "convenient," and "expedient." Such statements now appear as justifications for, rather than explanations of sex differences. Although the texts claimed to be compilations of accumulated knowledge, they were, in Ehrlich's opinion, nothing more than "collections of folklore and stereotyping" in their considerations of women. "The female viewed by the American male sociologist of the family, belongs at home, ministering to her husband and children and foreswearing all other interests." (*Ibid.*: 430) Women's labour-force participation was analyzed only in terms of its effect on the family.

The most significant challenge to the ideology of motherhood was the increased labour-force participation of married women. In 1941, 4.5 per cent of married women were in the labour force; by 1951 it was 11.2 per cent; and by 1961, 20.8 per cent. During the 1970s the two-income family became the norm. In the 1980s, the proportion of mothers of infants and young children in the labour force crossed the 50 per cent mark. (See Table 2.1.) Rising standards of consumption and economic expansion in the service and information sectors were the push and pull factors that encouraged married women to seek employment. They were attractive to employers because they were available, appropriately educated, and, above all, cheap. As the number of employed mothers became too high to ignore, attitudes about maternal employment began to soften. "Experts" began to question the assumption that maternal employment was damaging to children, or that nonmaternal care was necessarily second best. (Margolis, 1984)

The other change that did not fit with traditional thinking about women's family roles was the dramatic increase in marital separation and divorce. While more Canadian marriages still end in death than divorce, the divorce rates have risen dramatically in the last three decades. In 1968,

TABLE 2.1

LABOUR FORCE PARTICIPATION RATE OF WOMEN, BY FAMILY STATUS AND AGE OF YOUNGEST CHILD, CANADA, 1976-1988

	WOMEN LIVING WITH SPOUSE			WOMEN WITH NO SPOUSE AT HOME		
	With Pre-school Age Child(ren) (0-5 Years)	With Child(ren) 6-15 Years	Without Children Under 16 Years	With Pre-school Age Child(ren) (0-5 Years)	With Child(ren) 6-15 Years	Without Children Under 16 Years
	%					
1976	34.9	49.0	43.5	43.9	58.7	40.7
1977	36.6	50.8	44.3	46.8	60.5	39.5
1978	40.7	53.2	45.1	45.2	62.2	43.0
1979	42.1	54.6	46.3	49.6	63.0	44.1
1980	44.3	57.1	47.2	53.3	66.4	42.7
1981	47.1	60.2	47.7	51.3	67.8	45.4
1982	48.3	60.8	48.2	51.7	66.7	46.0
1983	51.6	61.5	48.6	51.0	65.5	47.4
1984	54.2	63.9	49.7	51.3	68.3	48.4
1985	56.7	65.6	50.1	54.0	69.2	48.6
1986	59.4	68.2	50.5	51.8	70.9	47.1
1987	60.7	70.6	51.5	52.8	71.5	48.5
1988	62.2	73.0	52.8	51.0	72.3	48.6

Source: *Women in Canada*, 1990, p. 80. Ottawa: Statistics Canada. Reproduced with the permission of the Minister of Supply and Services Canada, 1990.

long overdue changes to divorce legislation were introduced, and the divorce rate rose predictably. In 1968 the crude divorce rate (defined as the number of divorces per 100 000 married people in the population) was 54.8. It jumped to 124.2 in 1969, and continued to rise during the 1970s and doubled between 1970 and 1982. (See Table 2.2.) By age 54, about one-third of adult Canadians have divorced at least once. (Devereaux, 1987) Now, fewer Canadian households are married couples and their children, and more households consist of single people, childless couples (both married and unmarried, homosexual, and heterosexual), and lone parents and their children.

CHANGING ATTITUDES

Davis and van den Oever (1982) argue that rising divorce rates, declining fertility, and increased female labour-force participation make traditional roles more "costly" for women. Thus, both women and men (either because they see the rationale or simply out of self-interest) are more inclined to adopt more egalitarian views about women. Attitude studies

TABLE 2.2

DIVORCES AND DIVORCE RATE, CANADA, 1970–1987

	Number of Divorces	Divorce Rate[1]
1970	29 775	621.0
1971	29 685	607.2
1972	32 389	649.0
1973	36 704	719.7
1974	45 019	860.1
1975	50 611	942.4
1976	54 207	985.6
1977	55 370	988.9
1978	57 155	1 004.0
1979	59 474	1 028.7
1980	62 019	1 053.7
1981	67 671	1 129.2
1982	70 436	1 164.4
1983	68 567	1 125.2
1984	65 172	1 061.9
1985	61 980	1 003.5
1986	78 160	1 255.2
1987	86 985	1 372.2

1 Divorces per 100 000 married women aged 15 years and over.

Source: *Women in Canada*, 1990, p. 18. Ottawa: Statistics Canada. Reproduced with the permission of the Minister of Supply and Services Canada, 1990.

over the past two decades reflect this transition, although it seems that many Canadians remain ambivalent about women's paid employment.

Gibbins, Ponting, and Symons (1978) found two-thirds of their sample of Canadians agreed with the statement, "When children are young, a mother's place is in the home." There were no significant male/female differences in responses. Furthermore, only one out of five Canadians disagreed that "although a wife's career may be important, she should give priority to helping her husband advance his career." The authors found that both age and education influenced attitudes toward women. Younger and more educated respondents were more apt to express nontraditional views. Nevertheless, there seems to be a considerable gap between expectations and attitudes on one hand and demographic trends on the other.

Monica Boyd (1984) looked at changing attitudes to women as measured by thirty years of Canadian public opinion polls. She found a growing acceptance of women's employment outside the home but concern over the implied loss of traditionally defined domestic responsibilities. (*Ibid.*: 1) The polls show an increased (if reluctant) social acceptance of gainful employment for married women. In 1960, two-thirds of those polled thought that "married women should take a job outside the home if they had no young children." Only 5 per cent thought women should take a job outside the home if there were young children to care for. By 1987, most Canadians (almost 90 per cent) thought that married women should work if they did not have young children, but only 47 per cent agreed if children were present. (Canadian Gallup Poll, March, 1987) Over half the respondents in 1973, and again in 1982, said that the increased labour-force participation of married women has had a harmful effect on family life. (Boyd, 1984) By 1988, the percentage had dropped slightly to 48 per cent. (Canadian Gallup Poll, February, 1988) Younger and better educated Canadians are less apt to define the effects as harmful.

If adults are ambivalent, it is no wonder that children grow up with unrealistic assumptions about the possibility of marital disruption or the necessity of paid work. A recent study of young Canadian schoolchildren found that most girls expected to marry and become mothers, and they assumed that husbands would be providers. "There do not seem to be any unmarried mothers, deserted wives, widows or divorcees among the imaginary women Canadian schoolgirls expect to become." (Ellis and Sayer, 1986: 56) Adolescents, particularly those who have experienced living in a single-parent household, are somewhat more realistic about their future lives. Most adolescents in Baker's (1985) study expected to be married eventually. One-third of the girls expected to be full-time homemakers, although half of the boys expected this of their future wives. A few anticipated the possibility of divorce, yet most were unrealistic about its implications.

CONCLUSION

This chapter has looked at changes in women's economic and maternal roles from pre-industrial times to the present. In pre-industrial rural households, women's economic contributions were fundamental to the family's economic well-being. While far from equal partners, in practice or in law, men and women depended on each other for survival. Women's work centred on the home, where they could nurture and care for infants. Older children were jointly supervised by husbands and wives. With industrialization and the increased dependence on wage labour, the nature of women's economic contributions changed. From Confederation to World War II, married women's lives focused on home and children. The idea that women were naturally and primarily suited to maternity developed in response to the particular economic and demographic conditions of this period.

Even in the early years of the twentieth century, the contradictions inherent in the ideology of motherhood were apparent. No amount of social philanthropy could disguise the economic instability of working-class family life or the need for additional income provided by women and children. Middle-class women, too, were drawn to the labour force by expanding opportunities. For these "career women," the price of economic independence was usually celibacy and childlessness. Continued expansion of the service sector began to draw married women into the labour force, first on a part-time or temporary basis. More recently, marital instability, inflation, rising standards of consumption, and changing expectations have made labour-force participation the norm for married women.

The demographic, economic, and attitudinal changes of the last decades have profoundly altered family life. Most Canadians (about 90 per cent) eventually marry, but at any point in time about 40 per cent of adult women are unmarried. While the media might lead us to believe that singles are a young, affluent group, the reality is that most are older widowed women (because of sex differences in longevity, the tendency for men to marry younger women, and the fact that more men than women remarry after divorce or widowhood), most of whom are poor. An increasing number of households are lone-parent women and their children. Women whose life choices have been based on the assumption that men will provide lifelong economic and emotional security are economically vulnerable. Based on current patterns of marriage, divorce, and life expectancy, 84 per cent of Canadian women "can expect to spend a significant portion of their adult lives in husbandless households where they will have to support themselves and often their children as well." (National Council of Welfare, 1990: 15) This includes 13 per cent of women who never marry, 30 per cent who separate or divorce, and 41 per cent whose lifetime marriages end in widowhood. (*Ibid.*) Social attitudes have not kept pace with demographic and economic shifts, and social policies have lagged behind the needs of many women and children. Social science, too, has ignored the contradictions in women's lives. Until recently, mainstream sociology took for granted a "division of labour" among family members, treated women's paid work as secondary and transitory, independent living and childlessness as exceptions to the norm, and homosexuality as deviant.

The next chapter looks at the implications of the contradiction between the ideology of motherhood and the reality of labour-force participation for most women. While ostensibly women can choose marriage, parenthood, and/or a career, these decisions are (as the title of Gerson's [1985] book suggests) *Hard Choices*.

3 FEMINISM AND THE DILEMMAS OF FAMILY LIFE

In the postwar years changes in longevity and in marriage and childbearing patterns have had profound implications for the organization of women's lives. Women today marry later, and an increasing number choose to remain independent. Contraceptive technology has made parenthood a choice for the vast majority of women. At the same time, motherhood has become more challenging financially, socially, and psychologically. Proportionately more marriages end in divorce and an increasing number are remarriages for one or both partners. Rising divorce rates and an increased number of children born to unmarried women mean that increasing numbers of children are raised in lone-parent families, with severe economic consequences for both women and children. Although married women are more apt to be employed rather than full-time housewives, women still work in a limited range of jobs for which they receive low pay relative to similarly educated and experienced men. Employed women experience considerable tension trying to balance income-generating and family-related work. Women have increased their commitment to the labour force but continue to shoulder the "burden" of domestic and childrearing responsibilities. Husbands and fathers have not made a corresponding commitment to active involvement in family life. The contradiction between the assumed primacy of the wife/mother role coupled with the reality of extensive labour-force participation creates a dilemma for all women. This chapter looks at the implications of this contradiction. The first section explains the growth of the women's movement in the 1960s as a response to changing economic and demographic conditions. The impetus for the movement came from two directions: middle-class professional women and women involved in the radical student movement. The second section focuses on the implications for employed women and their children of our cultural ambivalence about maternal employment. The third section looks at the consequences of the assumption that women should expect to be economically dependent on men.

THE FEMINIST CRITIQUE OF MOTHERHOOD

According to Hamilton (1988: 3), the nature of family life in the postwar years created the preconditions for the women's movement of the 1960s and 1970s. Given the contradiction between the ideology of motherhood and the economic realities of women's lives, it is not surprising that a central issue of the women's movement was a critique of the family and the institution of motherhood. Feminists challenged pervasive heterosexism, the definition of motherhood as women's biological destiny, and the notion that mothers alone be responsible for the care and nurturance of children. They pointed out that since very little of women's lives are spent pregnant or giving birth, women should hardly be defined in terms of these capacities. They objected to ways motherhood was all-encompassing. Women "mother" not only children but men, bosses, the sick, the elderly, and needy people in general. (Levine, 1983: 30) Where the ideology glamorized motherhood, feminists exposed the darker side of motherhood: its isolation and low social recognition, and the costs to mothers in terms of guilt, frustration, fatigue, and stress.

Ostensibly women in the 1960s had choices regarding education and employment, but social pressures continued to push women in the direction of marriage and motherhood. The media, especially women's magazines, all but ignored women's employment, continuing to portray women as they had in the 1950s—as homemakers, consumers, mothers, and wives. Male and female jobs were advertised separately, and discriminatory practices in the labour force were commonplace. Expectations rose as more women attended universities and colleges, but few women were able to translate their education into opportunities in the labour force. Women, it was then assumed, were not interested in careers. The fact that most employed women worked in dead-end, part-time, or temporary jobs was evidence that this was what women wanted; and that women were paid less, did most of the housework and child care, or lived in poverty if they were divorced or widowed were overlooked. Public policy reinforced this contradiction by providing welfare assistance to single mothers and widows while ignoring structured inequality in the labour force and the need for child care or pension coverage.

In the 1960s, challenges to these restrictions came primarily from two sources: the established women's organizations and the women's caucuses of New Left groups. Understandably their concerns were different. The middle-class professional women members of groups, such as the Association of Business and Professional Women or the Canadian Federation of University Women, were primarily concerned with barriers to equality of opportunity in the labour force. They were motivated by the need for fair treatment and confident of the ability of existing institutions to change to meet the needs of women—once these needs were recognized. When the Report of the Royal Commission on the Status of Women was published in 1970, its 167 recommendations became the focus of reform. In keeping with the premise of *equal* rights, more attention was paid to ensuring equal treatment for men and women than to the unique needs of women as mothers. At the time it seemed important to emphasize the similarities between men and women and downplay biological differences. Overcoming discriminatory practices in the labour force took priority over supports for working women like paid maternity benefits and child care.

Women involved in campus-based peace movements were both younger and more politically radical than the liberal feminists. For these women the most important issues were freedom of sexual expression and the right to reproductive choice. The issues of contraception and abortion were inseparable: without access to birth control, women had to resort to abortion to terminate an unwanted pregnancy. Before 1969 all abortions were illegal in Canada, so women either risked an illegal (and sometimes life-threatening) abortion in Canada or travelled outside of the country to have an abortion.

Firestone (1970) and other radical feminists thought that reproductive technology would separate reproduction from the patriarchal family and "free women from the tyranny of their reproductive biology." In the two decades since Firestone's book was published, medical advances have indeed made artificial insemination, surrogate motherhood, embryo replacement, and embryo transfer possible. But they have not led to the social transformation Firestone envisioned. Far from increasing women's control of reproduction, technological advances in this field have made motherhood an increasingly public issue. Certainly, medical advances have made parenthood possible for some infertile women and men, but the screening of potential mothers for suitability, the fact that sperm donors and surrogate mothers are paid, and that legally binding contracts are signed have all separated women from decisions about and the experience of both pregnancy and childbirth. Contraception, abortion, the rights of the unborn, and, increasingly, new reproductive technologies are, as McDaniel (1988: 178) argues, among the most politically contentious issues of our time.

In the 1960s the women's movement focused on freedom from compulsory motherhood and all that this implied at the time, and freedom to enter the labour force on equal terms with men. Not surprisingly, women who benefited most from these initiatives were young, independent, and childless.[1] Marshall's study (1987: 7) of women in male-dominated professions in Canada found that these women were "more likely than women in other occupations to have never married, or if married, to have had fewer children or to be childless." She concluded that for many women (unlike men) "the decision to pursue a career may mean limiting marital or parental options." (*Ibid.:* 11) In the United States, 90 per cent of male executives 40 and under are fathers, but only 35 per cent of their female counterparts are mothers. (Brown *et al.*, 1989: 82)

---

[1] Highly educated women typically marry later, if they marry at all. The longer women postpone marriage, the more likely they are to remain single for life. (About one-half of single, 30-year-old women and two-thirds of single 35-year-olds will never marry. (Nagnur and Adams, 1987: 4–5)) Highly educated career women are also the most likely to postpone or forego childbearing. Currently, 15 to 20 per cent of Canadian women are childless. (Eichler, 1988: 228).

The majority of women, struggling with what we now call the "double day," juggling the demands of children and jobs, undoubtedly benefited from improved contraception and efforts to reduce discrimination in the labour force. But neither the pressures of *combining* employment and family life nor the concerns of full-time mothers were addressed. Demands for social supports for working mothers, although important issues for both liberal and radical feminists, were overshadowed by the focus on discrimination in the labour force and reproductive freedom. Failure to deal directly with the structural constraints of motherhood created a rift in the women's movement and left the movement as a whole open to criticism from the New Right. (Hewlett, 1986.) Betty Friedan, whose book *The Feminine Mystique* (1963) provided an early catalyst for the movement, and who served as the first president of the American National Organization of Women, was a vocal critic. In *The Second Stage*, (1982) she criticized the movement for ignoring the family and for giving insufficient attention to workplace policies to accommodate the needs of parents.

In the last two decades, the New Right has countered feminist demands for legal equality by reaffirming traditional family values. Defining themselves specifically as pro-family and antifeminist, many in the New Right blame the women's movement for creating current tensions in family life. (Eichler, 1986) The New Right's main concern is the breakdown of the family and the deterioration of values on which traditional family life is based. Drawing support from religious conservatives, the Right to Life Movement, and the political right, antifeminists stress the centrality of women to family and family to society. (Chafetz and Dworkin, 1987: 57) Any policies that upset this balance are seen as threatening to society in general. Antifeminists oppose nonmarital, nonprocreative sexuality (Eichler, 1986) (including homosexuality), divorce, reproductive control, and publicly supported day care. Antifeminists in the United States opposed the Equal Rights Amendment, which would have given women legal equality. Similarly, antifeminists in Canada opposed entrenching women's rights in the Constitution.

Antifeminists in both countries have rallied most intensely behind the abortion issue.[2] Erwin's (1988) survey of members of Canadian antifeminist groups found abortion to be their central concern. Almost all (99.5 per cent) of the respondents said it was the reason they became involved in antifeminism. Most are members of both pro-family and anti-abortion groups. Pressure from anti-abortion groups in Canada resulted in a reduction in the number of therapeutic abortions done in hospitals and clinics in the mid-1980s. (McDaniel, 1988: 182) However, in January 1988

---

[2] It should not be inferred that all feminists are necessarily pro-choice. There are some who define themselves as feminist and anti-abortion.

the Supreme Court of Canada decided that the 1969 abortion law was unconstitutional and that abortion was a private decision between a woman and her doctor. Since then, lobbying by both anti-abortion and pro-choice groups for new abortion legislation, and the media attention this has received, suggest that the issue is far from settled.[3]

Antifeminists hold the women's movement responsible for the deterioration of the family. They ignore the fact that both increases in labour-force participation and climbing divorce rates pre-date the contemporary women's movement, and both of these occurrences have more to do with large-scale economic shifts than changing attitudes.[4] The majority of Erwin's respondents (89 per cent) feel that feminism has devalued motherhood, and 86 per cent feel it has undermined the traditional family. Yet 63 per cent feel feminism has helped women in the workforce! (*Ibid.*: 271) Economic and demographic changes in the past two decades make the desire to return to traditional family living a moot point. Most women do not work out of choice: they work because of economic necessity—they are widowed, divorced or separated, or their husbands' earnings are low. Inflation has eroded real incomes such that it is difficult for families to thrive on the earnings of a single breadwinner. In the absence of social supports for employed parents, especially female lone parents, we have experienced, as Janet and Larry Hunt (1982) predicted a decade ago, a widening gap in the standard of living between households with children, and childless households.

The women's movement's focus on reproductive choice and labour force equality in the 1960s was a reaction to historically specific conditions. As British feminist Lynne Segal (1987: 14) sees it, "Feminists were over-reacting to what we saw as the shackles of conventional femininity, but we uncovered enough misery and bitterness in that world to warrant

---

[3] Advances in medical technology have added to the complexity of abortion debates in the last decade. Infants born as early as the twenty-third week of pregnancy can now be expected to survive, but in some cases abortions are allowed as late as the twenty-sixth week of pregnancy. At the same time, prenatal diagnosis has improved, raising new questions about the implications of selective abortion. Now, "the central question is not simply choice, but choice for whom and under what conditions." (Achilles, 1988: 291) Lobbying efforts by both anti-abortion and pro-choice groups for new abortion legislation were fueled by the media attention to two individual cases in the summer of 1989. Although the pregnancies of Chantal Daigle and Barbara Dodd were legally terminated, attempts by their partners to disallow abortion raised disturbing questions about the rights of fathers versus the rights of mothers to decide.

[4] Eichler (1986: 10) examined criticisms made by antifeminist groups of feminism in general and the National Action Committee on the Status of Women in particular. She found the antifeminist descriptions "blatantly inaccurate."

much of the reaction." By the late 1970s the context had changed. It was clear that rejecting motherhood to succeed in a man's world was not liberation. Instead of seeing motherhood as an obstacle to employment, feminists began to consider how the organization of paid work made parenting problematic. It was not, as Rich (1976) argued, the fact of biological reproduction that oppressed women, but the way motherhood was institutionalized. Despite the constraints and the ambivalence, many feminists were asserting that the experience of motherhood was a central and positive one. (Rossiter, 1988) The legislation of contraception, the medicalization of abortion, the isolation of motherwork, and the economic dependence of women and children made the *institution* of motherhood oppressive. That motherwork is assigned to women, without social recognition or support, is costly to women in emotional and economic terms. In the following paragraphs we will look at the implications of this assignment—for employed mothers who face the enormous responsibility of juggling the demands of paid and unpaid work, and for full-time mothers who work in isolation and leave themselves economically vulnerable now and as they age.

JUGGLING MOTHERHOOD AND EMPLOYMENT

The 1950s media image of the "Happy Housewife," which Betty Friedan (1963) found so objectionable, portrayed women as devoted wives and mothers. The "Superwoman" image of the 1980s has added accomplished professional to the picture. On the surface, this appears to be a step forward. It suggests that women can "have it all": a meaningful job, a devoted husband, and clever, well-adjusted children. But as Hochschild (1989) argues, the image has little to do with reality for most employed married mothers. More importantly, the image is a powerful model encouraging women to accept that the price of employment is the double day. "By defining the successful woman as one who is happily carrying this multiple burden and in addition suggesting that it was women who sought this change, the superwoman ideal de-legitimizes discontent." (Ferree, 1987: 162) The image implies that women are free to choose—career, motherhood ... or both. Granted, women today have much more control over decisions about education, employment, marriage, and motherhood than their mothers or grandmothers had. But these choices are circumscribed by conditions over which women have little control: financial need, the availability of child care, employment opportunities, and household responsibilities. "Characteristically for women ... the organization of their daily experience, their work routines, and indeed their lives are determined and ordered externally to them." Women's lives "have a loose episodic structure, lacking continuity and being singularly exposed to contingencies." (Smith, 1977: 19) As Epstein (1974: 650) pointed out, to suppose people do things because they want to is a peculiar bias in American sociology. Current living and working arrangements are often the consequence of other life events (e.g. divorce) and so cannot be assumed to always reflect an active choice. Assuming that choices are freely made and that juggling is simply the price women pay overlooks the structural constraints that frame the decision in the first place. In fact, it is a choice between "seriously flawed alternatives." (Duffy, Mandell and Pupo, 1989) Most employed mothers work for financial reasons, and they are ambivalent about the price they and their families pay for the money they earn. They see their work as "involuntary, permanent, contingent and unplanned." (*Ibid.*: 21)

How do women balance or choose between the competing demands of paid employment and motherhood? Kathleen Gerson (1985, 1987) explored this question by interviewing women who moved into young adulthood in the 1970s. By interviewing a diverse group of similarly aged women from different class backgrounds, Gerson was able to discover "how and why their contrasting commitments emerged over time." (1987: 271) Four general patterns emerged. One group (about 20 per cent of the sample) anticipated, and were able to pursue a traditional course giving priority to domestic life. The second group (about 30 per cent) had, like the first group, anticipated a full-time domestic role, but these plans changed because of circumstances in their adult lives. The third group (less than 20 per cent) anticipated and followed a nontraditional path, rejecting a full-time domestic role. Some rejected parenthood as well. The final group (about 30 per cent) expected a nontraditional path, but when this proved unsatisfactory, reassessed their goals. These women experienced "falling employment aspirations and began to see the home as haven." Because social conditions make it difficult for women to make equally strong commitments to family life and to gainful employment, each woman was required to seek an individual solution. Whether women were able to follow their early expectations or not depended on how they negotiated four key aspects of their social environment: the presence or absence or a stable supportive partner; blocked or enhanced job opportunities; economic need; and their perceptions of the costs and benefits of the traditional choice. (*Ibid.*: 273) These factors reflect widespread economic and family life shifts, which, Gerson argues, makes it difficult to explain the choices in terms of socialization, biology, or male dominance. The women Gerson described had different childhood experiences and role models and responded to these in different ways. Gerson concluded that "women experience psychic conflict over the choice between family and paid work because structural arrangements make it a choice in the first place." (*Ibid.*: 279)

Most of the women in Duffy, Mandell and Pupo's (1989) study of married Canadian mothers believed in a traditional division of labour. Regardless of their employment status, they assumed that their husbands would be primary wage earners and that they would give priority to family life. Most of the full-time employees in this study did not grow up to anticipate labour-force participation. "Their childhood experiences and adolescent expectations, as well as their parents' aspirations for them were consistently traditional." (Ibid.: 21–22) They did not have long-term career goals. Nevertheless, when faced with the necessity of combining family and paid employment, these women coped admirably. While they were overworked and had little time for themselves, they saw these problems as temporary. They felt a sense of personal competency and efficacy (Ibid.: 40) and enjoyed the financial freedom they had.

Why do mothers accept the larger share of parenting responsibilities? Women who were socialized to expect traditional marriages have adjusted to the demands of paid work. Why have fathers not made the reciprocal adjustment to shared parenting? Rossi (1984) argued that fathers have very little preparation for the possibility of caring for infants or young children, are likely to feel awkward, and thus experience failure in their attempts to "help." Research investigating the interactions of fathers and infants suggests that men "tend to avoid high involvement in infant care because infants do not respond to their repertoire of skills and men have difficulty acquiring the skills needed to comfort the infant." (Rossi, 1984: 8) For Rossi the solution is to teach fathers about parenting and thus encourage their participation.

Risman (1987) argues that males lack fathering skills because of "situational exigencies and opportunities" rather than biology or socialization. When situational factors change, "divorced, widowed and even married fathers are capable of providing the nurturance that young children require despite their gendered socialization." (Ibid.: 28) Risman's research suggests that fathers will become more involved in parenting when structural constraints are reduced. These include the introduction of parental leave for fathers and flexible work schedules for both men and women. "Only when situational contexts change will parenting behavior among men become more similar to the parenting behavior of women." (Ibid.: 28) Fathers who attend prenatal classes, assist during labour, and who are present during childbirth seem to be more involved in the routine care of their infant children. Indeed, fathers are more likely to help with children than with housework.

Clearly the problem is more complex than unco-operative husbands. The lack of control women have over the organization of their work and family life reflects the internal dynamics of particular households, the lack of public support for child care, and the realities of market inequalities. Structured inequality in the labour force exacerbates the problem of soliciting help from husbands. Wives typically earn less than their husbands and work in jobs where the penalties for working to the clock, absenteeism, or exit and re-entry are lower. Consequently, it falls on wives more than husbands to stay home from work if children are sick, to let school and day care hours determine work hours, or to follow spouses in job transfers. These day-to-day decisions may well be made in a context of what is best for the family, not who has the power to decide. True, many husbands are reluctant to "help" with housework and child care, and some wives admittedly overcompensate for their ambivalent feelings about paid employment by doing the lion's share of domestic work. (Duffy, Mandell and Pupo, 1989) But even in homes where both husband and wife espouse egalitarian attitudes, housework and child care are mostly women's work because of externally imposed conditions like work routines. This allocation of work and the inequities that lie at its root cannot help but be observed by children. As children internalize these dynamics, the stage is set for the reproduction of gender dominance and subordination. As Duffy (1988: 124) observed: "Good wives do not need to be controlled by their husbands, they are controlled by a lifetime of appropriate gender socialization."

An important consequence of our cultural ambivalence about maternal employment is the failure to publicly support child care. In 1987 there were over 1.9 million children under age 13 who needed care, but only 243 545 licensed child-care spaces. (National Council of Welfare, 1988b) Most children of working parents are in unregulated day care, are cared for by relatives, or, we must assume, take care of themselves. Demand for child care far exceeds supply, so few parents have a real choice of day-care arrangements. Regulated child care is both expensive and in short supply. Subsidies are available to low-income families, but most families who qualify do not get the service they are entitled to because there are simply not enough licensed spaces. (*Ibid.*)

In response to recommendations of the Royal Commission on Equality in Employment (Abella, 1984), the Canadian government has taken the first tentative steps to developing a national strategy on child care based on proposals to increase tax breaks for parents and increase subsidies for child care. (National Council of Welfare, 1988b)

Recently, labour organizations, such as the Canadian Labour Congress and the Canadian Union of Public Employees, have developed formal policy statements on child care. The CLC's statement reads: that "publicly funded, non-profit, high quality care be recognized as a basic social service which should be available to all parents who choose to use it." (quoted in Mayfield, 1990: 114) Some unions have bargained for child-care programs; others have provided seed money to create work-based child care. With or without union prodding, about 100 Canadian businesses have established work-based child-care programs. (Mayfield, 1990)

Because of declining fertility and the aging of the population, children make up a smaller proportion of the population. The percentage of the Canadian population under 18 years of age has declined throughout the twentieth century, and there are proportionately fewer households with

FIGURE 3.1

PERCENTAGE OF CHILDREN UNDER AGE 16 BELOW THE POVERTY LINE, 1980–1986

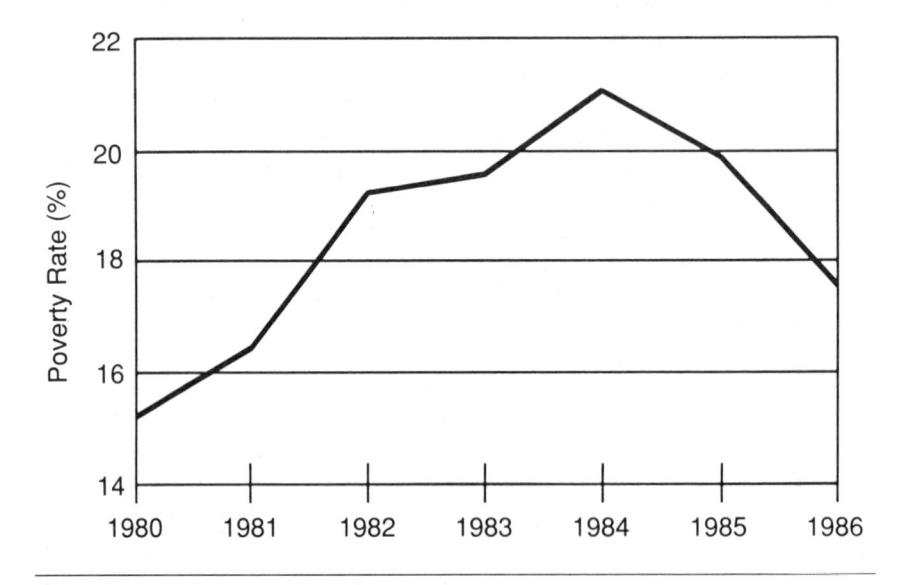

Source: National Council of Welfare, Poverty Profile, 1988, p. 27. Ottawa: Minister of Supply and Services.

children. "In a situation where so few adults feel any direct personal stake in the quality, or even the availability of essential services for children, it is easy for these services to atrophy and decline." (Pifer and Bronte, 1986: 8) American children are more likely than their parents' generation to commit suicide, perform poorly in school, be obese, and show other signs of physical, emotional, and mental distress. (Fuchs, 1988) In Canada in 1986, one child in six lived in poverty. [5] The majority of these children (60.1 per cent) lived in two-parent families. (National Council of Welfare, 1988a: 26–29)

---

[5] Statistics Canada bases its annual low-income cut-offs at the level where 58.5 per cent of gross income is spent on food, clothing, and shelter. The average for Canadian families is 38.5 per cent. National Council of Welfare uses the "low income line" to define poverty levels for families and individuals.

THE DARK SIDE OF ECONOMIC DEPENDENCE

Inequalities in the labour force create a double jeopardy for women. They enter a segregated labour force and work in jobs for which they receive low pay relative to equally qualified and talented men. Married women's earnings augment their husbands' wages but are not enough to be self-supporting. So, although women make a concrete contribution to the household, universal pay differentials make it very difficult for most women to have economic independence outside of marriage without experiencing a drop in their standard of living. Many women have sacrificed education and career for marriage and children, accepted geographical moves at the cost of their own careers, left the labour force to raise children, and/or accepted part-time or reduced job responsibilities to be available to their children. Within a marriage, these seem to be reasonable trade-offs. Outside of marriage they become costly barriers. Women who stay at home as full-time housewives leave themselves economically vulnerable in the short and long term. In the short term, they risk considerable financial hardship if their marriage fails. In the long term, they risk poverty in old age. The two groups most susceptible to poverty are unmarried mothers of young children and unmarried older women who have been homemakers most of their married lives.

Since 1970 there has been a dramatic increase in the number of lone-parent households in Canada and the United States. In the United States, half of all children will live in a fatherless home before they reach the age 18 years. (Glick, 1984) Two factors account for this increase: an increased number of births to unmarried women and an increase in divorce. In Canada in 1983, one-sixth of all births were to unmarried women, a fourfold increase of the stable patterns from 1930 to 1960, but far lower than in the United States. Some independent women have chosen to become mothers by bearing or adopting children. For others, particularly adolescent mothers, childbirth seems more closely related to a lack of contraception. Teenage mothers face a difficult future because of interrupted education and poor job opportunities. Forty per cent of American female high school dropouts cite pregnancy or marriage as the reason for leaving school.

In Canada, divorce rates increased dramatically following the 1968 liberalization of divorce legislation. These increases continued throughout the 1970s and declined in the early 1980s. By 1986 the divorce rate had risen again. Increases in divorce and in the number of children born to unmarried women mean an increase in the number of female-headed, lone-parent households. Since women are more likely to retain custody of their children and are less apt to remarry, the growing number of lone-parent households are mostly female-headed. In Canada, more than half of all divorces involve at least one dependent child. (Eichler, 1988: 243) In most cases (over 75 per cent), custody goes to the mother. Both divorce and premarital pregnancy are more common in the United States, and so there are far more single-parent families there. Currently about one-quarter of all American households are female-headed lone-parents compared to about 13 per cent in Canada. (Moore, 1987) In Canada, 57 per cent of these women are separated or divorced, 28 per cent widowed, and 15 per cent never married. (*Ibid.*)

The fact that there are fewer single mothers in Canada does not make the economic circumstances they face less problematic. Poverty for many women begins with single parenthood, although many divorced women were poor before their marriage ended. Low-income couples have a higher separation rate than middle- and high-income couples. Many are trapped in a cycle of poverty—truncated education, early marriage, poor housing, poor job prospects, and marital breakdown. In 1987 the poverty rate for single-parent mothers in Canada was 57 per cent. (National Council of Welfare, 1990)

Clearly, the most pressing issue facing single mothers is finances. In the best of circumstances single mothers with secure, well-paid jobs and support systems for child care will be financially disadvantaged compared to two-earner families. However women with these advantages are exceptions. Most women are not in a position to assume financial responsibility for raising children alone, and most absent fathers do not contribute to the support of their children. Without the economic and emotional support of another adult, time and money pressures create a stressful situation for divorced women and their children. Whatever the emotional and psychological consequences of separation and divorce (and we know that these are great [Eichler, 1988: 248]), it is clear that the economic consequences are far greater for women than for men.

Most women experience divorce as a severe economic crisis. The term "feminization of poverty" was coined by Diana Pearce (1979) to describe the connection between increased divorce and increased poverty among women. In examining the consequences of no-fault divorce in California, Weitzman (1985) found that, overall, women and minor children experienced a 73 per cent decline in their standard of living, while their former husbands experienced a 42 per cent rise. According to Weitzman (1985: xiv), "the major economic result of the divorce law revolution is the systematic impoverishment of divorced women and their children. They have become the new poor." Although divorce rates in California are much higher and the legislative assumptions somewhat different, it is important for us to pay attention to these consequences. Very few women in either Canada or the United States receive alimony, and child support awards are woefully inadequate. If husbands default, the onus is on wives to collect delinquent payments, and few women have the resources to pursue this. Raising the standard of living for the large number of "economically fatherless" children means breaking the poverty/welfare/low-income job cycle. A major public policy challenge is to recapture for these children the economic support of their absent fathers.

Divorced or widowed homemakers find labour force re-entry very difficult because of lack of confidence, labour-force inexperience, and age discrimination. For older women, the combination of agism and sexism is a "double whammy." (Posner, 1980) Their skills are not rewarded in the job market; what little job experience they may have is outdated, and they have no seniority. Mothers of young children with little labour-force experience find it difficult to find a job with enough earning potential to cover their child-care expenses. Child-care responsibilities and limited job opportunities force lone-parent mothers to rely increasingly on welfare rather than employment to survive economically. Either alternative will mean a life of poverty.

Although Canada is a relatively young country (demographically speaking) when compared to the United States or most of Europe, our population too is aging. Life expectancy increased by approximately twenty years in this century, and women outlive men by several years. At the turn of the century, there were more older (over 65) men than women. This ratio reversed at mid-century, and by 1981 women made up almost 60 per cent of those over 65. (National Council of Welfare, 1984b: 9) In 1986 there were 138 women for every 100 men aged 65, and there were more than twice as many women as men aged 85 or older! (Devereaux, 1987: 37) Sex differences in longevity make the likelihood of widowhood high. In 1986 about two-thirds of women over 75 and four-fifths of those over 85 were widows. (Priest, 1988) Canadian women outlive their husbands by an average of ten years. Few elderly widows remarry simply because there are fewer similarly aged men (and it is still unusual for women to marry younger men), and most of these men are already married.

Because women now reaching old age have an inconsistent record of labour-force participation, there is a high probability that they will end their lives in poverty. In 1986 one elderly Canadian in five lived below the poverty line—an improvement over 1981 when one-quarter of elderly Canadians were poor. (National Council of Welfare, 1984b) However, the reduced risk of poverty among the elderly has benefited families more than singles and men more than women. Approximately 70 per cent of the elderly poor in both Canada and the United States are women. (See Table 3.1 on page 42.)

Poverty among elderly women is an issue of economic dependence not longevity. The size of an individual's retirement income depends on where they have worked, how long they have participated in the labour force, and how much they have been able to save. Retirement income in Canada is often referred to as a three-tiered system: Old Age Security (OAS), Canada and Quebec Pension Plans (C/QPP), and employer-sponsored pensions and other private sources of income. First, OAS is a universal benefit paid to all Canadians at age 65. The federal Guaranteed

TABLE 3.1

THE ELDERLY POOR, BY FAMILY STATUS AND SEX, 1986

	Number	Poverty Rate	Percentage Distribution
In Families			
Women	67 900	7.9%	47.2%
Men	76 000	8.5%	52.8%
Total	143 900	8.2%	100.0%
Unattached Individuals			
Women	276 300	46.1%	82.3%
Men	59 400	31.9%	17.7%
Total	335 700	42.7%	100.0%
All Elderly			
Women	344 200	23.5%	71.7%
Men	135 800	12.5%	28.3%
Total	480 000	18.8%	100.0%

Source: National Council on Welfare, Poverty Profile, 1988, p. 40. Ottawa: Statistics Canada. Reproduced with the permission of the Minister of Supply and Services Canada, 1990.

Income Supplement (GIS), introduced in 1967, and Spouse's Allowance (1975) as well as provincial programs, such as the Guaranteed Annual Income Supplement (GAINS) in Ontario, provide additional benefits to the most needy. Approximately half of all OAS recipients also received full or partial GIS in 1985. Second, the Canada and Quebec Pension Plans are earnings-related public pensions, introduced in 1966. Employed Canadians contribute a percentage of income to the fund and subsequent retirement income is based on salary and number of years worked. Full C/QPP benefits require forty years of employment or self-employment. Spouses are entitled to a portion of benefits when a wage earner dies. Finally, about half of the work force have private pension coverage. Typically, these are higher paid workers who are also most able to save or invest in preparation for retirement.

Employed women are penalized by their interrupted labour-force participation, frequent job changes, part-time work, and the fact that women typically work in sectors of the economy where private pension coverage is rare. Less than 40 per cent of employed women have private pension coverage (*Women in Canada*, 1985) Typically, neither part-time workers nor workers in the trade and service sectors are covered, and women outnumber men on both counts. Only Canadians with a history of consistent labour-force participation, preferably with a single employer (and one with good pension coverage) will benefit from all three tiers. It bears repeating that housework brings no work-related benefits, no disability or unemployment insurance, no health benefits, and, most importantly, no pension coverage. Married homemakers share their husbands' pension benefits as long as he lives, but will only receive C/QPP benefits as survivors. Few private pension schemes have survivor benefits, and those that exist are paltry. The underlying assumption of the three-tiered system is that homemakers will be provided for in retirement as they have been until that time. But the vast majority outlive both their husbands and the pensions. Many rely solely on OAS, a system designed to supplement, not constitute, pension income. By definition this group will live in poverty.

Not only divorced and widowed women fall between the cracks of a system that assigns homemaking and caregiving to women yet fails to economically support this assignment. Although these women are most affected, all women live under the same cloud. As Bergmann (1987: 218) pointed out, the problem of displaced homemakers (as divorced and widowed women who have devoted themselves to the home have been called) affects married women also because they and their husbands know that, in the case of marital breakdown, her social and economic position will be far more negatively affected than his. This awareness gives husbands added interpersonal power. Marriage and motherhood create unequal structural opportunities for men and women. The assumption that women are primarily responsible for domestic maintenance and mothering and men for economic security means that women do not have access to economic resources on the same basis as men. Consequently, they are subordinates in all aspects of life. (Hartmann, 1981)

Economic dependence is further structured for immigrant women by immigration policy—particularly for those who speak neither English nor French. Usually one member of an immigrating family, inevitably the husband, applies for immigration as an independent. He in turn sponsors his wife and children who enter the country as family-class immigrants. As such, women and working-aged children are ineligible for government-sponsored language and skills-training courses provided free to the "household head." (Ng, 1988) Without language training, employment options are limited to jobs in a particular ethnic-linguistic labour market or jobs that depend on little verbal instruction or interaction. (Boyd, 1988: 322) These jobs are inevitably poorly paid and rarely carry benefits. Consequently, immigrant women's economic dependence is reinforced.[6]

Many feminists have drawn a connection between women's economic dependence and their passivity and emotional dependence. Because women assume the primary responsibility for domestic work, and because it is assumed that this is their primary role, they are economically vulnerable. When unable to depend on a man's economic support, women

---

[6] Women who are sponsored immigrants also face the prospect of deportation if their sponsor is deported.

inevitably face financial hardship. If it is true that women are (as Gloria Steinem so aptly put it) "only one man away from welfare," then it is no wonder that women and men see women as emotionally vulnerable. Even if a woman is employed, the segregated labour force makes it difficult for her to have control over the economic conditions of her life. "Her economic dependence is reflected in emotional dependence, passivity and other 'typical' female personality traits. She is conservative, fearful, supportive of the status quo." (Benston, 1969: 20) As Smith (1977) explained, what is described as backwardness is nothing more or less than a defence against a situation over which she has no control.

Women's experiences of family life are not unidimensional; they are complex and contradictory. Family life is not uniformly oppressive. We feel intense love; we also feel resentment and frustration. Some women are more in control of the conditions of their lives than other women, and control changes over the life course. In extreme cases, feelings of submission and dominance may culminate in violence. Since so many instances of wife abuse go unreported, it is difficult to determine just how extensive the problem is. Using records of doctors, lawyers, social workers, and the police, MacLeod (1980, 1987) estimated that one in ten Canadian women are beaten by their husbands or partners. This however may be a conservative estimate. MacLeod's data reveal the following chilling statistics: half of the battering husbands and one-third of the battered wives were beaten as children; up to 80 per cent of abused wives report being beaten during pregnancy. Family violence may be more visible in working-class homes, but wife battering transcends all racial, ethnic, and socio-economic groups. Women clearly have no alternative but to remain in an abusive relationship when they are economically dependent on men; isolated in the home with their children, fearful of physical retaliation, when there is minimal social recognition given to the problem of wife battering and when the agencies who do become involved seem more dedicated to the sanctity of marriage than to the safety of the victim. But, as MacLeod's more recent study (1987) found, for many battered women the solution is more complicated than simply ending the relationship. While these women did not want to live with abuse, in many cases they wanted to continue the relationship. The dynamics of interpersonal power are complex and contradictory, even when expressed as violence. MacLeod's point is that unless we understand the ambiguities and contradictions in the lives of battered women, we will be ill-equipped to offer the kind of prevention program that will be useful.

CONCLUSION

We have come to expect that one of the family's main functions is the satisfaction of emotional needs. In Zaretsky's view (1976: 30), a search for a meaningful personal life is an important result of the ennui created by the conditions of work in advanced capitalism. "Much of this search for personal meaning takes place within the family and is one reason for the persistence of the family in spite of the decline of many of its earlier functions." As wives and mothers, women have shouldered much of the responsibility for this search. Men may indeed find the family a retreat from the world of work, but women have little time for leisure or emotional regeneration. Mitchell (1973: 158) phrased it well when she said that "woman's task is to hold on to the unity of the family while its separate atoms explode in different directions."

The tension between income-generating work and family responsibilities has taken a toll on women in the last decades of the twentieth century. To combine labour-force participation, domestic work, and child care is exhausting; to be marginally or intermittently employed is risky and leaves women economically vulnerable now and as they age. It is no wonder that many women have chosen to remain single and childless.

The women's movement and feminist analyses that have developed out of it have done a great deal to rephrase questions of family life. As Bergmann (1987: 1) has stressed, we can only capture what was good about the traditional family through reforms that take into account its current realities. It attests to the influence of feminism that reproductive choice, family violence, and the feminization of poverty are now openly debated. The agenda for the 1990s includes new ways of distributing economic resources, new habits of distributing domestic responsibilities, new schedules of work, and new services to meet the needs of men and women in different family situations. Feminist theory, it was argued in Chapter 1, is an iterative process. What appeared as a simple lack of control over the conditions of their lives, imposed by a patriarchal society, is now understood to be a more complex dynamic. Women may find the family to be an oppressive institution, yet love their own husbands; they may find child care isolating and tedious, yet wish to spend time with their children. Women experience a "fundamental dualism" in family life.

> The family is simultaneously an important source of emotional and material support and a source of oppression. How that contradiction gets played out and which side of the contradiction is most salient are shaped by larger systems of domination and subordination. Thus different groups of women experience the contradiction differently because the relationship of the family to the political economy varies by race, class and family formation. (Glenn, 1987: 368)

In chapters 2 and 3 we have focused on one side of the inequality equation: the reproduction of motherhood. The other side of the equation is paid employment. Motherwork and housework form the bridge. Chapters 4, 5, and 6 are about the work women do. It is hard to escape the assumption that only paid labour deserves the label "work," although no one who does domestic work would make such a claim. The invisibility of housework finds expression in the oft repeated phrase "just a housewife." Chapter 4 deals with women's unpaid work at home. Chapters 5 and 6 are about paid employment. Although I have analytically separated child care, paid, and unpaid work, these are not easily separated from a woman's point of view. The amount of energy women devote to paid employment or volunteer work is determined by family responsibilities. At the same time, the quality of family life is closely related to the demands of a paid job.

4 HOUSEWORK

Housework is the shared experience of most women, whether or not they do other work. About one-third of all Canadian women are full-time homemakers. The rest have two jobs: one paid and one not. Nevertheless, the most striking feature of housework is its lack of public recognition. Very little academic attention has been paid to the analysis of housework, to how women view the job, or to the relationship between housework and industrial capitalism. In a sense, the work women do in the home has slipped between the cracks of social science theory. Because housework has been defined as a private service to the family, policymakers too have ignored the social and economic contributions of housework and parenting. This lack of attention both reflects and contributes to the general devaluation and trivialization of housework. "A real pressure underlying the work of the homemaker is lack of validation. The work is private: there is no audience beyond the family and the work is personalized for the family members who rate it as they please." (Daniels, 1987: 407) Housework is not yet included in Gross National Product calculations, although estimates in Canada and other countries place its value at between 35 and 40 per cent of the GNP. Ironically, the study of domestic labour as work has received more attention as fewer people do it full-time.

The nineteenth century definition of the home as a haven reinforced the idea that what goes on to make it so is not work but the essence of womanhood. In many ways, little has changed in over a century.

> Industrialization has had these lasting consequences: the separation of the man from the intimate daily routines of domestic life; the economic dependence of women and children on men; the isolation of housework and childcare from other work. Hence, through the allocation to women of housework and childcare, through modern definitions of the role of housewife and the role of mother, industrialization has meant the restriction of the women-housewife to the home. The restriction is psychological more than physical. Today's housewife can, and does, leave the four walls of home for factory, office, school, hospital or shop, but her world is permanently divided from the world of men. The institutionalization of the housewife role as the primary role for all women means that an expansion of their world outside the home is retarded by the metaphor, and the reality, of the world looked at through the window over the kitchen sink. (Oakley, 1974: 59)

In the last decade, labour-force participation has become the norm for Canadian women. Yet the organization of household work has not changed to accommodate the demands of paid employment. Domestic work continues to be done in isolation, primarily by women, without pay and without social recognition. A significant contribution of feminist scholarship has been to make visible the work women do as housewives and mothers. This chapter focuses on women's unpaid work. The first part of the chapter looks at ways housework was changed by industrialization, both materially and ideologically. As families became dependent on men's wages and as technology eased the physical burden of housework, the economic value of housework diminished and the work women did at home became less visible—although no less time consuming. The second section looks at the nature of housework today and the differing frustrations experienced by full-time and part-time housewives. The final section focuses on ways of coming to terms with these dilemmas to alleviate both the burden of the double day and the economic dependence of full-time housewives.

THE EVOLUTION OF DOMESTIC LABOUR

The industrial revolution was a transition period in both the ideology and the practice of domestic labour. Chapter 2 described pre-industrial family life as based on home production. Although men and women did different kinds of domestic work, the work of each was essential for family survival; and for everyone, work was physically demanding. "Given the burdens of home production, women were left with little time for the jobs that are labeled housework today." (Margolis, 1984: 15) House cleaning was an annual event, clothes were rarely washed; meals were simple and their preparation took everyone's involvement. The word "housework," referring to work done in the home, did not even become accepted terminology until the middle of the nineteenth century. (Cowan, 1987: 165) By this time family life had begun to change in response to industrialization. The desire to purchase manufactured goods created the need for cash, and the increased number of factories created more opportunities to earn cash. Families became increasingly dependent on men's earned wages and less on the home production of all family members.

The change from farming and home production had a greater initial effect on the household work of men. (Cowan, 1987: 167) For example, the grinding of corn, which had been done by men was no longer necessary after milled flour became available. There were no substitutes for women's skills of cooking, sewing, or caring for the young and sick members of the family. True the work became less physically exhausting, but it was still time-consuming labour. As Cowan (1987) points out, laundry increased since manufactured cloth could stand more frequent washings than homespun. Cooking was easier on coal stoves than it had been on open fireplaces, but without electricity or running water, meal preparation and household maintenance still took a great deal of time. Sewing was easier with ready-made cloth and, after 1860, sewing machines, but women and children's clothes were typically homemade not store bought. These changes of course did not happen overnight. The introduction of new products to the market and new sources of energy to power them was a gradual process. The separation between the public sphere of paid employment and the private domestic sphere evolved gradually as more men left home during the day for paid employment.

Middle- and upper-class urban housewives were the first to benefit from the availability of manufactured products for household consumption. By the end of the nineteenth century middle-class housewives were able to buy whatever products and services they needed. They were further relieved of the physical demands of housework by the presence of a domestic servant. Over time the responsibilities of middle-class housewives had shifted from the household management of home production to the management of child care and consumption. Although all women were influenced by the cult of domesticity, domestic life for upper- and middle-class women was very different from working-class life. Rural and working-class households retained their pre-industrial character for a longer period. For the working class, wage labour was less reliable and many families depended on the (sometimes intermittent) economic contributions of everyone in the family. Rural households still grew and processed much of the food they ate well into the twentieth century. Many rural and working-class families were unaffected by new consumer products because they simply could not afford them. Without these products or the help of domestic servants, housework was indeed hard work.

The ideology of separate spheres reinforced the separation between private and public life, work and family. Women were thought to be emotionally and psychologically suited to their responsibilities as guardians of the homefront, as men were suited to their responsibilities as breadwinners. Margolis (1984), who studied prescriptive advice for women from pre-industrial to present day America, found a change in advice beginning in the 1830s. Before then, household guides were primarily directions for making household products and were directed at men and women. The advice that began to appear in the 1830s had a different tone and was written for women. "Like motherhood, housework was elaborated and exalted and women advised that their responsibilities were far more awesome than the mere physical maintenance of their families." (Margolis, 1984: 119) The home was her arena, and she was being described as naturally suited to the responsibility of its maintenance and the care of her family. Few men or women challenged these cultural definitions unless driven by economic need.

More than a century ago a group of American feminists identified the isolation of housework in individual households as a contributing cause of women's subordination. (Gilman, 1898) These women, whom Hayden (1981) called "material feminists," challenged two characteristics of industrial capitalism: "the physical separation of household space from public space, and the economic separation of the domestic economy from the political economy." (Hayden, 1981: 1) For these women the solution was to collectivize housework, reorganizing both the work and the workplace. Their proposals included communal nurseries, laundries, kitchens and eating areas on one hand, and multifamily, kitchenless houses on the other. Their goal was to mechanize and socialize domestic labour. Since they defined home and family as women's concerns, their reforms focused on the idea that women should assume control over these areas. Thus they did not see, as many women do today, spousal sharing of domestic labour as a solution.

Between 1890 and 1920, some 5000 American women and men participated in experiments to socialize domestic work. They organized consumer co-operatives, including dining clubs and cooked-food delivery services. They designed kitchenless houses, multifamily residential units with facilities for communal cooking and housekeeping. They experimented with public and co-operative kitchens—the first of which opened in Boston in 1890. Magazines such as *Women's Home Companion* and *Ladies Home Journal* joined the campaign by promoting kitchenless houses and co-operative home-service clubs. But by the 1920s, several important social forces combined to frustrate the initiatives and innovations of the material feminists. The growth of monopoly capitalism; with that, the movement of homes and factories to the suburbs and government support of home ownership (in part to stabilize the industrial work force) changed the face of the urban environment, alleviating the crowded conditions of the urban core. By the 1920s the mass production of refrigeration, washing machines, electric appliances, vacuums, and so on and the utilities to power them were generally available to individual households. Consumer credit was introduced in the 1920s making these products available to more households. Home ownership through long-term mortgages became a standard of success and stability, tying men to the labour force and women to the home. Appliance and automobile manufacturers and the building and advertising industries seemed to conspire to reinforce a gendered division of labour in the family. Magazines were influenced by the growing impact of advertising on their industry and began to actively promote consumption, particularly of home appliances. "Housework became conceptualized as a personal task made easier by the purchase of an ever-increasing array of products which women bought because they wished to care for their families in the best, most modern way possible." (Rosenberg, 1986b: 94) The ideal of the individual household, bolstered as it was by the notion of dual spheres and the increased affordability of products to make it more welcoming, was too well entrenched to be successfully challenged by the material feminists. Their ideas remain as radical today as when they were first proposed.

The domestic science movement was far more influential than material feminism in determining the future of household labour. The domestic science movement was born of the concerns that preoccupied reformers in the late nineteenth and early twentieth centuries. Middle-class women were motivated by their belief in the need for proper standards of homemaking. "The recently discovered germ theory of disease propagation made dirty clothes or a dirty house seem tantamount to family neglect, as public health nurses and doctors tied childhood illness and high infant mortality rates to mother's ignorance of the need to keep their households and children clean." (Prentice *et al.*, 1988: 122–123) By applying principles of scientific management to the home, women could learn to run their households efficiently, taking advantage of the technological improvements that were increasingly available to them. Training was key, and so there was great support for teaching young women the principles of nutrition and hygiene.

As appliances, prepared foods, cleaning products, and no-iron clothing became available and their relative cost dropped, they became common features of Canadian homes. But technology has been a double-edged sword. Clearly, housework is easier now, but women's economic contribution to the household is less obvious and has become less valued. From the 1920s until the 1960s the responsibilities of housework increasingly focused on managing consumption. Because fewer homes employed domestic servants, middle-class housewives welcomed the appliances and prepared foods that made housework easier. In articles and advertising, women's magazines emphasized the benefits of labour-saving products for improving housekeeping standards (Fox, 1990) and allowing more time to devote to husbands and children.

HOUSEWORK AND MOTHERWORK TODAY

Housewives today, regardless of their employment status, assume responsibility for child care and household management. They do most of the shopping, cooking, and cleaning, and they co-ordinate the family's activities. Housework is their responsibility, whether they do it themselves or arrange for it to be done by others. Most of these activities, from monitoring homework to running errands, from car-pooling to entertaining business associates, falls outside of what we normally call work. For women, it is the intangible parts of housework like giving emotional support, the care of young and old family members, or the creation of a pleasant living atmosphere that women find most satisfying, yet these are generally dismissed as what women *are*, not what they *do*.

"Motherwork is the culturally organized set of tasks that are part of feeding, clothing, nurturing and socializing a child (or children) until he or she can leave home and become self-supporting." (Rosenberg, 1986a: 40) Although conception and birth are highly regulated by law and medical practice, once a child is born, child care is a private affair. It is also hard work. Caring for infants is demanding, physically and emotionally, and the experience bears little resemblance to the way motherhood is glorified in the media. Rosenberg (1987: 188), describing the incongruity women feel when faced with the demands of infant care, suggested the following analogy: "It's as if one were hired for a new job with the understanding that the job description would be so vast and so vague as to be undoable, that little assistance would be provided, and that any errors would be the employee's sole responsibility." Much is expected of mothers, but the work is not socially recognized (except by empty platitudes) or supported. "Even the concept of housework as work leaves what we do as mothers without a conceptual home." (Smith, 1979: 154)

Housework is no less time consuming now than it was when homes had few "labour-saving" appliances. Vanek (1974) found that housewives of the 1960s spent as much time doing housework as their grandmothers had, although they allocated their time differently. One of the most time-consuming of household jobs is shopping. By the 1970s, housewives were spending the equivalent of one working day a week shopping. (Vanek, 1974: 117) "The automobile brought with it the woman driver and the suburbs. The peddler disappeared and so did the milkman, replaced by the supermarket—and the woman who drove there to shop." (Cowan 1987: 172) In buying consumable products for the home, housewives support the enterprises that manufacture and distribute them. According to economist J.K. Galbraith (1974: 33), were it not for the service housewives perform as consumers, "all forms of household consumption would be limited by the time required to manage such consumption—to select, transport, prepare, repair, maintain, clean, service, store, protect, and otherwise perform the tasks that are associated with the consumption of goods." "Housework makes it *possible* [emphasis added] for people to be clothed, bathed, fed and refreshed." (Rosenberg, 1986a: 40)

In part, the increased amount of time spent shopping reflects a change in retailing. Economies of scale gave chain stores an edge over independents, and in their effort to compete, independents were obliged to introduce cost-cutting measures, including the introduction of self-service and the elimination of home delivery. (Glazer, 1987: 242–243) It was certainly more cost effective for retailers to substitute the labour of housewives for the labour of clerks. Advertisers encouraged self-service shopping by playing on the idea of choice (*Ibid.*: 245), an illusion that is maintained despite the increased concentration of ownership. For example, three corporations make most of the home cleaning and soap products available on the market today. They all produce a long list of products that are essentially indistinct, yet consumers are bombarded with testaments about the superiority of product X over product Y. "The real aim of advertising is not to promote Tide over Cheer, but to constantly assert the need for these products." (Rosenberg, 1986b: 97)

The effort women devote to housework depends to some extent on their families' economic resources. When inflation or unemployment reduces the family purse, household labour is intensified. In the early years of industrialization, working-class wives found ways to stretch and augment family income by minimizing expenses and earning supplemental income. Then it was possible for women to cut costs by doing without prepared foods and store-bought clothes, or growing and preserving food, or earning extra cash by taking in boarders, doing laundry, or sewing. Today, women's magazines are full of suggestions about how housewives can "stretch" the family income. Invariably these suggestions require an increase in the amount of time spent cooking, sewing, shopping, and so on. But there are fewer opportunities for housewives today to save money by simply working harder. Indeed, if the Consumer Price Index is an indication, sewing clothes, or making food "from scratch" is *more* costly. (Armstrong, 1984: 104) Although housewives can save money by shopping carefully, doing their own cleaning and mending, and so on, they will not make an appreciable difference to their standard of living unless they enter the labour force.

For full-time housewives, financial insecurity is a key issue. As housewives, women are financially dependent on the ability and goodwill of a provider. If the breadwinner is unable to work, loses his job, dies, or if the marriage breaks up, full-time housewives face considerable financial hardship. For the most part, they have little control over the economic conditions of their lives. Without an income of their own, they are not in a position to provide for their own economic security. Most housewives find it very difficult to translate their homemaking experience into labour-force equivalents. They receive little economic recognition for the work they have done raising children or supporting their husband's career. No-fault divorce has worsened the lot of many housewives. (Weitzman, 1985) The majority of "displaced homemakers" face two unsavory options: social assistance or a low-paying, low-skilled job. As we shall see in Chapter 6, this description fits the jobs most employed women hold. The older a woman is, the more she is economically vulnerable

In her study of working-class families in Flin Flon, Manitoba, Luxton (1980: 168) described the frustration housewives face because they lack control over the cost of purchases or the money they are allotted to buy them. For these women choices were further restricted because they lived in a one-industry town. Three-quarters of the women in Luxton's study responded to family financial difficulties by taking in work. Most of these women, like generations before them, took in boarders to supplement family income or provide a source of pocket money. Others provided child care, took in laundry, baked, gave haircuts or home perms, sewed, knitted, gave lessons, or sold products such as Avon or Tupperware. Activities like these are not restricted to working-class communities; middle-class communities have well established "hidden economies" based on women's labour. In suburban communities many women who do not have full-time jobs babysit, teach crafts, music, kindergym, women's fitness, or sell a variety of products through home parties.

Contrary to what we might think, Duffy, Mandel and Pupo (1989) found full-time housewives were not more traditional in their thinking than employed mothers. Their decision to work at home was not influenced by traditional socialization, nor did they believe that women generally should be at home. (*Ibid.:* 50–52) These women expected to re-enter the labour force and simply felt the benefits of staying home in the short run outweighed the costs. However, the decision to be a full-time housewife was more complex than simply weighing costs and benefits. It depended on the availability of alternatives for employment and child care, economic need, and spousal support. Not surprisingly, many women feel considerable ambivalence about housework. While housewives found much of the work to be dull and repetitive, they derived a great deal of satisfaction from "being there" for their children. They also appreciated that they had more job control than employed mothers. On the other hand, housework and motherwork *are* stressful, and can be dangerous as well. (Rosenberg, 1986a, has carefully documented the physical dangers of home-cleaning and other products and appliances used regularly by housewives and domestic workers.) Two-thirds of Kome's (1978, 1982) Canadian sample said that they would be happier doing something else. They had little time for themselves and many were bored. Many full-time housewives feel isolated and suffer from low self-esteem. As more women enter the labour force, the isolation of the full-time housewife is increased. (Ferree, 1980)

WOMEN'S DOUBLE DAY

Increasing numbers of women combine domestic and paid work. Now the typical married woman is in the paid labour force, and full-time housewives are a minority. In 1988, 59.1 per cent of married women and 65.9 per cent of mothers (married and unmarried) of young children were in the labour force. (Women in Canada, 1990: 79–80) Three-quarters of employed women work full-time. Employed housewives manage by soliciting help from husbands and children; subcontracting as much work as they can afford to; redefining their needs; relying more heavily on convenience foods and meals out; and squeezing the remaining work into the time available. They do this juggling because generally speaking the *organization* of housework has been unaffected by technical innovations or married women's labour-force participation. In a content analysis of a new magazine for employed women, Glazer (1980b) found that solutions to the dilemma of how to manage a job and cope with housework and child care depended on women's initiative. Women could increase efficiency by intensifying their work, delegating, or hiring others to do certain jobs. Very clearly, household efficiency is assumed to be a woman's responsibility. Women have adjusted the rhythm of their lives to the demands of paid work, but there has been no reciprocal adjustments on the part of husbands. And husbands are not given any encouragement to change by a society that blithely assumes that individual families are responsible for the care and maintenance of their members. Most domestic work done in private households and most of the hours spent shopping, running errands, cooking, doing laundry, and cleaning are spent by women. Even child care (which was brought into the public sphere more than a century ago with compulsory education) is a private family arrangement. Only 13 per cent of children of employed mothers in Canada are cared for in regulated day care.

In most families it falls on the shoulders of women to get the housework done or supervise a substitute. Studies done in Canada (Meissner *et al.*, 1975; Michelson, 1985; Kome, 1978, 1982) confirm that married men spend far less time doing housework and caring for children than married women. The suggestion that husbands may require more housework than they contribute (Hartmann, 1981: 381) will be no surprise to many wives. Hochschild (1989) averaged estimates from the major studies of the hours spent in paid employment, doing housework, and taking care of children for married men and women. She found that women work roughly 15 hours a week more than men—which amounts to an extra month of twenty-four hour days a year! "Most women work one shift at the office or factory and a 'second shift' at home." (*Ibid.*: 4) Not surprisingly, employed women have less discretionary time than either employed men or homemakers. They also sleep less and consequently are more apt to suffer from physical and emotional exhaustion.

To be sure, two-career couples with high-paying jobs and paid household help manage relatively well. But these couples are a minority. Most working couples can't afford the luxury of a nanny or a housekeeper, so they must cope by squeezing the work into the time available. When women hire others to babysit or do housework, they face a different kind of dilemma. For many women, these services are expensive in comparison to their own paycheques. Yet the poor pay received by babysitters and housekeepers reinforces the low status of the work and further exploits the women who do it.

"Women are apparently not, for the most part, able to translate their wages into reduced work weeks, either by buying sufficient substitute products of labour or by getting their husbands to do appreciably more housework." (Hartmann, 1981: 381) In some cases, women are unwilling to upset the fragile balance of their relationship by pressuring husbands to do more work. Although the relative size of his paycheque is not the determining factor in the extent to which husbands contribute to housework, couples cannot help but recognize their relative economic power. The wage gap and the inequitable consequences of divorce represent what Hochschild (1989: 252) calls a "tacit threat." At least one woman in Luxton's (1986a) study of two-earner, working-class families had been beaten for suggesting that her husband help with domestic chores. While few women suffer consequences this severe, all housewives have the extra job of soliciting "help." Because our culture is ambivalent about men's responsibilities to share domestic work, wives are obliged to negotiate what help they can. This negotiating work simply adds to an already stressful and responsibility-packed day. Husbands, for the most part, resist the extra burden, playing on their incompetence and inexperience. Some women find it's just not worth the effort. (Luxton, 1986a) Others find they are obliged to be manipulative to overcome the passive resistance of their spouse and are understandably resentful. (Hochschild, 1989; Luxton, 1986a) "If women want their husband's to begin doing domestic labour, they must be prepared to take responsibility not only for overcoming male resistance but also for helping men overcome both the accumulated years of inexperience and the weight of traditional assumptions about masculinity." (Luxton, 1986a: 26) Not surprisingly, very few couples actually *share* housework: only about 20 per cent of the couples in Hochschild's study did. In their cases, both had made career sacrifices, and neither had much leisure or personal time. On the other hand, these couples were happier than couples where domestic work was not shared.

It is no wonder that in two-income households pressure to share housework is a contributing cause of marital tension. (Blumstein and Schwartz, 1983) "In his Toronto study of quarrels during the first five years of marriage, family counsellor Ed Bader was surprised to find housework emerged as the number-one problem, causing more squabbles than sexual differences, in-laws or money problems." (Kome, 1982: 19) Hochschild (1989: 189–190) found the problem of the "second shift" affected both men and women, although the strains were greater for women because they worked harder. Husbands who share housework do so at some cost to their careers and their personal time; those who don't help are affected indirectly by the resentment and detachment of their overworked wives. One of the most interesting findings of Hochschild's research was the importance of *recognizing* spouses' efforts at home. "When couples struggle, it is seldom simply over who does what. Far more often, it is over the giving and receiving of gratitude." (*Ibid*.: 18)

Recent studies show a shift in attitude toward sharing housework, if not behaviour. In 1976, 57 per cent of Canadians felt that husbands should share housework. In 1986, most Canadians (81 per cent), men and women alike, felt this way. (The Canadian Gallup Report, March 10, 1986) On the other hand, the same survey found that more husbands *say* they help than wives say they *get* help. Many couples, it seems, believe in sharing housework, but few actually carry out this belief. Why are men so resistant to change? Is this a transitional stage as Hochschild (1989) suggests? Janet and Larry Hunt (1987) argue that the problem of male resistance may be more deeply rooted. The Hunts suggest that the movement of married women into the labour force has not been without cost to the quality of family life. Employed women have very little energy for the physical and emotional caretaking work wives did in the past. There are no adequate market substitutes for this kind of care, and men have not been able to fill the gap. Their days at work are equally stressful, they lack experience as caretakers, and they receive no social supports for their attempts. As the Hunts argue, unless both men and women see that family needs have been sacrificed to corporate interests, corporate interests will remain unchallenged and family life continue to erode.

THE VALUE OF HOUSEWORK

Although housewives receive room and board, clothing, a certain derivative social standing, and other socio-emotional rewards, they have no job security, no retirement, and no pension. Indeed, few homemakers ever "retire." Given that most men live out their lives in family settings, we can assume that for many women domestic work becomes more demanding with age because it inevitably includes the care of an ailing spouse. The Report of the Royal Commission on the Status of Women (1970: 40) recommended that changes be made in Canadian Pension Plans "so that the spouse who remains at home can participate in the Plan." This recommendation has not been implemented. Allowing voluntary contributions to C/QPP has been suggested as a way to acknowledge the economic contribution of housework and provide older women additional income security. Practically, however, the option would only be available to higher income families, and these are not the women at greatest risk. The 1983 Parliamentary Task Force on Pension Reform suggested that pension credits be assigned to homemakers for the years that they stayed home to care for children under eighteen, or for dependent, infirm adults. Now, women who leave the labour force to care for children under the age of seven receive continuous C/QPP coverage. (National Council of Welfare, 1990: 102)

In analyzing the financial implications of providing pensions for full-time homemakers, the National Council of Welfare (1984a) concluded that they would create more inequities than they alleviated. Affluent widows who were lifetime homemakers would benefit as much as low-income widows. Single women and women who have combined domestic work and labour-force participation would be ineligible, regardless of need. For these reasons, and because the number of full-time, full-life homemakers is declining, it seems more promising to provide for widowed homemakers in other ways. The fact that increases in need-based supplements to OAS have raised the standard of living for this group over the past decade makes a case for continued expansion of these benefits. Since 1987, C/QPP pension credits earned during marriage must be divided equally at divorce; if separated, wives and women whose common-law relationship has ended may apply for the splitting of credits. As demands for equitable divorces, homemakers' pensions, and other supplements increase, more attention has been paid to estimating the value of work performed at home.

Ironically, studies in both Canada and the United States find that housework receives a relatively high prestige score when compared to other occupations. Eichler's (1977b) Canadian study and Bose's (1980) American study found that housewives ranked in the middle of the prestige scale. On Eichler's scale, housewives were ranked as having equal or higher prestige than the 25 "leading" female occupations, with the exceptions of nursing and teaching. They were ranked higher than housekeepers by a considerable margin. Not surprisingly, a housewife's status is closely related to her husband's occupation. Wives of physicians had a score of 81.5 compared to a ranking of 37.1 for wives of elevator operators. On the other hand, *The Dictionary of Occupational Titles* published by the United States Department of Labour ranks some 22 000 occupations. "Each occupation is rated on a skill scale from a high of 1 to a low of 887. Listed at the 878 level are homemakers, foster mothers, childcare attendants, home health aides, nursery school teachers and practical nurses." (Scott, 1984: 317)

While not considered work by economists, household labour is the "world's largest service industry." (Kome, 1982) Since substantial contributions to the economy are provided by the services performed in the home, many people have argued that these should be included in calculations of the Gross National Product. The GNP is an annual calculation of the value (measured at market prices) of the goods and services produced in a particular society. The GNP is used by policymakers to measure cyclical changes in economic activity. Including housework would signal the value of the work performed and provide a data base for policy decisions. Since the value of some services currently included in GNP calculations are imputed, there is no reason not to include housework—the lion's share of which is done by women—as well. Estimates of the value of household work in Canada placed its value at between $131 and $138 billion for 1981. (Swainamer, 1986) This would constitute 35 to 40 per cent of our GNP and is consistent with estimates from other countries. Some opponents claim that the addition of housework would misrepresent economic well being and create problems when doing cross-national comparisons. Others object because an economic accounting of housework would be limited to those services that could be purchased in the market. Because there is no market equivalent for the intangible parts of housework, they would be excluded in the estimates. Yet these intangibles are the very skills housewives feel are their most important contributions.

Much of what constitutes housework, the cooking, cleaning, laundry, and errands, can be measured in terms of market value. There is no doubt that when the work is done publicly, it is indeed paid. There have been several attempts to catalogue the core tasks and the time spent doing housework to estimate the monetary value of housework.[1] Time-use studies usually estimate the replacement cost (that is, the hourly wage if the work is performed outside the home) of each separate function or household duty. One of the first of these estimates was done by the Chase Manhattan Bank in 1965 and published in a pamphlet entitled "What's a Wife Worth?"[2] According to the bank's figures, the average American housewife not employed outside the home spent a total of 99.6 hours a week at jobs such as nursemaid, laundress, cook and dishwasher, housecleaner, and maintenance person. The bank calculated the value of these services at the going rate and arrived at a weekly pay of $259.34, or an annual salary of $13 485.68—in 1965 dollars!

Proulx (1978) used time-budget data for Halifax and Toronto families to estimate the amount of time women spent doing housework. She found that full-time Canadian housewives with two children, the youngest of whom is in school, spent 49 hours a week doing housework. The annual estimated replacement cost in 1977 dollars was $9742.64. One of the difficulties in calculating these estimates is that housewives often perform several functions simultaneously. Mothers of young children cook, shop, clean, wash and iron, all while caring for their children. Such overlaps are often left out of replacement cost estimates. More fundamentally, trying to fit housework into traditional occupational models misses the essence of how women define their work. (DeVault, 1987: 179)

For over a century it has been argued by some feminists that women, like any other service workers, ought to be paid for their household work.[3] There can be no doubt that payment for housework would be a concrete recognition of the social value of the work. Respondents in Kome's Canadian study felt that the lack of remuneration for housework meant that "the rest of the world, the family and they themselves undervalue their work." (Kome, 1978: 38) Payment for housework would acknowledge the value of childrearing, emotional support, and the countless other services

---

[1] For a detailed discussion of ways of estimating the value of housework see Hawrylyshyn (1978). The two most common methods are replacement cost and opportunity cost. Replacement cost evaluates the hourly wage of each task if the work is done outside the home. Opportunity cost is established by what a woman might earn if she were employed outside the home. Potential earnings are determined by education, qualifications, and previous work experience.

[2] This article has been frequently reprinted. It is found in Evelyn and Barry Shapiro, *The Women Say/The Men Say*. (New York: Dell Publishing Co., 1979)

[3] Manitoba was the first province to introduce Family Allowance (or Mother's Pensions as they were then called) in 1916. These were small subsidies to help needy widows. Divorced and unmarried mothers were not generally eligible. The other provinces followed Manitoba's lead, until the program as a whole was taken over by the federal government in 1944. At that time, Family Allowance became a universal payment.

housewives perform—not only for their families, but for society as a whole.

Opponents argue that paying for housework is regressive. Lopate (1974) suggested five reasons women ought not devote their energies to this issue. First, such emphasis detracts attention from investigating the nature of the work itself—including alternative arrangements for doing it. Second, the strongest demand for payment for housework came from Italy, where the labour-force participation of women is far lower than in North America. Third, payment for housework would not essentially alter the existing class structure and implementing such measures creates additional tax burdens. Fourth, Lopate argues, women need not have their labour transformed into a commodity to have its value accepted. Finally, she argues that payment for housework does nothing to alter the existing sexual division of labour.

Eichler (1988: 250) has suggested a way out of this dilemma. The first strategy is to separate the socially useful work from the privately useful work that housewives perform and ensure state support for the former. The second strategy is to provide a safety net of short-term policies (labour force re-entry programs, economic support for widows) to compensate women for the structural disadvantage they have experienced.

In the 1970s, feminists anxious to establish a material basis for women's oppression, tried to analyze domestic labour in Marxist terms by focusing on the productive and reproductive value of housework. (Armstrong and Armstrong, 1985) Some argued that by producing the next generation of workers and socializing them appropriately, women did create labour power. It was also argued that women's domestic work maintained the present work-force, and their cooking and sewing created consumable products for the home. Although the domestic labour debate was abandoned before it was resolved, European women, sparked by pamphlets written by Selma James and Mariarosa dalla Costa, formed the Wages for Housework Campaign in the early 1970s. This group, which now has an international following, has the goal of gaining recognition and compensation for the unwaged household and community work women do. At the 1985 Decade for Women Conference in Nairobi, this group successfully co-ordinated an initiative to include women's unpaid work in GNP calculations. The job of implementing the decision remains. In April 1989, a bill to include women's unwaged work in Britain's GNP was introduced.

CONCLUSION

Mothers and housewives are not a homogenous group. While most have in common the responsibility for housework, their working conditions will vary with household income, the number and ages of children, the presence or absence of a spouse, his or her willingness or unwillingness to share the workload, and the nature of work-force demands. Very few women now are housewives for the long term. Social and economic conditions are such that this is rarely a viable option. Most women have labour-force experience before they become mothers and return to the labour force soon after the child's birth. Women now take fewer and shorter breaks from paid employment to care for children. The relentless burden of the double day is thus felt most by mothers of young children who are in the labour force full-time. In a sense, employed mothers pay the price of overwork now for long-term economic security. If their marriage ends, because of either death or divorce, they will be less financially vulnerable than women with little labour-force experience. At retirement, they will be less subject to the risks of poverty faced by older women now because they will draw on their own pensions.

Although many men are more involved in childrearing than fathers were in the past, we are a long way from a situation where shared family and domestic responsibilities is the norm. Nor has the organization of housework changed substantially. Typically the routine care and feeding of family members is carried out in private households, and this work is orchestrated or done by women. Unless we challenge the organization of domestic work, as the material feminists did a century ago, we are left to conclude that the solution to the double day depends on women's ability to solicit help. Some women successfully enlist "help," and these couples say they are happier. But for many women soliciting help is hard work. The fact that women continue to do household work, regardless of employment status recreates a gendered division of labour. Women, men, employers, and policymakers act as if this is the expectation. Children grow up expecting the pattern to repeat for them.

As described in Chapter 2, the ideology of separate spheres and the ideology of motherhood developed in response to particular economic conditions in the nineteenth century. The idea that women were naturally best suited to mothering and homemaking and men to paid work was the core of this belief. The fight for a family wage and for protective legislation governing women's paid work were framed in this context. Although economic reality contradicted the ideology of separate spheres for many families, this reality did not undermine its strength. Women's double day is a legacy of this thinking. Indeed women have always had a double day of productive work and work for the home.

> Even during the purported height of dual spheres, many women participated in productive work throughout their lives, but the location of that work in the home, in a husband's business, or on a family farm reduced its social visibility. Thus men's and women's spheres were never fully separated, except for some white, native-born, middle-class couples. (Bose, 1987: 282)

The economic inequality in the labour force perpetuates women's double day. The size of the wage gap means that family economic prospects are enhanced when men devote their energies to paid employment. Male resistance to household work is therefore (in part) structured by workplace demands. Because men typically earn more, they will risk more if they violate workplace norms by imposing family needs and schedules on work routines. Unless we challenge this aspect of the structure of work so that men are free to father, mothers will never be free of their double day. The segregated labour force, the wage gap, and workplace policies that make mothering but not fathering easier recreate a gendered division of labour at home and reinforce women's economic dependence in the long run.

Women's responsibility for domestic labour is the backdrop for the examination of women's labour-force participation in the following two chapters. Most women anticipate and participate in paid work in the context of the double day. They, their husbands, and their employers assume that it will be so. For women it is a vicious circle.

5 HISTORICAL TRENDS IN WOMEN'S PAID EMPLOYMENT

The changing economic role of women is perhaps the most important change in the lives of Canadian women in the twentieth century. Women's labour-force participation rates have increased from 14.4 per cent in 1901 to 57.4 per cent in 1988. Yet for the most part, women continue to work in a limited range of jobs for which they receive low pay compared to men. In order to understand how well established these patterns of segregation and low pay are, we will begin by stepping back in time. This chapter will describe women's paid work from the mid-nineteenth century until the mid-twentieth century; Chapter 6 will focus on present patterns. An important undercurrent in both chapters is the way women's employment has responded to economic fluctuations and the changing demands of the labour force. The first part of this chapter looks at general trends in women's employment; the second part focuses on particular occupations —domestic servants, garment workers, teachers, clerical, and sales personnel. The first two jobs, both extensions of homemaking activities, were typically done by working-class women. Teaching, clerical, and sales jobs were originally done primarily by men. Rapid expansion (in the case of clerical work) and low pay (in the case of teaching) led to the recruitment of women. In the space of a few years they became established as work appropriate for women. Before discussing these, and the economic shifts that led to women's employment in these particular fields, we will discuss some of the difficulties of doing any historical analysis of women's work.

HISTORICAL ANALYSIS: PROBLEMS AND PROSPECTS

Canadian history, as usually told, is the history of men of British origin; a history of public life in which few women participated. (Burnet, 1986: 2) What women did was not (until recently) a subject of particular interest. To study the history of women's work is to encounter the same problems feminists in all fields of study have experienced. On one hand is the straightforward need to redress the balance by focusing on neglected areas of study. But to write a compensating history is only part of the goal. The aim is to write a history of women from women's point of view. The more we understand the world view of the data collectors and the constraints of the data collection system, the more expertly we can assess the evidence. In the past, sociologists have been accused of uncritical acceptance of secondary analyses done by historians. Familiarity with the data will enable us to avoid this in future.

TABLE 5.1
FEMALE POPULATION AND LABOUR-FORCE PARTICIPATION, CANADA, 1901–1961

Year	Female Population (000s)	Labour-Force Participation Rate
1901	1 957	14.4%
1911	2 521	16.6%
1921	3 184	17.7%
1931	3 875	19.4%
1941	4 097	22.9%
1951	4 792	24.4%
1961	5 962	29.3%

Source: Statistics Canada, 1982.

The most systematic data on women's paid work are found in the Canadian decennial census and in the monthly Labour Force Surveys. The first census was taken in 1851. At that time Canada was a British colony with a population of 2.5 million. More than 85 per cent of the population lived in rural areas. Because most people lived and worked on independent farms, employment statistics were not systematically gathered in the first enumerations. Although data was gathered in selected communities, it was not until 1891 that labour-force information was collected for the country as a whole. In 1891, 11.4 per cent of Canadian women over fourteen were gainfully employed. Subsequent enumerations added information on correlates of female labour-force participation; immigration status in 1911; age in 1921; and marital status and pay in 1931. The Labour Force Survey, based on a sample of the population, was initiated in 1945. It was published quarterly until 1952, and monthly thereafter.[1]

Census data describe a gradual pattern of increased labour-force participation since 1901 (see Table 5.1). Since annual data was not collected until 1945, we do not know the extent to which participation rates responded to short-term economic shifts. During World War II, women's labour-force participation showed dramatic increases that are not reflected in the decennial census. It is quite likely that similar fluctuations exist for earlier periods, although we have know way of knowing their magnitude.

Although official surveys provide a great deal of information to the researcher, their use involves some serious drawbacks. The major difficulty is that census data underestimate women's economic activity. Unpaid labour in the home has never been included in labour-force statistics. Because of the nature of domestic day labour and sweatshop work, or sweat-

---

[1] The Canadian Labour Force survey is based on a sampling, by area, of the Canadian population; it currently includes 56 000 households. The survey is also the principal source of data on the seasonal and annual fluctuations that indicate how women's work is susceptible to economic shifts.

ing, it is likely that many women who did this work were not counted in official estimates. The same is true of women agricultural workers. Nor was it clear to census takers whether farm wives were *employed*. Two surveys conducted in Saskatchewan in June 1946 arrived at very different estimates of the number of female agricultural workers in the area. The labour-force survey estimate was 103 000. The census figure was 8000. (Pool, 1978) Notwithstanding such mechanical problems, these surveys provide a wealth of useful data.[2] But to understand the meaning of the work women have done, it is necessary to look to more qualitative sources.

In the last quarter of the nineteenth century, Canada was coping with the universal problems of newly industrializing countries. Politicians faced the dilemma of balancing the need to develop Canada's manufacturing industries with the demands of labour reformers. Between 1880 and 1930 there were several investigations of working conditions in mills and factories.[3] The employment of women and children was one of the is-

---

[2] Problems of definition abound. Both the census and the labour-force survey have been revised and updated. Changes in conceptualization create discontinuities and discrepancies in the data; the lack of standardization makes comparisons difficult. For example, the census has not always used the same definition of labour-force participation as has the labour-force survey. The census originally used the concept "gainfully employed"; the labour-force survey used the concept "labour force," which included those actively *looking* for work. In 1951, the census adopted the terminology of the labour-force survey and subsequently adjusted figures back to 1921. Although the resulting differences are small, the numbers do not coincide.

Changes in categorization present another problem. In 1951, the census examined sixteen occupational groups. They looked at thirteen in 1961 and at twenty-one in 1971. Furthermore, current systems of occupational classification tend to be sex-biased. (Pool, 1978) Multiple jobs are not categorized; persons with more than one job are classified according to the job at which they spend the most time, but we cannot estimate the extent to which women may combine part-time jobs to create full-time work.

[3] Some of the more important reports and commissions are:
- 1885: Royal Commission on the Sweating System in Canada
- 1889: Royal Commission on the Relation of Labour and Capital
- 1889: Royal Commission to Inquire into Industrial Disputes in the Cotton Factories of the Province of Quebec
- 1892: Scott, Jean Thomson, "The Conditions of Female Labour in Ontario." Toronto University Studies in Political Science
- 1909: Royal Commission on Cotton Factories' Industrial Disputes
- 1914: British Columbia Report on the Royal Commission on Labour
- 1916: Ontario Commission on Unemployment
- 1935: F.R. Scott and H.M. Cassidy, "Labour Conditions in the Men's Clothing Industry"
- 1938: Royal Commission on the Textile Industry
- 1970: Royal Commission on the Status of Women in Canada

sues addressed. These reports provide an insight into the meaning of women's work, although they are shrouded in Victorian images of women's proper place in society. Of the several commissions investigating the sweating system, mostly in the cotton and textile factories, the most thorough was the Royal Commission on the Relations of Labour and Capital of 1889. One unique aspect of the Labour Commission, as it was popularly called, was the effort made to solicit views from labour reformers and from men and women of the working class. The Labour Commission remains the most complete view of Canada's industrial activity of the late nineteenth century.[4]

A Canadian historian examined the two reports and four volumes of evidence of the Labour Commission to ferret out information about the work done by women. (Trofimenkoff, 1977a) Of the more than two thousand witnesses, only 102 women were called before the commission. Most of the women preferred to testify anonymously; and most needed encouragement to speak. Consequently, the report is much clearer about how men—commissioners, employers, or fellow labourers—viewed women's work than about how women themselves saw it. It is a challenge to sort out the perceptions of those who claim to speak for women from the perceptions of women themselves. The attitude of men toward women's factory work is clear from the evidence: reformers, trade unionists, employers, and fellow labourers saw women's employment as undesirable at best. The extent to which women shared this view is less clear.

Because official reports give us little of the flavour of working women's lives, historians have turned to journals, diaries, letters, magazines, newspapers, court transcripts, parish records, and any other available resource to find out more about women's day-to-day lives. These resources have been used in writing biographies, in studies of particular occupations, and in regional histories. They give us a better understanding of the sexual division of labour, and power and authority relations. The main drawback is that such accounts are scattered and representative of small segments of the population. Women who were literate, who enjoyed the luxury of leisure time, and who were motivated to communicate their experiences were few and far between on the Canadian frontier.

---

[4] Although the original report is not easily accessible, it was recently edited and reprinted. See Greg Kealey, editor, *Canada Investigates Industrialism* (Toronto: University of Toronto Press, 1973). The edition is a useful tool for anyone doing cross-cultural research into the early days of industrialism. The book's index contains page references for female labour.

WOMEN'S PAID WORK IN THE NINETEENTH CENTURY

Until Confederation, Canada was a sparsely populated colony whose economy was based on farming, fishing, lumbering, and fur trading. Ontario and Quebec were the most populous provinces and were the first to industrialize. In the last quarter of the nineteenth century massive immigration increased Canada's population. Immigrants were drawn to the frontier by the promise of land, and they were drawn to the cities by the prospect of work. Rural land shortages in Ontario and Quebec also encouraged urban or westward migration. Industrialization proceeded at an uneven pace—geographically and economically. Movement to the cities brought affluence to some and poverty to others. Home production continued to characterize rural settlements, while the cities of Montreal, Quebec, Kingston, Toronto, and Hamilton were developing centres of trade and commerce. It was not until well into this century that the majority of working people actually worked for wages. (Phillips and Phillips, 1983: 2)

In the nineteenth century, the rural economy was primarily based on home production, although only the most isolated farms were literally self-sufficient. Both men and women earned money to buy things the family did not produce themselves. Farmers earned seasonal income in the fur trade, lumbering, or fishing; their wives sold or exchanged any extra vegetables, butter, cheese, eggs, or whatever they produced. Unmarried daughters (and some widows and married women) worked in the homes of wealthier neighbours if their labour was not needed at home. In fact, Bose (1987: 271) argues that in pre-industrial United States, rural white and native American women were more likely than men to participate in the cash economy. As Canada became more urbanized and more industrialized, home production generally declined and with it women's economic contribution to the household. Married women lost the income-earning possibilities they previously enjoyed on family-operated farms. "In general there was a decline in skilled work for farm women and a resulting decline in the money a farm woman was able to earn, leaving her with little visible or recognized economic input." (Prentice *et al.*, 1988: 118)

The economic expansion in the last half of the nineteenth century created opportunities for paid employment for men and some single women. New immigrants and rural migrants moved to urban areas in search of work. Urban living and working conditions left much to be desired, and many working-class families lived on the edge of poverty. Average industrial salaries for male workers were not enough to support a family. (Phillips and Phillips, 1983: 7) It was not until the 1920s that male wages for unskilled work amounted to a family wage. (*Ibid.*: 18) Industrial accidents, illness, job insecurity, and economic recession meant that working-class families could not rely solely on the male breadwinner's earnings.

The interdependence of family members, which was a key to survival in rural Canada, was also crucial as working-class families adjusted to an economy based on wage labour. "Gainfully employed daughters who lived in their parents home committed a high proportion of their income to the family economy underwriting not only their share of the family budget but also the educational costs of their brothers." (Danylewycz, 1987: 67–68)

In 1931, when the marital status of the female labour force was first calculated, only 10 per cent of employed women were married. Presumably, the numbers were even smaller in the nineteenth century. Katz and Davey's (1976) study of Hamilton, Ontario, found that between 1851 and 1871, 97 to 98 per cent of employed women were single. Hamilton may not be typical because it did not have many textile manufacturers. A higher proportion of married women worked in the textile manufacturing centres of Quebec. Jean Scott's (1892) study of working women in Ontario found few employed married women, although some did seasonal work in the canning industry. Without modern conveniences, including utilities, domestic work was far too taxing to allow women to work outside the home. Even in the most needy families wives worked only as a last resort. Indeed there were often legal restrictions placed on the employment of married women. If the family needed money, married women did jobs that could be managed in the home. Women tended to move in and out of the labour force, buffeted by childbearing, family need and the availability of work. Nevertheless, women's labour-force participation was more widespread than official statistics suggest. Employment statistics do not include the thousands of women who did day work in other women's homes or who worked in their own homes keeping boarders, sewing, doing laundry, or piece-work for the garment trade.

During this period, child labour was more important than maternal employment as a supplementary source of income. Cities like Montreal depended on both child labour and an extensive "putting out" system (home production) involving all family members. "Factories advertised for families ... offering the inducement that children would remain under the family's supervision while allowing the mother to earn an income, although this was really designed to get a whole family of workers for the price of one living wage." (Phillips and Phillips, 1983: 8) The employment of women and children was highest in textiles and food processing where opportunities were greater. In 1871, women and children made up 42 per cent of the industrial workforce in Montreal and 34 per cent in Toronto. (Phillips and Phillips, 1983: 8) Conceding the reality of women's employment, several Roman Catholic religious orders in mid-nineteenth century Quebec established child-care facilities to enable women to work in factories. (Cross, 1977)

In urban areas there were more employment opportunities for single women, an increasing number of whom worked until marriage. The 1921 census was the first to calculate labour-force statistics by age. In that year, 70 per cent of working women were between the ages of 14 and 24 years. The majority of employed single women worked in domestic service until well into the twentieth century. In the last half of the nineteenth century, an increasing number of single women worked in manufacturing and a significant number were teachers. Factory work was preferable to domestic service because it gave women more freedom. Later, as clerical and sales opportunities expanded, single women moved into these jobs as well. Otherwise, employment opportunities for women were very narrow. Some single women moved west, attracted by the demand for farm help, domestic servants, teachers, and we may assume, the possibility of marriage. But there were more opportunities in eastern cities and urban life promised more independence and more excitement. Low salaries were justified because women worked in unskilled jobs and because their employment was a short-term interlude before marriage. Because so many single men were attracted by opportunities on the frontier, single women outnumbered single men in urban centres in the east. Many of these women never married, so for them labour-force participation was anything but temporary. Wherever they worked, women earned less than 60 per cent of what men earned, even when, as was often the case, they worked longer hours.

The following account of the employment status of women in the community of Kingston, Ontario, in 1861 (Davitt, *et al.*, 1974: 75) gives a good indication of the kinds of jobs women did in nineteenth-century Canada.

There were 7091 women and girls:

- 1200 of whom were in school
- 75 of whom were dressmakers and tailors
- 30 of whom were milliners
- 22 of whom were seamstresses
- 32 of whom were teachers
- 9 of whom were laundresses
- 2 of whom were midwives
- 538 of whom were servants

Unmarried Roman Catholic women had an important option not available to their Protestant sisters. Convents in Quebec provided social services and education for young women. Entering convent life offered an alternative to marriage or spinsterhood as well as a meaningful vocation and the chance for social mobility. Convents were also attractive because they looked after the lifelong material needs of their members and cared for them in illness and old age. (Danylewycz, 1987) The decision to enter a convent was not irreversible: young women could enter as novitiates and leave if they weren't happy. In the last half of the nineteenth century an increasing number chose the convent life over marriage. By 1921, 9.1 per cent of single women in Quebec were members of religious communities.

(*Ibid.*: 17) For women who wanted to teach, the working conditions in convents were far better than in public schools where salaries were low and lay-offs common. Since convents were self-managed, sisters had unique opportunities to exercise leadership or work in fields like carpentry or engineering if they chose. Teaching sisters had the chance to move beyond the classroom to administrative posts. (*Ibid.*: 96) There were also opportunities for educational advancement. Sister St-Leonard du Port Maurice was the first women in North America to receive a Ph.D.

THE EARLY TWENTIETH CENTURY

The early years of the twentieth century were prosperous ones in Canada. Industrial expansion and corporate mergers created the foundations of our present economic structure. Larger businesses employing more people made record-keeping an increasingly important function. Inventions such as the telephone and the automobile changed the nature of urban life. Health and educational facilities served more and more Canadians. The labour market expanded and the number of women in the labour force climbed as more women were recruited to clerical and sales jobs.

The prosperity of this period ended just before the World War I. Canada was in an economic recession when war broke out. For the first years of the war, additional labour requirements were filled by the existing unemployed. Labour shortages during World War I were never as acute as during World War II. According to a 1916 Ontario Commission on Unemployment, there were an estimated eight to ten thousand unemployed women in Ontario in 1914 and 1915. It was not until 1916 that it became necessary to actively recruit women. Conscription did not begin until June 1917. Although it is generally believed that wartime employment opened new doors for women, this view is somewhat exaggerated. To be sure, there were jobs available for female workers during the latter half of the war, but the demand was temporary and mostly in occupations such as office work and light factory work. Some women did work in munitions, but this was the exception rather than the rule. Conditions of work deteriorated during this period. Employers used the war as an excuse to lengthen the working day for both men and women. Wages were low for all workers, but women were paid less than men.

Following the war, Canada experienced another period of prosperity before the Depression of the 1930s. Clerical and sales work began to overtake domestic service or manufacturing as the most suitable jobs for women. By 1931, half of all employed women worked in service or clerical jobs. By the 1920s it had become quite acceptable for middle-class women to work for a few years before marriage. As Canadian women's magazines of the 1920s suggested, a short period in the labour force was a good experience. It would make women better wives and mothers and prepare them for the "exigencies of spinsterhood and early widowhood." (Vipond, 1977: 118) "The 1916 Report of the Ontario Commission on Unemployment stated that one of the advantages of nursing as a career was that a trained nurse was better fitted to marriage by virtue of her training in health care, diet, cleanliness and so on." (Coburn, 1974: 155) Employment was understood to be temporary and secondary to the ultimate goal of marriage. Magazines made it clear that married working women were exceptional. "Time after time when a proficient businesswoman was mentioned in a magazine article, it was pointed out that despite her success she was `still at heart a woman'." (Vipond, 1977: 123) On the surface it seemed that employment opportunities for women expanded. But, domestic service was still the leading job category, and whatever work women did, they received less pay than men.

Canadian magazines in the 1920s showed no ambivalence regarding pay. "In general, the popular magazines simply reported that the differential existed, warned women to accept it and not be resentful, and explained why it was so." (Vipond, 1977: 119) The reasons given were standard: women were temporary members of the labour force; men had to earn more in order to support their families. The plight of the woman working to support herself or others was ignored.

The Depression meant a backward step for women's economic independence. Subtle and not-so-subtle pressure deterred women's employment. Public opinion supported the idea that women who were otherwise supported ought not work; they would be taking a job from someone with dependents to support. Because no yearly national data are available for this period, it is difficult to estimate the effect of the Depression on women's employment. The statistics that are available indicate that women's unemployment rates were lower than men's. But married women are often excluded from unemployment figures, as were women who did day work or sweating. We should hesitate to conclude, therefore, that the Depression was less difficult for women than for men.

The next section looks at conditions of work for women during this period of industrial growth. Without access to training or education, women worked in jobs that were either natural extensions of their homemaking and nurturing skills or that were rapidly expanding and in need of an inexpensive labour pool. The strongest motivation to hire women was that they were cheap. If they became organized, or otherwise bothersome, employers would simply replace them. The assumption that their work was temporary provided a rationale for paying women low wages. Women, too, assumed that their work was temporary, and they were for the most part not in a position to act collectively to improve their working conditions.

In 1891, the ten leading female occupations were: servant, dressmaker, teacher, farmer, seamstress, tailoress, saleswoman, housekeeper, laundress, and milliner. (Department of Labour, 1964: 1) From 1901 to 1971, six

TABLE 5.2

PERCENTAGE DISTRIBUTION OF WORKING WOMEN BY LEADING OCCUPATIONAL GROUPS, CANADA,[1] 1901–1961

Occupational Group	1901[4]	1911	1921	1931	1941[5]	1951	1961
	%	%	%	%	%	%	%
Clerical	5.3	9.4	18.7	17.7	18.3	27.5	28.6
Personal Service	42.0	37.1	25.8	33.8	34.2	21.0	22.1
Professional	14.7	12.7	19.1	17.8	15.7	14.4	15.5
Commercial and Financial	2.4	6.8	8.5	8.3	8.8	10.5	10.2
Manufacturing and Mechanical[2]	29.6	26.3	17.8	12.7	15.4	14.6	9.9
Other[3]	6.0	7.8	10.1	9.6	7.7	11.9	13.6
Total[3]	100.0	100.1	100.0	99.9	100.1	99.9	99.9

1 Includes Newfoundland (1951 on), but not Yukon and Northwest Territories.
2 Includes stationary enginemen and occupations associated with electric power production.
3 Includes armed forces.
4 10 years of age and over in 1901; 15 years of age and over 1911–1961.
5 Not including active service, 1941.

Source: Department of Labour, Canada: *Women at Work in Canada*, 1964: 28.

occupations accounted for at least 50 per cent of the Canadian female labour force: dressmakers and seamstresses, servants and maids, nurses, teachers, office workers, and saleswomen and clerks. (Calculated from Connelly, 1978: 92–93)

CONDITIONS OF WORK

DOMESTIC SERVICE

From the earliest years of European settlement, until World War II, domestic service was an important source of income for working-class women in Canada. In 1825, an estimated 14 per cent of the urban work force in Quebec were women. Most of these were domestic servants. (Lavigne and Stoddart, 1977: 131) In 1891, 41 per cent of the female labour force were domestic servants. (The corresponding figures for the next sixty years are: 1901, 34.3 per cent; 1911, 26.9 per cent; 1921, 18.1 per cent; 1931, 20.2 per cent; 1941, 17.9 per cent; 1951, 7.6 per cent.) Given the nature of the work, it is likely that these figures underrepresent the number of women doing domestic work. The turnover rate for domestics has always been high. The "servant problem" (shortage) existed as early as the 1870s in Montreal. (Cross, 1977: 71) Most domestics were young women who saw their work as a short-term way to support themselves until they married or found other work.

If annual figures of the number of domestics were accurately known, they would parallel other indices of the country's economic well-being. When jobs were plentiful, women chose factory work over domestic service. During times of economic recession (or times of personal crisis) women entered domestic service as other options dwindled. It was not unusual, especially during the Depression, for married women in the Finnish community to work as domestics and men to be "househusbands." (Lindstrom-Best, 1986: 36) Many domestics had little choice of occupation. They were drawn from a group that included immigrant women, workhouse children from Britain, and Canadian children who had no one to support them.

Even in the nineteenth century, Canadian women preferred factory or shop work to domestic service. Between 1851 and 1871 the percentage of employed women in Hamilton doing domestic work dropped from 72 per cent to 47 per cent. (Katz and Davey, 1976: S96) At the same time, the proportion of women doing industrial work rose to about one-third. Although the pay for domestic service was relatively good, since room and board were included, and domestic work was not subject to seasonal layoffs, most women found the conditions of work unattractive. They resisted the lack of privacy, companionship, and free time; the low status and long hours. (Scott, 1892; Leslie, 1974: 86) They had few opportunities to meet other young people and no possibility to advance. Some who remained in service for a long time lost the opportunity to marry and have their own families. Lindstrom-Best (1986: 43) suggests that the high rates of illegitimacy in Montreal in the 1930s may indicate that some women made a deliberate decision to have a child outside of marriage.

Canadian-born women were reluctant to enter domestic service and needed strong encouragement to do so. Major women's organizations, such as the National Council of Women, "championed the professionalization of domestic service." Their "support of the household science movement was motivated in part by the hope that the public school system might train girls for employment in bourgeois homes." (Stoddart and Strong-Boag, 1975: 41) It was, however, newly arrived immigrants who filled the need. By 1911, 35 per cent of all domestic servants were immigrants. (Phillips and Phillips, 1983: 12) Church groups, women's groups, and the government recruited and sponsored immigrant girls and women by offering passage loans and guarantees of employment. Domestic service took care of two of the pressing concerns of new immigrants: where to live and where to work. (Lindstrom-Best, 1986: 37) It also gave these young women a chance to learn Canadian customs. In the best cases, employers were surrogate families, but this was rare. The federal government bent immigrant regulations and worked with steamship booking agencies to make travel arrangements for young women who promised to work as domestics. Many travelled to Canada in conducted parties organized by groups like the British Women's Emigration Association. By the 1920s, the Canadian government had become active in all phases of recruitment.

> The new women's division of the Department of Immigration sent staff officers to Britain authorized to give final approval in the selection of British domestics. In Canada it established a chain of Women's Hostels to receive the domestics who travelled in conducted parties and were placed in situations by the new government employment service. (Barber, 1986: 61)

The largest group of immigrant domestics came from Britain—over 170 000 between 1900 and 1930. (Barber, 1986: 56)

Industrialization and the introduction of electricity and labour-saving equipment into private homes reduced the heavy demands of housework and the need for domestic help. Over time, fewer and fewer homes employed domestic servants. Domestic workers today have more independence than domestics had in the past, but the work is still isolated and unprotected. The work of cleaning women, nannies, and babysitters remains low status and poorly paid, and those who do it are vulnerable to exploitation. Since the number of European immigrants willing to do this work could not satisfy the demand, the Canadian government began in the 1950s to actively recruit Third World women. Currently, women entering Canada as domestics are given temporary employment visas which effectively ensure that they don't do other work. "In 1978, 12,483 temporary employment visas were issued for domestic work in Canada.... In 1982, there were more than 16,000 visas issued, despite the fact that unemployment in Canada had been rising at an alarming rate." (Silvera, 1983: 15)

The very nature of the job means that standard conditions of employment are difficult to impose. Legislation now covers wages and hours of work, but these are difficult to regulate. Many employers simply ignore the rules. Domestics are in a weak bargaining position because of their immigration status and because they live with their employers. The nature of the work and the working relationship remain insurmountable barriers to effective collective action.

SWEATING AND FACTORY WORK

The word "spinster" originally referred to the operators of spinning wheels: often unmarried women who lived with their parents or siblings and took on spinning as their contribution to the household. From the early years of the Industrial Revolution, textile and clothing manufacture were key sources of employment for women. Before the sewing machine appeared in Canadian homes in the 1860s, some women were employed as seamstresses, sewing by hand at home. The demand for hand-sewing decreased with the introduction of machine-made clothing. The ten leading occupations for women in 1891 included dressmaker, seamstress, tailoress, and milliner. Clothing was manufactured in factories, small shops, and private homes. Most of the sites were not regulated by Factory Acts, and working conditions were miserable. A good part of the industry was based on a system of subcontracting referred to as "sweating." Under the sweating system, women and children sewed in their own homes or in small shops for a middleman who sold the completed goods to a manufacturer. In some cases, collectors went from house to house picking up the finished products. Some women returned the work themselves, using baby carriages to carry the heavy bundles. Mackenzie King estimated that three-quarters of the clothing made in Montreal was produced under the sweating system, which employed an estimated ten thousand French and Jewish women. (Lavigne and Stoddart, 1977: 135) This fragmentation made it difficult to regulate wages or conditions of work. It also made it impossible for women to organize.

Sweating was controversial enough by the 1890s to warrant a parliamentary investigation. According to the Royal Commission on the Sweating System (RCSS), the number of women engaged in the ready-made garment industry exceeded the number of men. Sweat shops were poorly equipped and poorly ventilated, and many were fire hazards. Factory Inspector Brown, reporting to the RCSS in 1885, made the following comment: "I will tell you of a place; over the Army and Navy stores on King Street. I went into the shop and could hardly breathe for steam, heat and the smell from the gas irons. I could hardly even see the girls." Although he added that this situation was unusual, it seems that conditions had not improved by the time the Royal Commission on the Textile Industry (RCTI) published its report in 1938. "The physical working conditions in several sections of the textile industry appear very unpleasant to anyone visiting a plant for the first time." (RCTI, 1938) The Commission reported problems of dust, heat, humidity, fumes, and gases—problems that continue to present serious health hazards to the 200 000 women who work in the garment and textile industries in Canada today.

Women who sewed at home earned very little but had the one advantage of being able to care for young children. Even as some stages of textile manufacture became mechanized, the homework system continued because of the constant availability of a cheap source of labour. The market was subject to seasonal fluctuations, and so the work was sporadic. When demand was high, the hours were long, but there were often periods of unemployment. In many ways the conditions of homework have changed little in one hundred years. Women working in the garment industry today still do home sewing in conditions reminiscent of the nineteenth century. (Johnson, 1982; Gannage, 1986) The first steps to regulated homework in Canada were not taken until the 1930s.

The isolated nature of the work and the vulnerability of the workers still make homework a difficult industry to regulate. Homeworkers have always been drawn from the most vulnerable sectors of the labour force. They have little alternative but to accept the poor pay and appalling working conditions. "As a system of employment, the homework system is founded on economic need, cheap labour and a lack of available childcare services for working parents." (Johnson, 1982: 98) Most of the estimated 100 000 homeworkers in Canada today are immigrant women, many of whom speak neither English nor French, and who are unfamiliar with legislation governing their work.

Women factory workers have always been paid much less than men. In the nineteenth century, wages were insufficient for most women factory workers to live on their own. (Trofimenkoff, 1977a) In 1895, the chief inspector for Quebec reported that he found many young girls working from seventy-five to eighty hours a week; the weekly wage ranged from fifty cents to three dollars. When the Mayor of Toronto was asked by a Labour Commissioner if he believed that low wages would drive women to prostitution, the Mayor replied, "A good woman will die first." (Trofimenkoff, 1977a: 79) Women were customarily paid by the piece, and received no money when materials were not available or when the machinery broke down. Both the Labour Commission and the RCSS reported that a system of fining for fabricated flaws in the work was common. "A woman brings in her work. The foreman says 'That does not go,' and pretends to find some defect. He checks so much of her money. If she does not take what he gives her he says 'There is no more work for you'." (RCSS, 1885)

Working-class families were caught in a classic bind. Women and children were forced to work to augment the inadequate wages of men. Yet this reserve of cheap labour kept wages low. (Copp, 1974: 44) Out of necessity, women accommodated themselves to the fluctuating demands of the industry; they had no choice. As a consequence, their bargaining position was weak. Women workers often had to accept part-time work, piece-work, homework, and unskilled jobs in the labour-intensive garment industry. (Macleod, 1974: 309)

Reformers, including the NCWC, concentrated on eliminating child labour and protecting the health and morality of unmarried women.[5]

---

[5] None of the reforms suggested by the Royal Commission were carried out through Dominion legislation. Although seven Dominion factory bills were prepared between 1880 and 1886, none was passed. The reluctance to enact Dominion legislation was partly due to the laissez-faire orientation of the British North America Act, by which social legislation was considered outside the realm of the federal government. The lack of uniformity between the provinces in terms of labour legislation was another problem that existed well into the twentieth century. As late as 1919, a Dominion–Provincial Commission was appointed to study the matter of unifying and co-ordinating provincial legislation and establishing certain standards.

Factories employed female inspectors to monitor conditions, but their main concerns were to keep the sexes separated during working hours to ensure propriety and protect the morals of working women. Morality was thought to be a serious issue where men and women laboured under the same roof. Yet the Labour Commission of 1889 was forced to conclude that there were no signs of serious immorality in Canada's factories. But as Trofimenkoff (1977a) has pointed out, commissioners were not asked about morality; they were asked about factory conditions. Inspectors focused on such things as separate toilet facilities, seats (to protect reproductive organs during the long hours at work), and cleanliness. They supported measures such as different departure times for men and women. When commissioners were asked about sanitary conditions, they discussed sanitary conveniences. Separate closets for men and women became a virtual obsession, which tells us more about the middle-class Victorian world view than about factory conditions in the 1890s. (Trofimenkoff, 1977a) Commissioners neatly avoided the crucial social and economic questions raised by the factory system and women's place in it.

During the early years of industrialization working-class women worked in domestic service, sweating, or factory work. By the beginning of the twentieth century, women with formal education could add teaching, office work, or retail sales to their list of options. On the surface, these jobs conferred some status and better working conditions. Yet they had much in common with domestic and factory work.

WOMEN'S PROFESSIONS

The assumption that women's place was in the home provided a rationale for restricting educational opportunities. Women, it was thought at the time, were morally superior but physically and intellectually weaker than men. They would, it was believed, distract the male students. Consequently women were, for the most part, excluded from jobs that required advanced education or training. (Teaching was the single exception.) Generally women did not benefit from the expansion of higher education in Canada in the late nineteenth century. Indeed, women did not receive degrees until Mount Allison University became a degree-granting institution. Since women could not receive training in law, medicine, or commerce, they were effectively kept from practising. In the case of medicine, the exclusion of women was particularly ironic. Women had long assumed responsibility for the health of the family, and in the eighteenth century it was women who practised midwifery and surgery. Women like Emily Stowe, who wanted to practise medicine, had to go outside Canada to be trained. Her daughter was the first woman doctor to graduate from a Canadian medical school. Even with a medical degree, women had difficulty gaining clinical experience, and they had trouble attracting enough patients to earn a living. (Prentice *et al.*, 1988: 132)

Until the 1930s, nursing in Canada had more in common with domestic service than with other professions.[6] Most nurses came from working-class homes because the difficult working conditions and low pay made the work unattractive to middle-class women. Nursing schools were connected to hospitals and as such provided a constant source of unpaid labour for the institution. For example, in the early 1900s the entire staff of the Toronto General Hospital were unpaid nurses in training. (Coburn, 1974) This system provided limited job opportunities for graduate nurses. The majority did home nursing, and thus faced sporadic employment and long periods without work. The pay was low and, needless to say, the job held little security.

When Martha Hamm Lewis was admitted to teachers' training school in New Brunswick in 1849, she was instructed by her principal to "enter the classroom ten minutes before the male students, sit alone at the back of the room, always wear a veil, leave the classroom five minutes before the end of the lesson and leave the building without speaking to any of the young men." (MacLellan, 1972: 6) It was not until twenty-six years after Martha Lewis started teacher training that a woman received a university degree in Canada. Grace Anne Lockhart was awarded a Bachelor of Science degree from Mount Allison University—the first woman in the British Empire to earn one.

In December 1936, *Maclean's* magazine published an article entitled "Is the School-Marm A Menace?" The author, who had been a school principal for more than twenty years, began by voicing a general concern for the educational system. He identified the "weakest feature in the system" as "the woman teacher." "The sisters took that field and made it their own, partly to get away from household duties, partly for the salary and prestige, and largely because it gave them greater chances to land an eligible mate a cut above the village swain." The author described what he identified as the consensus of opinion of school superintendents and inspectors of women teachers. They were, he said, "Immature, exceedingly young, with a low standard of professional training, little or no cultural background, lacking experience and unable adequately to profit by experience with no vision and little professional pride." (Woollacott, 1936: 19)

In the first half of the nineteenth century, women who taught did so privately in their homes. Public teaching was a male responsibility. Later, as the household school declined, women moved into public-school teaching. By the 1880s, women dominated the teaching field. From 1895 until 1930, at least 75 per cent of elementary and secondary school teachers in Canada were women. (Statistics Canada, Historical Statistics of Canada, 1982) As demand rose and conditions improved, teaching again

---

[6] Florence Nightingale resisted the professionalization of nurses claiming that "nurses cannot be registered or examined any more than mothers." (Coburn, 1974: 156)

became an attractive occupation for men. The proportion of women teachers has declined every census year since 1931. In 1980, less than one-half of all teachers in Ontario, from kindergarten to grade thirteen, were women. (Taylor, 1980: 56) For a century, teaching provided women with one of the few opportunities for professional status; but teaching is once again becoming a male occupation.

Women's early dominance of teaching had little to do with their assumed suitability: it was simply a matter of economy. Women teachers were inexpensive to hire. Although categorized as a "professional" occupation in the census, teaching in the nineteenth century was anything but. Classrooms were crowded (there were sometimes more than one hundred children) "and standards of conduct, clothing and hygiene were not high." (Davitt *et al.*, 1974: 89) Training was haphazard and certification requirements often waived. Male teachers received less pay than day labourers, and women received about half the salary of their male counterparts. In 1883 the mean annual salary for urban male teachers in Quebec was $737; for women it was $217. Similar differences existed well into the twentieth century. (Danylewycz, 1987: 58) In rural areas across Canada the pay for both men and women was much less. Roberts (1976: 31) reported that, at the end of the nineteenth century, teachers in Toronto were paid less than were letter carriers, subordinate clerks, or charwomen. "Teachers frequently had to bid for jobs with the city awarding the contract to the lowest tender." (*Ibid.*: 31) Low pay for women was justified because women teachers were less apt to be certified, and because they usually left teaching when they married. Indeed most women teachers were single. In 1895 the Toronto Board passed a motion prohibiting the employment of women who had husbands to support them! (*Ibid.*: 31–32) That many single women had family responsibilities, or that many male teachers were also single men whose turnover rates were equally high did not challenge the blatant pay discrimination.

OFFICE WORK AND RETAILING

Less than a century ago, clerical and sales jobs were male domains. Early in the twentieth century, office work became an alternative in the small but expanding list of occupations suitable for women, and the number of women who entered the clerical field increased dramatically. One bank in Toronto increased its female staff from 200 to 8000 in two years. (Roberts, 1976: 26) In 1891 there were 862 women working in Canadian business and professional offices. By 1911 there were 25 438 women; by 1921 there were 91 016 women doing office work throughout the country. (Davitt *et al.*, 1974: 98) By 1921, clerical work replaced domestic service as the primary female occupation in Canada. In 1901, more than three-quarters of all clerical workers in Canada were men. By 1921, 40 per cent were women, and by 1951 almost 60 per cent were women. (Connelly, 1978: 93)

The pattern was similar in the United States. According to the 1870 census, there were seven women stenographers and typists; by 1920 there were half a million. (Kanter, 1977: 26) These changes in occupation became part of the rhetoric of women's magazines: "In 1900 the *Ladies Home Journal* was urging women to stay out of offices, but by 1916 the same magazine was glorifying the feminine traits of stenographers; their ability to radiate sympathetic interest, agreeableness, courtesy." (*Ibid.:* 26) In both countries, wartime needs accelerated the feminization of clerical jobs.

The rapid expansion of white-collar work, which began in the latter part of the nineteenth century, enabled women to move into these fields. The growth of industrial capitalism gave rise to a corresponding growth in office bureaucracies. The small office with a handful of male bookkeepers and clerks gave way to the larger office staffed by women. "The entry of women into the office coincided with the proliferation of many new fragmented, routine jobs in the lower reaches of administrative hierarchies." (Lowe, 1980: 366) From the employer's point of view, women were perfect candidates for these jobs. They were well-educated, conscientious, and would accept low pay. As with needlework, a machine paved the way. This time it was the typewriter, which first appeared in 1873. The Remington Company trained women to demonstrate the new machine, so from its inception, typing became defined as "women's work." (Glenn and Feldberg, 1984: 321) As early as 1880 in Canada, the YWCA set up training programs to introduce women to the new machines and to train them in office practice. The YWCA also provided day-care arrangements for women who sought the training. (Davitt *et al.*, 1974: 129)

New technologies and the growth of retailing created other job opportunities for women. Four per cent of working women were in merchandizing occupations in 1891. By 1911 this had increased to 12 per cent. (Phillips and Phillips, 1983: 17) As Roberts (1976: 28) notes, many women took up shop work because they had no other skills. It was a job open to women of all ages. As in all areas of employment, women's wages were lower than men's. Salesmen at Eatons earned $10 to $12 a week; saleswomen earned $6 to $8 a week. (RCRLC, 1889) Although these white-collar jobs held little opportunity for women to advance, they were more attractive than domestic service or factory work. Furthermore, opportunities in the latter areas declined in the twentieth century. In the early years, clerical workers earned more than teachers, and the working conditions were far superior to factory work, nursing, or domestic service.

ROSIE THE RIVETTER

World War II had a more dramatic effect on women's labour-force participation than World War I had. More women were gainfully employed, more employed women were married, and more women worked in nontraditional jobs. The media gave women war-workers the name "Rosie the Rivetter." Women worked in heavy industry, in farm labour, and in munitions. They flew airplanes and drove trucks. Age was no barrier to employment. One Ontario plant boasted 287 grandmothers in its employ. (Manpower Review, 1975: 7) Despite these examples, attitudes about women's nature and women's place did not change dramatically during World War II. "Women's increased job opportunities during the war were not a recognition of their right to work, but rather a convenient source of labour for both private industry and public service." (Pierson, 1983: 25)

Women were drawn into the labour force only as required. As quickly as the need for workers diminished, women were ousted from their positions. At the beginning of the war there were 3.8 million Canadians in the work force and an overwhelming 900 000 unemployed. For the first two years of the war, this pool of unemployed, primarily males, met the needs of the expanding labour market and the needs of military recruiters. By 1942, this source was depleted and women began to be recruited.

The Armed Forces were anxious to employ women in support positions in order to free men for combat. In the summer of 1941, both the Air Force and the Army established women's divisions; the Navy followed suit in 1942. In total, almost 50 000 women enlisted—approximately 2 per cent of the adult female population under forty-five. (Pierson, 1983) But far more women were employed in civilian jobs: in service, manufacturing, agriculture, or as part of the Women's Voluntary Services.

In September 1942 there was a compulsory registration of all women, married or single, in the 20- to 24-year age bracket. Recruitment began with the most mobile—single women—and only much later resorted to the least mobile—married women with children. Recruitment was the job of a body called the National Selective Service (NSS), established in 1942. Perhaps understandably, the Canadian government and its agent the NSS were single-mindedly concerned about the war effort. Women's rights were not an issue. For women to work during the war was considered a patriotic duty. According to the associate director of the NSS in charge of the Women's Division, the key words were service and sacrifice. The NSS launched several campaigns to mobilize women. Each campaign was directed at a less mobile source of female labour than the previous one.

> Measures to assist in the campaign included establishment of special job information and placement services for women, the provision of hostels and other housing arrangements, payment of transportation costs to work, the provision of medical and recreational facilities, nurseries to care for children and training programs. (Manpower Review, 1975: 7)

These incentives, including tax breaks to married women, were introduced as needed, and were promptly discontinued after the war.

For the first time in Canadian history large numbers of married women worked outside the home. In 1939 there were 638 000 women in the labour force, an estimated 10 per cent of whom were married. In 1944 there were

1 077 000, an estimated 35 per cent of them married. By 1947 the figures had dropped, and they remained low until 1954. Since 1954 participation rates have increased annually, but they did not exceed the wartime high until the late 1960s.

To get women back into their homes was easier said than done, but the problems were well anticipated. The Advisory Committee on Reconstruction appointed a subcommittee in January 1943 to study the problems facing women in the transition from war to peace. At the war's end, the immediate problem was to encourage women to leave the labour force to "make room" for the demobilized troops and other men whose jobs would cease with the war. But the problem was not simply to get women out of the labour force and get men in; there were 37 000 service women to consider, in addition to the 265 000 women engaged, directly or indirectly, in war production. (Pierson, 1977b) The subcommittee on Post-War Problems of Women calculated that, excluding ex-servicewomen, there would be approximately 180 000 self-supporting women without jobs as a result of postwar economic dislocation. *(Ibid.)*

COLLECTIVE ACTION

During the first half of the twentieth century the ideology of separate spheres dictated that women's place was in the home. Reformers were more concerned about issues of health and morality that the rights of working women. In 1922, the Quebec Department of Labour referred to women's labour-force participation as "one of the sad novelties of the modern world." (Prentice, 1978: 74) Unions also accepted the prevailing view of women and did not rally behind the plight of working women. They focused instead on securing a family wage for men. In 1898, the Trades and Labour Congress of Canada called for the *abolition* of child and female labour in all branches of industrial life. (White, 1980: 15) (In 1914 the CLC had a dramatic turnaround, arguing instead for equal pay for equal work.)

In the nineteenth century few Canadian workers were unionized. By 1911, only 5 per cent of the labour force were union members. (White, 1980: 1) Because most unions restricted their membership to skilled workers, women, whose work was defined as unskilled, were ineligible for membership. One exception was the Nights of Labour, a union open to skilled and unskilled workers, men and women. Most male union members saw women as competitors and preferred to fight for a family wage than to support the cause of working women. Although men and women generally worked in different jobs, the feminization of (and consequent wage erosion in) teaching and clerical jobs were examples of what might occur in other fields. Moreover, even skilled craftsmen were largely unsuccessful in having their demands met. In 115 of 287 strikes in Montreal in the first two decades of this century, employers totally rejected the workers demands. (Copp, 1974) Employers were extremely hostile to unions and didn't hesitate to fire or blacklist union activists. (White, 1980: 10)

Several characteristics of women's work were obstacles to unionization. Most importantly, the female labour force was highly fragmented. The majority of employed women worked as domestic servants. The realities of day-to-day life—fear of retaliation, isolation, long hours—made it virtually impossible for domestics to organize. Early attempts to unionize were quickly thwarted. (Leslie, 1974) Industrial workers, too, were unlikely to act collectively. Most textile and garment workers worked long hours in sweat shops or in their own homes, isolated from one another. Many domestics and factory workers were immigrants from Europe or rural Canada and so were further separated by culture and language. (White, 1980: 9) Turnover was high in these jobs, and troublesome workers were quickly replaced. "This constant turnover of women workers was a crucial deterrent to unionization. Given the context of powerful employer opposition, maintaining a union in the face of constantly changing membership was extremely difficult." (White, 1980: 8–9) Social attitudes, employer opposition, union weakness, and worker insecurity were effective barriers to union organization among women. (*Ibid.:* 10) Despite these obstacles, there were occasions when women actively supported striking men or organized on their own behalf. (Frager, 1983) Women teachers, nurses, and domestics, as well as textile and service workers did organize and act collectively, although their demands were rarely met. For example, in 1907, 400 nonunionized Bell Telephone operators went on strike to protest poor working conditions, low wages, and long hours (Sangster, 1986), and Toronto dressmakers went out on strike in 1931. (Macleod, 1974)

THE EARLY POSTWAR YEARS

In 1954, after a brief postwar low period, labour-force participation rates for women began to rise again. In 1961, women made up slightly more than one-quarter of the labour force: 30 per cent of women were gainfully employed and 45 per cent of these women were married and living with their husbands. Half of this group had children under 16. (*Women at Work in Canada*, 1964) Participation rates for women in 1961 were higher for women in their late 30s and 40s than for younger women. In the 1950s, married women typically left the labour force when their children were born and re-entered when their children reached adolescence. As we will see in the next chapter, many married women still leave the labour force when they have children, but they leave for far shorter periods of time.

Economic need met opportunity with the continued expansion of the service industry. Early in the twentieth century most work was in agriculture or manufacturing. But, beginning before World War I, the labour market changed due to the expansion of public services, such as education, health, and welfare, the growth of financial services, including banks and insurance companies, the growth of retail sales, and increased concentration in the hands of fewer and larger corporations. More and more service-sector jobs and fewer jobs in agriculture, primary industry, or manufacturing were created by these changes. In the post-World War II period these trends have accelerated. Technological innovations in farming, mining, and manufacturing made it possible to increase productivity without increasing the number of workers. While technology affects jobs in the service sector too, much of this work is still labour dependent. Some of these jobs (teaching and selling for example) depend on interpersonal relationships. In others, the price of labour is low enough to forestall the expense of mechanizing the work.

As Table 5.3 shows, there was little change in occupational concentration over the first half of the twentieth century.[7] According to the 1961 census, of the ten leading female occupations accounting for 62.7 per cent of the female labour force, women outnumbered men in all but one: farm labourer. Even within these occupations there was a distinct pattern of segregation by age. "In general, women clerical workers tend to be young, while the women in personal service occupations (with the exception of hairdressers and waitresses) tend to be older. School teachers are a bit older than average, while nurses are considerably younger (partly due to the inclusion of the group still in training)." (Department of Labour, 1964)

Part of the age difference may be accounted for by differences in education. Women with elementary-school education worked in the service and manufacturing sectors. Women with some secondary education worked in clerical and service jobs; women with high-school education worked in clerical, professional, and technical jobs. The differential effect of education for men and women was also becoming fixed during this period. Education became a more important determinant of labour-force activity for women than for men (in part because men work in the kinds of jobs in which formal education is less important than on-the-job training and experience).

---

[7] For a short period of time, labour-force segregation was a mixed blessing for women. Beginning in 1958, unemployment rates for men increased, while rates for women have been low until recently. One reason for the difference is that the demand for clerical and service workers continued during this period, and most women sought jobs in these fields. (For example, between 1951 and 1961 there was a 63 per cent increase in the number of female teachers in Canada; the increase met the needs of rapidly expanding educational systems.) Another reason for the lower unemployment figures for women is that when women return to the role of full-time housewife after leaving the labour force, their unemployment is hidden from statisticians.

TABLE 5.3
TEN LEADING OCCUPATIONS OF WOMEN IN CANADA, 1961

Occupation	Number	Per Cent	Women as Percentage of All Workers
Stenographers, Typists and Clerk-Typists	209 410	11.9	96.8
Clerical occupations, n.e.s.	165 613	9.4	51.2
Sales Clerks	133 234	7.6	58.0
Maids and Related Service Workers, n.e.s.	120 161	6.8	88.1
School Teachers	118 594	6.7	70.7
Bookkeepers and Cashiers	98 663	5.6	62.6
Nurses, Graduate and In-Training	81 868	4.6	96.8
Farm Labourers	66 081	3.7	29.7
Waitresses	61 802	3.5	78.6
Sewers and Sewing Machine Operators	50 592	2.9	90.5
10 Occupations	1 106 018	62.7	66.3
Total Female Labour Force	1 763 862	100.0	27.3

Note: Including Newfoundland, but not Yukon and Northwest Territories.

Source: Department of Labour, Canada: *Women at Work in Canada*, 1964: 26.

CONCLUSION

Although this discussion of the history of women's paid work has been brief, it demonstrates the extent to which current patterns are entrenched. Since the early years of industrialization, most employed women worked in unskilled, low-paying jobs in which the vast majority of workers were other women. In the first half of the twentieth century, increasing numbers of women entered the paid labour force, and until World War II the vast majority of these women were single. The combination of inflation, improvements in household technology, smaller family size, a shorter work week, continued expansion in the clerical and service sectors, and changing attitudes have encouraged the employment of married women since mid-century. Women have always responded to the fluctuating needs of the economy. They have been drawn into the labour force as needed and eased out when the need abated. (Connelly, 1978) In the next chapter it will be clear that the problems identified here have not yet been resolved.

6 CURRENT PATTERNS OF LABOUR-FORCE PARTICIPATION

In a liberal democracy it is assumed that everyone has the opportunity to advance if they have the corresponding talent and ambition. In other words, individuals create their own chances for upward mobility, primarily through hard work. Differences in labour-force activity of men and women are more comfortably attributed to lack of desire than lack of opportunity. Thus, it is unpopular to argue that women face discrimination in the labour force, particularly when they have made such evident progress in the last two decades. Yet the persistence of occupational segregation and low pay challenge these assumptions. In this chapter we will first review the major trends in women's paid employment in Canada, then consider the factors that reproduce gender inequality in the labour force, and finally look at the policy implications of this analysis.

LABOUR-FORCE TRENDS

The dramatic increase in female labour-force participation is one of the most important economic trends of this century. Table 6.1 shows the labour-force participation rates of women in nine industrialized countries. In 1960, Canada ranked lowest among these countries, and by 1970 we placed only seventh. But in 1981, Canadian women had the third highest participation rate among these countries—behind Sweden and the United States. During this period, Canadian rates continued to rise, while they were falling in West Germany, Italy, and Japan.

Canadian census data shows a gradual increase in female labour-force participation from 14.4 per cent in 1901 to 29.3 per cent in 1961.[1] (See Table

---

[1] Most analyses of the Canadian labour force are based on data from either the Decennial Census or the monthly Labour Force Survey. Detailed census calculations are based on a sample of Canadians—those who completed the "long forms." In 1971 this was one in three households, and in 1981 it was a 20 per cent sample. The obvious disadvantage of the census is its infrequency. Furthermore, because of the magnitude of the data base, special studies exploring the interrelationships among key variables are often not published until several years after the enumeration.

The Labour Force Survey is a monthly sample of 55 000 households representative of the noninstitutional civilian population aged fifteen or older. By definition, the labour force includes people who are either currently working or looking for work. Those not in the labour force include students, retired people, housewives, and "discouraged workers." Discouraged workers are no longer actively seeking employment.

TABLE 6.1
FEMALE PARTICIPATION RATES IN NINE INDUSTRIALIZED COUNTRIES, 1960, 1970, AND 1981

	1960	1970	1981
Canada[1]	30.1	38.3	51.6
United States	37.7	43.3	52.1
Australia	—	40.4	45.5
Japan	52.7	49.3	46.7
France	41.6	40.1	43.1
West Germany	41.2	38.4	38.5 *
United Kingdom	39.5	42.0	46.6 *
Italy	33.8	26.8	29.9 **
Sweden	—	50.0	60.5 *

* Preliminary figures.
** Rate in 1980.
1 The rates for Canada in this table, which are drawn from the Labour Force Survey, differ slightly from those in other tables, which are based on census data.

Source: C. Sorrentino, "International Comparisons of Labor Force Participation, 1960–81," *Monthly Labor Review* 106, no. 2 (February 1983).

5.1 in Chapter 5.) It jumped to 39.9 per cent in 1971 and by 1988 was 57.4 per cent.[2] According to annual summaries, women's labour-force participation has climbed every year since 1953 following a brief tapering-off period after World War II. The participation rate for all women crossed the 50 per cent mark in 1980, and it is much higher for younger women. Even during the recession of the early 1980s when male participation rates dropped, the female rate continued to rise. The key factor in these increases is the increased employment of married women.

As we saw in the last chapter, until the 1950s the typical female employee was young, single, and childless, and worked in one of half a dozen fields. In 1951, fewer than 8 per cent of married women were in the labour force. In 1988 it was almost 60 per cent. In the space of just forty years the gap between the employment of married and single women has closed significantly and has all but disappeared for younger women. Indeed, the highest participation rates are for married women in the childbearing/childrearing years between 15 and 44. In 1988, the participation rate for mothers of children under three years was 58.3 per cent. Clearly, young children are no longer the deterrent to labour-force participation that Gunderson (1977) found them to be in his analysis of the

---

[2] Recent figures used in this chapter are taken from two Statistics Canada publications: *Women in Canada*, 1990, and *Women and the Labour Force*, 1990.

1971 census. The pattern of working until the first child was born, leaving the labour force to raise children, and re-entering when the children reach a certain age was characteristic of the 1960s. Since then the average length of time spent out of the labour force has shortened, and many new mothers return to work after a brief maternity leave. Since the 1950s the marital status and age profiles of employed women have changed, but the job profiles have not. The concentration of women in service occupations has changed little since these figures were first calculated in the 1891 census.

What accounts for the dramatic increases in employment in just three decades? Although they are extensions of long-term trends, recent increases are the result of a combination of demographic, economic, and ideological changes. Chapter 5 described the increased demand for women workers in the service sector of the economy. In the 1960s continued expansion, coupled with rising standards of consumption, and a decline in real wages encouraged the employment of married women. While demographic and economic changes pre-date the women's movement of the 1960s, increased awareness of sexual inequality contributed to changing attitudes. Until the 1960s, mothers of young children who worked outside their homes did so at the risk of social disapproval, and usually in the face of economic need. Now, women are an integral part of the labour force and most Canadians support women's right to work. On the other hand, the inadequacy of child-care space and the inflexibility of work structures suggest considerable social ambivalence about combining employment and domestic life.

Economic and ideological changes coincided with reduced family and household responsibilities, which "freed" married women for employment. As well, more women were remaining or becoming single. At any point in time, about 40 per cent of adult women (over 15) are single. Some have never married, some are divorced, and some widowed. Most of these women must support themselves and many have dependents. However, if we consider current rates of marriage, divorce, and longevity, far more women will at some point in their lives be unmarried, and consequently— we may assume—self-supporting. Of every one hundred teenaged girls today, eighty-seven will marry at some point, but one-third of these will divorce. Of those who remain married, over 70 per cent will outlive their husbands. (National Council of Welfare, 1990: 16) In short, the majority (84 per cent according to this estimate) of Canadian women will be economically self-supporting, either by choice or force of circumstances, for some period of their adult lives. In 1985, 39.4 per cent of employed women were unmarried; 18.5 per cent of these women were lone parents. (Connelly and MacDonald, 1990: 13)

Economic expansion in the postwar years fostered rising standards of consumption, yet real wages fell. More families found it difficult to live well on the earnings of a single breadwinner. In 1971, over one-third of all husband-wife families depended exclusively on the husband's income.

(Pryor, 1984) By 1981 this figure had dropped to one-sixth. During this period, the proportion of wives with employment earnings rose from 42.9 per cent to 63.4 per cent. Yet in the same ten-year period the proportion of *family income* contributed by wives increased very slightly—from 25.2 to 28.1 per cent. Pryor (1984: 102) concluded that the "family economic position would have deteriorated significantly without the escalating contribution of wives."

While the employment of married women cuts across all social classes, not surprisingly, poorer families are highly dependent on wives' earnings. In 1985, 60.1 per cent of employed wives were married to men whose annual income was less than $30 000. (Connelly and MacDonald, 1990: 13) "In many cases [wives'] earnings are essential to keep their families from falling into poverty or to prevent a substantial drop in their standard of living." (National Council of Welfare, 1990: 40)

OCCUPATIONAL SEGREGATION

Occupational segregation by sex is a universal characteristic of labour markets, although the types of jobs performed by men and women vary from society to society. As we will see in the following discussion, occupational segregation has important implications for the instability of women's work (because of the extent of part-time employment in the service sector) and income differences (because service sector jobs, which women dominate, are low paying).

Fox and Fox (1987) used the index of dissimilarity to measure occupational segregation in Canada from 1931 to 1981. The index of dissimilarity measures the difference between the percentage of the male and female labour force in each occupational category. The index can be interpreted as the percentage of women who would have to change jobs to eliminate occupational segregation. According to Fox and Fox's calculations, the index dropped from about 75 per cent in 1931 to about 60 per cent in 1981. In other words, in 1981, 60 per cent of all employed women would have to change jobs to eliminate segregation.

Table 6.2 lists the twenty-two occupational categories used in the census enumeration. These jobs fall into three broad categories: service occupations, primary extraction, and manufacturing. According to the table almost 80 per cent of all female employees in Canada in 1986 worked in six service sector jobs: clerical (32.9 per cent), service (15.3 per cent), sales (9.9 per cent), medicine and health (9.1 per cent), managerial (6.2 per cent), and teaching (6.2 per cent). The first three columns indicate the percentage of all employed females in each occupational category. The second set of columns give (for each occupational category) the percentage of all employees who are female. The first group of columns show women's concentration in particular service sector jobs. The second group show that women dominate certain occupational categories. Comparing the two

TABLE 6.2

FEMALE EMPLOYMENT BY CENSUS OCCUPATIONAL CATEGORY: 1971, 1981, 1986

	Percentage of all Female Workers			Women as a Per Cent of Occupation		
	1971	1981	1986	1971	1981	1986
Managerial, Administrative	2.0	4.2	6.2	15.7	24.8	31.5
Natural Sciences, Engineering, Math	0.6	1.2	1.5	7.3	14.1	17.4
Social Sciences	1.0	2.0	2.5	37.4	52.5	56.6
Religion	0.1	0.2	0.1	15.8	26.5	21.2
Teaching	7.1	6.1	6.2	60.4	59.5	61.3
Medicine and Health	8.1	8.3	9.1	74.3	77.6	78.4
Artistic, Literary, Recreational	0.7	1.4	1.5	27.2	39.8	42.1
Clerical	31.7	35.1	32.9	68.4	77.7	78.5
Sales	8.4	9.6	9.9	30.4	40.8	41.9
Service	16.1	15.4	15.3	49.3	52.3	52.7
Farming, Horticulture	5.4	2.2	2.3	31.4	21.1	23.1
Fishing, Hunting, Trapping	—	—	0.1	1.9	5.6	7.9
Forestry, Logging	—	0.1	0.1	2.1	6.3	7.3
Mining, Quarrying	—	—	—	0.6	2.2	2.1
Processing	2.0	2.2	1.8	17.8	22.2	22.4
Machining	0.4	0.4	0.3	5.7	6.8	6.9
Product Fabricating	5.1	4.7	3.9	23.7	24.4	22.9
Construction Trades	0.2	0.3	0.3	0.4	2.0	2.3
Transport Equipment Operating	0.3	0.6	0.7	2.4	6.5	7.8
Materials Handling	1.4	1.1	0.9	19.6	22.6	22.3
Other Craft and Equipment Operation	0.4	0.6	0.6	12.4	21.1	21.4
Not elsewhere classified	0.7	0.6	0.7	13.0	17.4	18.6
Totals		100.0	100.0	100.0		

Source: Calculated from Statistics Canada, 1981 Census, Catalogue 92-920. 1986 figures from Statistics Canada, 1990, Catalogue 98-125. Reproduced with the permission of the Minister of Supply and Services Canada, 1990.

pieces of information gives a good indication of the extent to which the Canadian labour force is segregated by sex. The most striking example is clerical jobs. Between 1971 and 1986 the proportion of employed women who worked in clerical jobs increased from 31.7 per cent to 32.9 per cent. Over the same period, clerical jobs became more sex dominated. In 1986, 78.5 per cent of all clerical workers were women.

Women have made significant inroads into what were once male-dominated professional and managerial fields. Marshall (1987) measured the movement of women into professional occupations in the 1971–1981

TABLE 6.3
WOMEN IN MALE-DOMINATED PROFESSIONS, 1971–1981

	Total Number of Women 1971	1981	Percentage Increase 1971–1981	Women as % of Total Growth in Profession 1971–1981	Women as % of Total Employment in Profession 1971	1981
Management Occupations, Natural Sciences and Engineering	70	800	1 042.9	7.6	2.7	6.6
Management Occupations, Social Sciences and Related Fields	760	3 805	400.7	54.2	33.8	48.2
Administrators in Teaching and Related Fields	6 445	9 120	41.5	41.2	21.5	25.0
Chemists	895	1 975	120.7	50.8	11.8	20.4
Geologists	145	795	448.3	23.2	2.9	10.3
Physicists	45	65	44.4	4.0	5.6	5.0
Meteorologists	40	90	125.0	27.0	4.9	9.0
Agriculturists and Related Scientists	330	1 220	269.7	31.8	5.1	13.2
Biologists and Related Scientists	830	2 330	180.7	36.4	26.1	31.9
Architects	125	560	348.0	14.0	3.0	7.7
Chemical Engineers	65	340	423.1	12.9	1.8	5.9
Civil Engineers	235	980	317.0	6.9	1.1	3.0
Electrical Engineers	205	1 000	387.8	6.7	1.3	3.7
Mechanical Engineers	100	380	280.0	4.5	0.8	1.9
Metallurgical Engineers	15	50	233.3	3.8	1.7	2.8
Mining Engineers	20	105	425.0	5.9	0.9	2.9
Petroleum Engineers	15	225	1 400.0	6.7	1.1	4.9
Nuclear Engineers	—	40	—	6.9	—	4.8
Other Architects and Engineers	140	1 640	1 071.4	15.0	4.0	12.2
Mathematicians, Statisticians and Actuaries	1 010	2 070	105.0	55.9	25.0	34.7
Economists	640	2 570	301.6	28.8	11.0	20.5
Sociologists, Anthropologists and Related Social Scientists	170	540	217.6	42.5	33.0	39.0
Judges and Magistrates	75	220	193.3	18.6	5.7	10.5
Lawyers and Notaries	860	5 390	526.7	24.9	5.2	15.5
Ministers of Religion	900	1 785	98.3	26.9	4.5	7.6
University Teachers	5 190	9 785	88.5	43.7	19.7	26.5
Other University Teaching and Related Occupations	1 525	6 170	304.6	55.0	30.3	45.8
Community College and Vocational School Teachers	3 280	13 770	319.8	45.3	33.0	41.6
Physicians and Surgeons	3 150	7 255	130.3	33.4	10.7	17.4
Dentists	330	860	160.6	13.6	4.9	8.1
Veterinarians	75	605	706.7	30.2	4.3	17.2
Osteopaths and Chiropractors	80	340	325.0	22.0	7.3	14.9
Pharmacists	2 540	6 090	139.8	78.3	25.3	41.8
Optometrists	105	365	247.6	52.0	6.7	17.7
Total	30 410	83 340	174.1	29.0	11.0	18.6

Source: Marshall, 1987, *Canadian Social Trends,* Autumn, p. 9. Reproduced with the permission of the Minister of Supply and Services Canada, 1990.

census period. She classified forty-six occupations as professional. Of these, thirty-four were male-dominated (at least 65 per cent of employees were men). Most professional women (78 per cent) work in occupations where they are a majority. The male-dominated professions with the highest numbers of women are pharmacy, university teaching, mathematics, management jobs in the social sciences, and optometry (see Table 6.3). Very few women work as physicists or engineers.

PART-TIME WORK

An important characteristic of women's labour-force participation is the extent of part-time or full-time but seasonal work. Because labour-force surveys ask people about their current employment status, women in seasonal or short-term jobs may be counted as full-time workers. Other evidence suggests less continuity in women's employment than official statistics imply. (National council of Welfare, 1990) Almost three-quarters (72 per cent in 1985) of all part-time work is done by women, and one-third of women (compared to 8 per cent of men) work part-time. Three interrelated trends affect women's involvement in part-time work: the expansion of the service sector; the increased number of service sector jobs that are part-time; and the concentration of women in part-time service sector jobs. Most employed Canadians (70 per cent in 1985) work in the service sector. (Gower, 1988) Over 20 per cent of these jobs (compared to 6 per cent of jobs in the goods producing sector) are part-time. (Burke, 1986) In 1975, 11 per cent of Canadians worked part time (Burke, 1986)—in 1987 it was 20.6 per cent. (Gower, 1988) The number of part-time jobs is growing faster than the number of full-time jobs.

The single advantage of part-time work is flexibility, which is why it once appealed to married women and continues to appeal to students and retirees. Part-time or seasonal work is often unskilled; therefore it is low paying and offers little opportunity for advancement. Part-time workers are rarely protected by legislation, nor are they generally unionized. From the employers' point of view, part-time workers are cost effective since they are paid less and receive no benefits (usually equal to between 33 and 40 per cent of salary). By employing part-timers, employers can cover peaks and troughs in business demand at the lowest cost.

In the early postwar years when full-time work for mothers was frowned upon, married women were encouraged into the labour force by part-time work opportunities. Then, it was an acceptable compromise allowing women to earn "pin money" without neglecting their families. But economic and demographic conditions have changed and "extra" income is not enough to support the needs of most women today. Now, many women take part-time work because they do not have alternatives for employment or for child-care, or because of extensive domestic responsibilities. In 1985, 19 per cent of married women part-time workers said they

TABLE 6.4
REASONS FOR WORKING PART-TIME, 1985

	MEN Single	Married	WOMEN Single	Married
	%			
Personal or family responsibilities	—	—	—	19.2
Going to school	62.3	7.4	57.7	1.4
Did not want full-time	—	38.8	10.2	53.4
Could only find part-time	29.3	43.8	30.1	24.9
Other	1.1	7.4	1.2	1.2

Source: Burke, 1986, *Canadian Social Trends*, Autumn, p. 13. Reproduced with the permission of the Minister of Supply and Services Canada, 1990.

worked part time because of personal or family responsibilities. Another 25 per cent said they could not find full-time jobs. (See Table 6.4.)

In the recession of the early 1980s, the number of part-time jobs and the number of involuntary part-time workers increased as many employers replaced full-time with part-time workers. Involuntary part-time work increased 374 per cent from 1976 to 1985. (Akyeampong, 1987) Regions with highest unemployment have the highest involuntary part-time work. (*Ibid.*) In 1975, one in ten part-time workers said they worked part time because they couldn't find full-time work. By 1986, four in ten were involuntary part-time workers. (*Ibid.*)

Part-time work (which in Canada is defined as less than 30 hours a week) is paid less in average hourly wages than full-time work. It is not much of a consolation to know that the male/female wage gap for part-time work is less than for full-time work: most male part-time workers are students! In the long term, retirement income is hampered by a history of part-time employment. Only 9 per cent of part-time employees are covered by employer pension plans. (Burke, 1986) Since contributions to C/QPP are income determined, part-time workers will receive lower benefits at retirement. Given these implications, increases in part-time work should be viewed with skepticism if not alarm.

UNEMPLOYMENT [3]

The economic recession of the early 1980s was felt more deeply in Canada than in the United States. In the 1970s unemployment rates in the two countries were similar. In the 1980s our unemployment was greater and

---

[3] It is still common to hear arguments identifying women's labour-force participation as a factor contributing to male unemployment. Sometimes this suggestion comes from official sources. A March 1980 publication of Statistics

our recovery slower. Before the recession, women's unemployment rates were higher than men's for adults over 24 years of age. The recession reversed this trend. Separating full-time and part-time unemployment rates shows how the recession affected women's and men's unemployment differently. (Clemenson, 1987) In the 1980–1986 period, women had higher full-time unemployment rates than men, but lower part-time rates. Women, it seems, preferred to settle for part-time work than unemployment. Women made up almost 70 per cent of the involuntary part-time labour force in 1986. (*Ibid.*)

The concentration of women in clerical jobs raises the important concern regarding future job displacement and unemployment because of microtechnology. It is difficult to assess the effect of technological innovations on clerical work because, within organizations, the transition has so far been gradual enough to deal with reduced needs for clerical staff by attrition, transfers, and normal turnover. Therefore, estimates of unemployment and displacement are based on the proportion of work that will become automated by job sector. Some predict a very gloomy picture of unemployment among clerical workers. The Canadian Union of Public Employees (CUPE) estimates the loss of 1.5 to 2 million jobs in Canada as a result of microtechnology. (Hickl-Szabo, 1983) Others are more optimistic and point out that the number of jobs created by industrial automation in the 1950s exceeded the number of jobs lost. The group most affected by job loss in clerical jobs are women with high-school education, for it is this group who dominate in clerical work. Providing labour-force information to students should thus be a major part of the strategy in planning for job displacement in this field.

INCOME DIFFERENTIALS

In 1985 female full-time employees earned on average $18 136 compared to an average of $27 675 for men. (*Women in the Labour Force*, 1986–87) The fact that women earn approximately 60 per cent of what men earn has been reported consistently over the past several decades. In 1911 women's wages were 52.8 per cent of men's. In 1985 they were 64.9 per cent. Table 6.5 shows that there is considerable variation by job sector when men's and women's earnings are compared. Twenty-five years of persistent lobbying on the part of women and legislation making wage discrimination illegal has had little impact on wages when measured at the aggregate level. The wage gap persists whether one looks at salaries or wages, full- or part-time work, or calculations based on an hourly, weekly, or annual rate.

Canada, *Canada's Female Labour Force*, posed the question: "Is the high rate of unemployment in recent years the result of the rapid entry of females into the labour market or is high unemployment simply due to the fast growth in the labour market plus changing economic conditions?"

TABLE 6.5
AVERAGE EARNED INCOME OF FULL-YEAR WORKERS BY OCCUPATION AND SEX, CANADA, 1985

Occupation	Women	Men	Difference Between Women's and Men's Earnings	Women's Earnings as a Percentage of Men's Earnings
Managerial	22 414	37 467	15 053	59.8
Professional	22 372	35 141	12 769	63.7
Clerical	15 927	23 915	7 988	66.6
Sales	12 771	25 040	12 269	51.0
Service	10 740	20 949	10 209	51.3
Farming	8 584	14 750	6 166	58.2
Processing and Machining	18 061	27 649	9 588	65.3
Product Fabrication	14 672	25 616	10 944	57.3
Construction	*	26 029	3 395	*
Transportation	14 575	24 610	10 035	59.2
All Occupations	16 903	27 788	10 885	60.8

Sources: Statistics Canada, Household Surveys Division.
Statistics Canada, Household Surveys Division, *Income Distributions by Size in Canada, 1984,* Ottawa, April 1986, Cat. No. 13–207, Annual.
* Sample inadequate for reliable estimate.

Source: Labour Canada, Women's Bureau. *Women in the Labour Force,* 1986–87 edition, p. 47. Ottawa: Minister of Supply and Services. Reproduced with the permission of the Minister of Supply and Services Canada, 1990.

Much of the wage gap can be explained by the segregated labour force. When male/female earnings are compared within occupational categories, the income differences are much smaller. The finer the categorization used the less the income differences, but the more the job segregation. Bergmann (1974) has suggested that this can be explained by the overcrowding of women into certain job categories as a result of employer discrimination. The result is a combination of high supply and low demand for female workers that depresses female wages. Women whose earnings are lowest work in female-dominated jobs. They are held there by processes that reproduce class and gender; processes deeply rooted in ideas about women's domesticity and women's employment.

The extent of the wage gap and of part-time employment among women means that increased labour-force participation has done little to alter women's economic dependence on men. Few women earn enough to support themselves or their dependents on their own.

THE REPRODUCTION OF LABOUR-FORCE SEGREGATION

Patterns of labour-force segregation and pay differentials have deep historical roots as we saw in Chapter 5. At their base are assumptions about women's economic dependence and our primary responsibility for child care and domestic maintenance.

Historically, women's employment has reflected the changing needs of the economy and women's own economic needs. For most of the twentieth century, women were drawn into the labour force by the expansion of certain jobs or pushed in by economic necessity. Because their paid work was defined as a short-term accommodation and secondary to domestic responsibilities, married women have constituted what Connelly (1978) refers to as the "institutionalized inactive reserve army of labour." Marx introduced the term "reserve army" to explain why wages were kept low in industrializing economies. As a reserve army, married women have been available to work in wartime, in times of economic prosperity with the expansion of certain occupations, and on a part-time or part-year basis in response to peaks and troughs in daily or seasonal business cycles. Discriminatory practices (firing women when they married, laying-off women workers first, regardless of seniority) have been accepted in the context of women's economic dependence. Indeed, in 1921 the civil service prohibited the employment of married women! (Archibald, 1970: 16) Paying women less than men has been common practice—justified because women were not primary breadwinners. It was not until 1964 in Canada that the practice of wage discrimination became illegal. Nor was there much incentive for employers to train or promote women, who were not assumed to be permanent members of the labour force. These early patterns go a long way in explaining why women continue to dominate part-time and temporary jobs—jobs which are typically poorly paid, and without benefits, pensions, or prospects for promotion.

The social expectation that women will continue to assume the major responsibility for child care and other domestic tasks persists despite major changes in both family and work. As long as women are identified with these responsibilities they will, as Glazer (1980a) argues, continue to be the economy's "shock absorbers." Such expectations affect the way women anticipate their employment, and the way they organize their public and private lives. Economic dependence and labour-force inequalities are further reproduced because spouses, employers, and policymakers share this assumption. In the following section we will look at ways education, employer attitudes, and social policy perpetuate occupational segregation and low pay.

EDUCATION AND TRAINING

Human capital theory has received a great deal of attention as a possible explanation of wage discrepancies—initially between blacks and whites, and more recently between men and women. According to Becker (1964), an early and major proponent of the theory, individuals make human capital investments in "activities that influence future monetary and psychic income by increasing the resources in people." Human capital is built up in the form of education (years of education) and on-the-job-training (usually measured in years of experience). Individuals assume the direct and indirect costs of these human capital investments. Because they are then assumed to be more productive employees, those with more human capital accumulation are rewarded in terms of higher wages. Differences in employee wages are therefore assumed to reflect differing amounts of human capital. In short, human capital purports to explain sex differences in income as a result of sex differences in education and on-the-job-training.

Human capital theory has considerable face validity. It is appealing to think that labour-force inequities could be rectified by increasing human capital. In fact, this assumption has resulted in policy initiatives to increase women's access to education and training. Unfortunately the solution is not that simple. In Canada women with higher educational qualifications have higher rates of labour-force participation, lower unemployment, and receive higher salaries relative to men than women with low education. Because labour-force participation for women increases with education, employed women are on average, better educated than employed men. But regardless of education, women receive lower wages than equally educated men. University-educated women who work full time earn only 67 per cent of what male graduates earn, and their salaries amount to only $1600 a year more than male high school graduates. (*Women in Canada*, 1985: 27)

Typically, women have had less job experience (that is, less uninterrupted time in the labour force) than men, and this may explain some part of the wage gap. On the other hand, younger women have fewer and shorter breaks. Furthermore, men receive greater returns for their experience than women do. (Ornstein, 1983) In a national sample, almost half of all women workers reported no interruptions in work experience, but they still received lower salaries than men in the same kind of work. (*Ibid.*)

When the majority of women high school graduates enter the labour force, they seek jobs as clerical workers. For women who take business practice courses there is a close link between the skills they acquire in high school and the skills needed to perform clerical work. In other words, it has been the high schools, not employers, who have taken responsibility for the training of clerical workers. It is reasonable to assume that employers will feel less committed to clerical workers because they have little invested in them and because there is a constant supply of well-trained women graduating from high schools across the country.

Anisef *et al.* (1980) compared starting wages of newly graduated Canadian men and women. This kind of measure would presumably isolate the effects of education from the effects of experience. But these researchers found starting salaries of women were 80 per cent of the starting salaries of equally educated men. The greatest salary difference existed between male and female high school graduates in an academic program. One of the main reasons for these differences is that men and women with similar education are recruited to different kinds of jobs. Women with high school education typically take clerical jobs. University-educated women are more likely to look for teaching, medical, or clerical jobs. Regardless of education, men find work in a much wider range of jobs. Generally, the problem is not the amount, but the type of education women receive.

FIGURE 6.1

WOMEN AS A PERCENTAGE OF BACHELOR'S AND FIRST PROFESSIONAL DEGREE RECIPIENTS, BY SELECTED FIELDS OF STUDY, CANADA, 1971 AND 1987

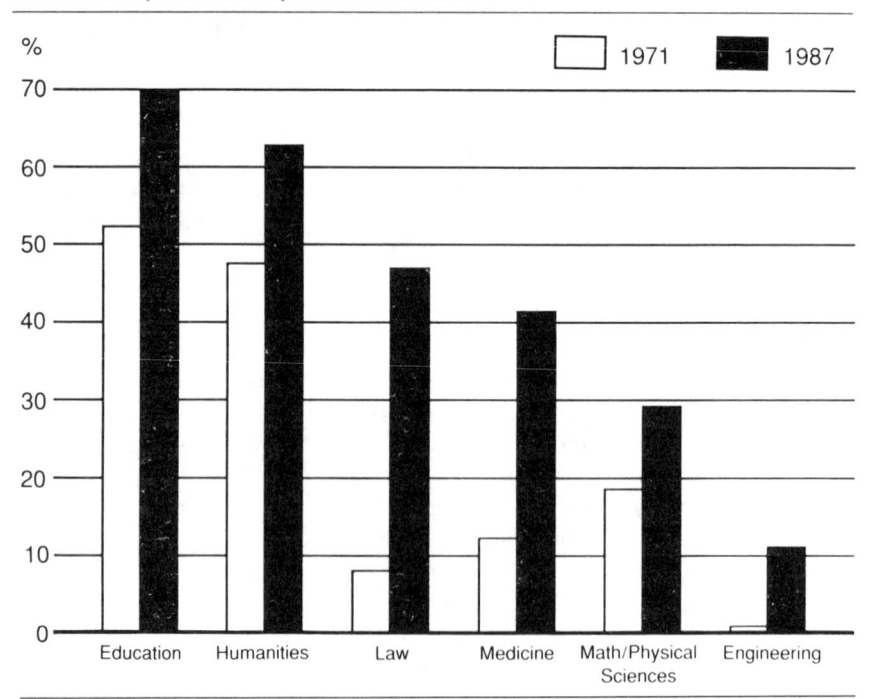

Source: *Women in Canada*, 1990, p. 47. Ottawa: Statistics Canada. Reproduced with the permission of the Minister of Supply and Services Canada, 1990.

High school enrolment patterns show that women are far more likely to take courses in certain subject areas, like business practice, and avoid other subjects, like mathematics. At the postsecondary level, the proportion of women students has increased, but again men and women gravitate to different areas of study. Fewer women than men graduate from professional or business schools, and proportionately fewer women continue to graduate school. In the last two decades there has been an impressive increase in the number of women enroled in courses in business administration, law, and medicine, although the numbers taking engineering, math, or science remain small. These choices both reflect interests developed as a result of early socialization and shape skills, interests, and occupational choices of adults.

Studies of young children show the extent to which sex typing of jobs becomes ingrained at an early age. Social-psychological theories of cognitive learning and reinforcement suggest how this process works. Children make early distinctions between males and females and thereafter categorize their observations in these terms. These early assumptions are reinforced by everyday experiences—in what we have called "the reproduction of gender." The pervasiveness of occupational segregation creates a catch-22 when we try to break the cycle. No matter what we tell children to discourage stereotypical thinking, they will inevitably observe women performing certain kinds of tasks and men performing others, they will characterize these as sex-appropriate behaviours and will define their own behaviour and aspirations in accordance with these observations.

A Canadian study (Ellis and Sayer, 1986) of young (aged 6 to 14) schoolchildren demonstrates this contradiction well. Girls in the study were aware that women *could* enter nontraditional jobs, but few indicated these as choices for themselves. "Many of them seemed to be saying 'Yes, women can become doctors, but I expect to be a nurse', or, 'Bank managers can be women as well as men, but I am going to be a teller'." (*Ibid.:* 55)

Observing the gender-relatedness of skills and jobs inevitably affects children from a very young age. For example, if they rarely see women doing certain kinds of work, for instance jobs requiring mathematical skills, they will come to believe that these jobs are not ones females usually excel at. Unless they are strongly encouraged or exceptionally motivated, they will not aspire to a career in mathematics. Of course the same holds true for young boys. It will matter little if young boys are encouraged by their "liberated" parents to value nurturing and feeling responsible for the domestic work they create if their experience of the world outside contradicts these ideas. Changing these processes depends on changing the structure of both family and work, since no matter how conscientiously parents and teachers try to instil values of sexual equality, the messages children receive from their own observations reinforce traditional patterns.

EMPLOYER ATTITUDES

When pay differences are analyzed, the variance that remains unexplained when occupation, experience, and education have been held constant is understood to be the effect of discrimination. Most analysts suggest a figure between 15 and 20 per cent. But, as Skolnick (1982: 117–118) points out, because education, occupation, and hours worked are also the effects of discriminatory practices, the total effect of discrimination is much greater.

Discrimination may be overt, as when individual employers make decisions about hiring and promoting people based on ascribed characteristics. It may also be more subtle.

> The most dangerous discrimination does not result from isolated individual acts motivated by prejudice, but from assumptions and traditions which have become an intrinsic part of the employment system. Established behaviors and rules, and organizational attitudes, policies and practices often embody a bias against disadvantaged groups that effectively excludes them from employment opportunities. This "systemic discrimination" exists even when there is no intent to discriminate. (Bruce, 1985: 53)

The idea that employers discriminate against women by paying them lower wages is inconsistent with one of the most fundamental tenets of economics. Most economic theory begins with the assumption that individuals are rational profit maximizers. Therefore, it is in the interests of employers to hire women if their wages are typically lower and if they are equally productive. In fact, it would make more sense to hire only women. The more females a firm hired, the higher the firm's profits would be. Eventually more firms would follow suit, increasing the demand for female labour and causing wages to rise with demand. In short, if employers acted out of rational interest, they would hire more women, and women's wages would consequently increase. Gunderson (1981) refers to the fact that this has not happened as the "economic paradox." Economists have tried to account for this economic paradox by attributing the wage differential to employer discrimination, suggesting for example that some employers who have a "taste for discrimination" (Becker, 1971) are willing to pay the price of the wage differential to avoid hiring women.

The attitudes of employers have a great deal to do with the kinds of jobs women fill in the labour force. The process whereby employers make judgements about women as individuals because of their beliefs about women as a group has been referred to as error discrimination (if the judgement is erroneous) or statistical discrimination (if the judgement is based on fact). For example, if employers believe women have higher turnover rates, they will be reluctant to hire them. In fact the evidence contradicts this assumption. Men and women have similar "quit" rates and are equally likely to quit a low-paying than high-paying job. To take another example, if employers believe women are less skilled than men in certain areas, for instance mechanical skills, they will hire only men for these jobs. In this way employers use ascriptive criteria to reduce the information costs associated with evaluating individuals. However, economists predict that statistical discrimination will eventually erode because of the presumed rational motivations of employers.

Several authors have pointed out the extent to which characteristics of jobs become associated with individuals most likely to perform these jobs. (Barron and Norris, 1976; Kanter, 1977) Dual labour market theory shows how these attitudes develop as a consequence of occupational segregation. The extent of occupational segregation suggests that men and women not only work in different jobs but also in different labour markets. The usual distinction divides the labour market into primary and secondary occupations. The primary labour market is characterized by jobs with relatively high wages, good working conditions, fringe benefits, stability and job security, and the opportunity for upward mobility. Jobs in the secondary labour market are poorly paid, with poor working conditions, and little stability, security, or opportunity for advancement. Because of these differences, there is little mobility from the secondary to the primary sector.

Barron and Norris (1976) argue that secondary-sector workers tend to acquire histories and attitudes that reflect the jobs they hold. Yet these histories and attitudes are often attributed to the individuals themselves and are used to justify the workers' location in the market. For example, the assumption that women have high turnover rates is stated "as though this were a property of women and not the jobs they occupy." Kanter (1977: 161) argues that lower levels of work aspiration and commitment are related to job opportunities. "Men with low opportunity look more like the stereotype of women in their orientations toward work." As I have argued in earlier chapters, the fact that married women work in jobs that have lower penalties for absenteeism or work to the clock, mean that they rather than their husbands accommodate work demands to family demands. In this way, social expectations and structured inequalities create a self-fulfilling prophesy.

UNIONS

The barriers to women's union participation in the first half of the twentieth century were described in Chapter 5. The conditions of work (isolation, long hours), the attitudes of employers and male union organizers, and women's own attitudes to their work meant that women had neither the inclination nor the opportunity to organize. Since mid-century union membership generally has grown and the number of women in unions has increased. The main factor in this growth was increased unionization in the civil service, where women make up a significant proportion of the employees. As Maroney (1987: 88) explains, the "top-down legislative conversion of provincial and federal staff associations into unions" affected a large number of women clerical and administrative workers. Following this large increase, union membership has stabilized. In 1971, 33.1 per cent of the labour force were union members; in 1982 it was 33.3 per cent, and it has climbed slightly since then. (Neill, 1988) (In the United States union membership dropped to less than 20 per cent during the 1970s. [*Ibid.*]) By 1985, one-third of unionized workers in Canada were women and 38 per cent of women were union members—up from 16.6 per cent in 1965. (Neill, 1988; Phillips and Phillips, 1983: 148)

Women's union activity reflects the segregation of the labour force. Women are concentrated in a limited number of unions, within which they are often a majority of the members. Forty per cent of unionized women belong to unions where women are the majority. (Phillips and Phillips, 1983: 148) Women are not proportionately represented on union executives, even in unions with relatively large female memberships. (White, 1980: 65–67) Consequently, it has been difficult to ensure that issues such as equal pay for work of equal value, sexual harassment, or paid maternity leave receive high priority.

Several recent strikes reflect increased activism among working-class women. (Maroney, 1987) The 1978 strike at Fleck Manufacturing in southwestern Ontario was a hardwon struggle for better pay and improved working conditions. Most of the employees were immigrant women working for very low pay in appalling conditions. The strike, which lasted six months, became a "test case for feminism." (Maroney, 1987) Feminist activists and UAW supporters rallied behind the handful of women strikers against intense resistance of the company. In the same year, women were centrally, if indirectly involved in a strike at the International Nickel Company in Sudbury, Ontario. Wives of striking steelworkers formed a "Wives Supporting the Strike" committee. This committee provided "material and social support for families of striking miners"; educated wives about the union to forestall their resentment about the strike; provided direct support by raising money and walking the picket line; and travelled outside the community to seek support. (Luxton, 1986b: 73–74)

Does union membership benefit women? The answer seems to be a qualified "yes." Unionized workers are paid more, and the wage gap is less for union than nonunion workers. Union members were less likely to lose their jobs in the recession of the early 1980s. (Neill, 1988) Unionized women are more likely than nonunionized women to have maternity leave beyond the minimum required by law, and some unionized part-time workers receive employee benefits rarely allowed nonunionized part-timers. (White, 1980) At the time of White's study (1980), the larger unions were committed (on paper) to eliminating sexual inequality among members, but few contracts reflected this commitment. For example, a Canadian Labour Congress policy statement recommends that both male and female workers should receive assistance "to facilitate the harmonious combination of home and work responsibilities" in the form of flexible working hours and shorter working days. (*Ibid.*: 68)

To summarize, the key factor in understanding labour-force inequality is occupational segregation. Women typically work in a narrow range of jobs, and in jobs where most employees are other women. In the early years of the twentieth century women were drawn into clerical jobs and to jobs in sales, teaching, and health care by expanding opportunities in these fields. These jobs quickly became defined as "women's" jobs. Occupational segregation is reinforced by gender socialization, educational experiences, and employer discrimination. At the root of these processes has been the assumption that employed women are wives and mothers first, employees second. Women, socialized to expect and accept prime responsibility for domestic tasks, do not envision the wide range of occupational choice available to men. Socialization, in subtle and not so subtle ways, reinforces traditional sex-role behaviour with the result that young women fall into an educational streaming process that further restricts their choices. By the time women have graduated from high school, differences in aptitudes and interests have been reinforced to the point that employers feel justified in using these as screening devices. These expectations and behaviours are so well entrenched that market forces will do little to change them without legislative encouragement. The following section reviews legislative attempts to deal with labour-force inequities.

POLICY IMPLICATIONS

Late nineteenth and early twentieth century reformers sought to protect women workers by restricting the conditions of their employment. Motivated by an unquestioned belief in the importance of women's responsibilities as mothers, reformers assumed women's paid employment was temporary. The goal of early legislation was to restrict the hours and conditions of women's work and to prevent exploitation. Early in the twentieth century employers were required to pay women a minimum wage (sufficient to support a single woman) and men a living wage (sufficient to support a family). (Niemann, 1984: 34) "This kind of differential calculation led to the pernicious habit of setting women's wages at a level of about two-thirds the amount set for men, a proportion which approximates the ratio of women's earnings to those of men even today." (Ibid.: 34) It was not until 1972 that lower minimum wages for women were finally disallowed in Canada! Whatever the short-term benefits of this early legislation, the long-term consequences were to reproduce occupational segregation and wage inequality. (Kessler-Harris, 1987)

Beliefs about separate spheres were challenged, if not dispelled, by economic changes from the 1930s to the 1960s. High male unemployment during the Depression exposed the weakness of a wage structure based on the idea of a family wage for men. Women's employment in "non-traditional" jobs during World War II challenged notions about women's ability or willingness to do men's work. The increased employment of married women in the postwar years and the mounting evidence that women could be as committed to the labour force as men, as committted to work as family, added fuel to mounting pressures for equal treatment in the labour force. Legislative initiatives, such as the ones spelled out in the Royal Commission on the Status of Women, were primarily directed at removing barriers and asserting claims for equal opportunity and wage parity.

The following paragraphs look at three policy initiatives: (1) equal pay policies; (2) employment opportunity policies; and (3) work-structure policies.

EQUAL PAY POLICIES

There are two points to keep in mind regarding equal pay legislation in Canada: jurisdictional coverage and the changing definition of equal work. Federal legislation covers all federal departments, agencies, Crown corporations, and corporations under federal jurisdiction. As such, it covers about 11 per cent of the labour force. Other workers are covered by provincial legislation. When equal pay legislation was first introduced (by the federal government and the provinces, separately) in the 1950s and 1960s, it required equal pay for equal, or "substantially similar" work. Its effectiveness depended on how "substantially similar" was interpreted by the courts. In 1950s and 1960s a very narrow interpretation was taken, and since small differences could always be found (Gunderson, 1985: 13), the legislation had little effect.

Quebec was the first Canadian jurisdiction to legislate a broader interpretation of equal pay—equal pay for work of equal value. Two years later, in 1977, the federal government introduced its *Human Rights Act*, which similarly requires equal pay for work of equal value. Manitoba, Nova Scotia, Prince Edward Island, New Brunswick, and Ontario now have similar requirements.

Equal pay for work of equal value has been a goal of the International Labour Organization (ILO) since its inception in 1919, although it wasn't until Convention 100 in 1951 that it was formally adopted as an international labour standard. Canada was slow to ratify this principle, but finally did so in 1972.[4]

> In ratifying Convention 100, Canada has made a binding international commitment to ensure the application of the principle of equal remuneration for men and women workers for work of equal value; to give effect to the provisions of the Convention through objective methods of job appraisal; and to

---

[4] Canada made another international commitment reiterating the goal of equal pay for work of equal value when the United Nations International Covenant on Economic Social and Cultural Rights was ratified in 1976. A third commitment to the same principle was made with the ratification of the United Nations Convention on the Elimination of All Forms of Discrimination against Women in 1981.

co-operate with employers' and workers' organizations in implementing the principle. (Niemann, 1984: 23)

Canada was thus committed to bringing its legislation into conformity with the ILO standard, although no timetable has been established.

The Chief Commissioner of the Human Rights Commission described the essence of the equal pay section of the Act as: "(a) men and women who (b) do work of equal value in (c) the same establishment, must (d) be paid equally." (Labour Canada, 1986a: 8) Labour Canada estimates that with full compliance this legislation can eliminate 25 per cent of the wage gap for employees covered (i.e. employees of the federal government or Crown corporations). (*Ibid.:* 4) Individuals, groups, or third parties may initiate complaints to the Commission, or the Commission may initiate its own complaint. (Labour Canada, 1986b: 11) Quebec legislation is similarly structured. Manitoba and Ontario have separate enforcement agencies. The legislation in these two provinces is more comprehensive in that there is strong pro-active component. Employers are required by law to take positive steps to reduce the wage gap. (*Ibid.:* 13–15)

Unions have been instrumental in the process of ensuring compliance with the law through collective bargaining and by registering complaints. (Labour Canada, 1986b: 17) As we would expect, employers in the provinces not covered by equal pay for work of equal value legislation have resisted attempts to pay women and men equally. In these provinces, union efforts have focused on pressure to enact similar legislation. (*Ibid.*)

Equal value is determined by comparing jobs in terms of: skill, effort, responsibility, and working conditions. Points are assigned in each area, and the total score is used to compare jobs. The major advantage of the concept of equal pay for work of equal value or comparable worth (over equal pay) is that it challenges the assumption that the work men do and the skills needed to perform in male-dominated jobs are inherently more valuable than women's work.[5]

Although the point system can be cumbersome, existing job accountabilities and job evaluations can often be used as a basis. Otherwise, job accountabilities can be created by a third party. In the United States (where the term "comparable worth" is used instead of equal pay for work of equal value), extensive comparisons have already been made. Examples of jobs judged by consultants to be of comparable worth include: typing pool supervisor and painter, senior legal secretary and senior carpenter, licenced practical nurse and electrician. (Royal Commission on Equality in Employment [RCEE] 1984: 251)

The first case settled by the Human Rights Commission involved a comparison of the work done by Library Scientists (65 per cent female) and historical researchers (75 per cent male) working for the federal gov-

---

[5] Changing preconceived notions of value are not unproblematic. (Gaskell, 1986)

ernment. The Commission determined that these jobs were indeed similar and resulted in a $2.3 million settlement. A second landmark case involved General Service federal employees. The laundry and miscellaneous service workers (most of whom were female) were paid substantially less than messengers, custodians, and building and store services employees, most of whom were male. Pay settlements in this case amounted to $17 million. (Labour Canada, 1986b)

EMPLOYMENT OPPORTUNITY LEGISLATION

Equal opportunity legislation is designed to combat discrimination in hiring, promotion, and conditions of work. The first antidiscrimination legislation in Canada, in the 1950s, did not specifically mention discrimination on the basis of sex. When Canada ratified ILO Convention 111 in 1964, a commitment was made to address sex-based discrimination, but no action was taken until the *Human Rights Act* was introduced. Human Rights legislation dealt with discriminatory practices by focusing on individual cases and employee initiative.

American Affirmative Action legislation was designed to counter systemic discrimination (defined on page 100). Instead of requiring employees to show that discrimination has occurred, employers are required to show that discrimination has not occurred. Title VII of the *American Civil Rights Act* prohibits discrimination in hiring, firing, employment, and benefits on the basis of race, colour, sex, or national origin. Further legislation requires any businesses doing business with the federal government to analyze their employee profiles for evidence of underrepresentation of women and minority groups. Businesses must then establish numerical goals and timetables for increasing representation of underrepresented groups. In other words, Affirmative Action "calls for positive steps to rectify past discrimination and inequalities which have become a structured part of the system." (Cohen, 1985: 23)

The Royal Commission on Equality in Employment (1984) preferred the term "employment equity" to affirmative action as a solution to systemic discrimination. In response to one of the Commission's recommendations, the federal government passed an *Employment Equity Act*, effective in June 1988. This Act applies to all federally regulated businesses of 100 or more employees and companies contracting with the government (for contracts exceeding $200 000). These companies must implement employment equity by identifying discriminatory employment practices and routes to their elimination. The law is enforced by the Canadian Human Rights Commission.

The effect of antidiscrimination legislation in both Canada and the United States has been minimal if measured in the aggregate. Although women in professional jobs have made progress (relative to professional men), the numbers are small and these women inevitably face what the media calls the "glass ceiling." In other words, women still do not have access to the top jobs. The majority of women have not experienced noticeable improvement in their economic well-being. The feminization of poverty has increased, and there has been little change in the wage gap or in occupational segregation. (Kessler-Harris, 1987)

Perhaps there are, as Kessler-Harris (1987: 532) suggests, two lessons to be learned from past legislative efforts. The first is that paying attention to the characteristics of one group of workers can overemphasize their special needs and result in discrimination. The second lesson is that ignoring differences tends to perpetuate existing inequality. With these in mind, two kinds of legislative initiative hold promise for the future: continued emphasis on equal pay for work of equal value (or comparable worth), and enabling policies that redefine established work structures for all employees. If more flexibility existed for all employees, it would not always fall on women to accommodate the needs of family to the demands of the labour force. (For American examples see Kamerman and Kahn, 1987.)

WORK STRUCTURE POLICIES

The preceding discussion has focused on legislation designed to reduce discrimination in employment practices and remuneration. Unquestionably, improving women's relative economic disadvantage is of fundamental importance. However, past experience has shown that (1) changes will be slow and (2) women who benefit first (and most) will be highly educated professional women without family obligations. Public policy has an important role to play in providing necessary support and incentive to create working environments where the care of families does not by definition take second place to work demands.

In the past, businesses have been more than willing to change the structure of work to accommodate women with family responsibilities. In the 1960s, the need for clerical and sales workers was met by creating part-time opportunities for married women. Some companies have introduced alternate career paths, flex-time, job sharing, and telecommuting to make it easier for women to integrate family and work. The controversy surrounding the idea of the "mommy track" shows how these woman-centred policies are fundamentally flawed.

In an article published in the *Harvard Business Review* (Schwartz, 1989) argued the merits of dual career tracks for women: one for "career primary" women, who place work advancement above family, and one for "career and family" women, who are willing to trade some career growth and compensation for time away from work. But because the "mommy track" (a term used by the media, not Schwartz) is based on the assumption that child care and family concerns are women's (not men's) concerns, it reinforces gender segregation and reproduces economic dependence. It further assumes that prevailing work values, which ignore family needs, are appropriate and that women, not men or work organizations, should be responsible for any integrating that is done. What is needed instead are work-related policies that apply to all workers and focus on the needs of working parents, not working mothers.

Flexible working arrangements such as staggered hours, compressed work weeks, job sharing, and part-time and at-home work are usually individually negotiated. In the last decade, a more generalized demand for flexible work has come from environmental agencies. In cities like Los Angeles, the need to reduce traffic congestion and pollution from automobile exhaust has created public pressure to reconceptualize some traditional assumptions about work. Continued pressure from working parents and from environmental agencies suggest that some change in work structures are inevitable.

Increased work flexibility raises some interesting possibilities regarding the integration of work and family. Imagine Couple A and B, both working full-time; A has a Monday to Thursday compressed week; B a Tuesday to Friday compressed week. A telecommutes on Wednesday; B on Thursday. Both have time off together and time-off alone. The needs of children, whether very young or school-aged, can be accommodated and responsibility for their care can reasonably be shared.

Gradually, the family responsibilities of men, and the resulting challenge to the work ethic, are being recognized by such mainstream business magazines as *Business Week*. Their cover story on the "Mommy Track" (March 20, 1989) concluded with the following comment:

> As the [baby] boomers age, more men as well as women may trade the next rung on the ladder for other rewards ... The challenge for companies is to provide flexibility and a rainbow of options so both men and women can raise their families as they see fit and still contribute.

It bears repeating that if flexible work policies are to have any real impact on the integration of family and work, there must first be a major reduction in the wage gap.

CONCLUSION

In making life choices, women confront what Oakley (1974: 8) refers to as "structural ambivalence." Until the 1950s and 1960s, women's experience of structural ambivalence amounted to choosing between marriage and motherhood (combined with sporadic employment) or full-time employment. Maternal employment was discouraged and discriminatory practices commonplace. As described in earlier chapters, liberal feminists focused on expanding women's options, gaining acceptance of the right to employment regardless of marital or parental status, and removing barriers to education and employment.

In the last two decades structural ambivalence has been complicated by economic need and marital instability. Now most women are gainfully employed. While the most blatant barriers to employment have been removed, social attitudes, educational streaming, the absence of child care, and the rigidity of work structures mean that women's employment decisions are far from freely made.

Persistent monitoring and lobbying on the part of liberal feminists and trade union activism on the part of socialist feminists have increased public awareness of labour-force inequalities and resulted in changes in legislation and policy. The next chapter looks at women's efforts to gain control over the conditions of their family and work lives through an increased voice in government and community activism.

7 THE WOMEN'S MOVEMENT AND WOMEN'S POLITICAL PARTICIPATION

The women's movement has been an important force of change in almost every society in the world. In Western societies we usually think of the women's movement as having two rather distinct phases or waves: the nineteenth century movement and the current movement. In this chapter we will consider both waves of the women's movement. Together, they constitute the major force of change in the ideas about women—and a major attack on structural barriers to sexual equality. The first section of the chapter provides a brief history of the first wave of the women's movement. One of the main goals of the suffragettes was the right to a political voice. The second section of the chapter deals with the extent to which this goal has been successfully achieved. The suffragettes established a tradition of exerting pressure through the political process. Political representation continues to be an important issue. Yet if political power is measured in terms of representation, women have made little progress. The third section of the chapter describes the current women's movement and the challenge of the New Right.

THE WOMEN'S MOVEMENT IN THE NINETEENTH CENTURY

During the second half of the nineteenth century, there was a wave of feminist protest throughout the Western world. Although individuals had expressed their dissatisfaction with conditions imposed on women before this time, in the mid-nineteenth century women began to act collectively. In England, women actively protested against working conditions, marriage and property laws, restricted educational access, and their exclusion from politics. Frustrated by their inability to initiate reforms through political appeal, women focused their energies on obtaining the vote. British women's protest was expressed first in marches on Parliament and civil disobedience. When these tactics failed, women turned to militancy and property damage. When arrested and imprisoned—as they were in great numbers—they responded with hunger and thirst strikes. Emmeline Pankhurst, one of the more militant British suffragettes, was jailed and released thirteen times in 1913. (Anderson and Zinsser, 1988: 366) In the United States, militancy and property damage were used only as a last resort. The Canadian movement was never militant; it was truly a battle of rhetoric. Canadian suffragettes seemed to follow Nellie McClung's advice: "Never retract, never explain, never apologize, get the thing done and let them howl."

In all three countries, gaining the vote began as a means to an end, but became a lengthy and tedious campaign. In the United States, the women's movement was partly borne of the abolitionist movement. When women were excluded as voting representatives at the World Anti-Slavery Convention held in London in 1840, it became clear that without the right to vote their protest lacked political clout. The 1848 Seneca Falls, New York, convention, which is said to mark the beginning of the women's movement in the United States, was a response to women's exclusion from the Anti-Slavery meeting. Delegates at Seneca Falls approved a "Declaration of Sentiments" modelled on the Declaration of Independence. Although the Declaration of Sentiments included a resolution to fight for the vote, this was not the most important issue. In fact, after the Civil War, the movement split because women could not agree to concentrate on suffrage. Women joined forces again in 1890 with the decision to focus on obtaining the franchise—a goal that was not reached for another thirty years.

The women's movement in Canada was influenced by developments in the United States and England. Several Canadian women had attended the Seneca Falls Convention. Suffragettes from both the United States and Britain spoke to large and receptive audiences in Canada, and Canadian women were inspired by their associations with individuals and organizations in these two countries. The beginning of the suffrage movement in Canada is said to be the founding of the Toronto Women's Literary Club in 1876 by Emily Stowe. (Cleverdon, 1974) The club's neutral name was deliberately chosen to avoid public ire. Seven years later it was renamed the Women's Suffrage Association. Emily Stowe had fought a personal battle to become certified to practise medicine. She was refused admittance to Canadian schools of medicine, but she received her degree in New York in 1868. Understandably, a key issue for Stowe was to expand educational opportunities for women. Like liberal feminists today, Stowe argued for women's rights on the basis of an assumption of sex equality. As described in Chapter 2, maternal feminists did not share this assumption.

Social historians refer to the period of 1880 to 1920 as a period of social reform. Indeed, the last quarter of the nineteenth century gave birth to a large number of women's organizations committed to reform. Some (including the Anglican Girls Friendly Society and the Young Women's Christian Association) focused on preparing young, single women for employment while protecting them from temptations and evils of urban life. Other organizations focused on eliminating child labour, improving working conditions, and a score of health and welfare reforms. "Organized pressure for the vote was thus allied with a broader reformist response to the rapid pace of industrialization, urbanization and the perceived decline of traditional values." (Bashevkin, 1985: 5) When reform groups took up the cause of women's suffrage, the movement gained a much needed national network—but at the cost of establishing an essentially conservative approach to the suffrage cause. (*Ibid.*)

Most women involved in reform movements were middle class. They were motivated by their belief that they, as mothers, were uniquely responsible for preserving family stability in the face of the social disruptions brought about by industrialization. They accepted, indeed celebrated, innate differences between men and women and argued for voting privileges as a way of ensuring that women's voices be heard. They argued that women were natural peacemakers who would "cleanse and purify the world by law."[1] (Nellie McClung, quoted in Savage, 1979: 26) Their demands were conservative by today's standards but at the time were met with considerable resistance. Opponents of female suffrage referred to women's inexperience, to their inability to take up arms for Canada, to their physical and mental shortcomings, and to the potential for undermining both women's femininity and the harmony of the home. (MacLellan, 1972: 14–15) Suffragettes countered with arguments about the positive influences woman's voice would have in government—particularly regarding moral issues. (*Ibid.*: 15)

Canadian women won the right to vote several years before British or American women. It took women's involvement in World War I to sway British and American public opinion enough to grant women the franchise. Granting Canadian women federal voting rights was a manœuvre to gain support for conscription, not a recognition of the claims of the women's movement. It was assumed that women with close relatives serving in the armed forces would vote in favour of conscription, and these women were given the vote—on behalf of their relatives—in 1917. Full federal franchise was granted to Canadian women in 1918. Winning the vote was, in many ways, an anticlimax; the press was too wrapped up in wartime issues to pay particular attention. (Trofimenkoff, 1977b: 197)

Between 1880 and 1900, most municipalities granted voting rights to all property owners, regardless of sex. (Bashevkin, 1985) Provincial voting rights were granted individually:

1916: Alberta, Saskatchewan, and Manitoba
1917: British Columbia and Ontario
1918: Nova Scotia
1919: New Brunswick
1922: Prince Edward Island

Newfoundland did not become a province until 1949, although women had gained the right to vote provincially in 1925. It was not until 1940 that

---

[1] The term "feminist" became widely used in the 1890s. (Kealey, 1979: 7)

women in Quebec were finally granted provincial voting rights.[2] Ironically, women had voting rights in Quebec, New Brunswick, and Nova Scotia long before Confederation in 1867. However, these rights were removed in Quebec in 1834 and later in the other two provinces.

Achieving the vote was perhaps the most visible concern of early feminists—but it was not the only concern. Women continued to participate in reform movements, and some were actively involved in the trade union movement. (Wade, 1980) Women's associations within political parties were involved in social reform issues and later in supporting women's candidacy for election. (Bashevkin, 1985) Gaining the right to vote was a small victory over prevailing attitudes toward women, but it did not significantly alter the tide of public opinion.

At the time, women's organizations were pushing (without success) for the appointment of women to the Senate. Only persons could be appointed to the Senate, and women were not persons. According to British Common Law "women are persons in matters of pains and penalties, but are not persons in matters of rights and privileges." Women could vote, they could run for public office, but they could not be appointed to the Senate. To obtain a ruling from the Supreme Court, women had to file a petition with five signatures for an order in council. Five women from Alberta met to draw up the document. The Supreme Court of Canada first upheld the ruling that women were not persons. Later this was appealed and reversed by the Privy Council in Britain in October 1929, "awarding" Canadian women full citizenship.

The first woman Senator, Cairine Wilson, was appointed in 1931. A *Maclean's* magazine profile (April 1, 1930) of Wilson was clear to point out that, along with her other accomplishments, "she is first, last and always a woman—a wife and mother of eight children."

Since Wilson's appointment, there have been twenty-six additional women appointed to the Canadian Senate. Twelve women are currently members. (Information Services, Canadian Senate, August 1990)

WOMEN IN ELECTORAL POLITICS

The first federal election in which Canadian women could vote was held in 1921. Four women sought election. One was successful. Agnes Macphail, from Grey County, Ontario, was the first woman Member of Parliament in Canada. In the 53-year period from 1917 to 1970, there were 134 federal and provincial elections. Of the 12 262 candidates, only 300 were women. Of the 6845 successful candidates, 67 were women. (RCSW, 1970: 339–340) The number of women candidates increases with each

---

[2] Although maternal feminists were adamant about the right to vote, they were ambivalent about women actually running for office. (Bashevkin, 1985: 15)

TABLE 7.1

WOMEN RUNNING FOR AND WINNING SEATS IN THE HOUSE OF COMMONS

Year	Number of Women Candidates	Women as Percentage of All Candidates	Number of Women Elected	Women as Percentage of All MPs
1920–1970	300	2.4	18	0.8
1972	71	6.4	5	2.0
1974	135	11.2	9	3.4
1979	195	14.6	13	4.6
1980	181	12.3	14	5.0
1984	214	14.8	27	9.6
1988	302	19.2	39	13.2

Source: 1920–1979 figures, Kopinak, 1980: 445. 1980 figures, Doerr, 1984. 1984 figures, Stewart, 1984. 1988 figures, Elections Canada Communication.

election, although it is still a small percentage of the total number of candidates. The number of women elected remains very small. (See Table 7.1.)

Mary Ellen Smith was the first woman in the British Empire to be made a cabinet minister. She was appointed in British Columbia in 1921. It was not until Ellen Fairclough's appointment in 1957 that a woman became a member of the federal Cabinet. Judy LaMarsh was the second federal appointee, in 1963. Further appointments at the federal level have been few and far between.[3]

Mary Ellen Smith's election to the British Columbia legislature in 1918 signalled two patterns that characterized women politicians for several decades: widow's succession and "fringe" party candidacy. Smith was elected to a seat previously held by her husband until his death. Interestingly, she did not initially run for the same party: her husband had been a Liberal, and she ran as an Independent on a women's rights platform. (Cochrane, 1977: 39) (Unlike Smith, and more recently Rosemary Brown of British Columbia, most women candidates avoid being identified as a one-issue [i.e. women's] candidate.) Between 1921 and 1970, six of the eighteen

---

[3] After the 1974 election three women were appointed to the Liberal Cabinet. Five years later, the Conservatives appointed only one woman, Flora MacDonald. During the 1980 government session there were two women cabinet ministers, three women parliamentary secretaries, and the first woman Speaker of the House. Six women were appointed to Cabinet following the 1984 election. Flora MacDonald and Pat Carney were given key Cabinet posts, which qualified them for membership in the powerful inner Cabinet.

women elected to the House of Commons were widows of former members; another was the wife of a former member. The phenomenon of widow's succession has all but disappeared today. In the 1960s and 1970s, there was only one such example. (Brodie and Vickers, 1982)

Women in Canadian federal and provincial politics have disproportionately represented the smaller or more radical parties, or they have run as Independents. The likelihood of success for "fringe" party candidates is very low—for men or women. In the five federal elections between 1974 and 1988, the proportion of women who were "fringe" candidates is as follows:

1974: 73/125, or 58.4%
1979: 106/195, or 54.4%
1980: 122/181, or 67.4%
1984: 83/214, or 38.7%
1988: 128/302, or 42.3%[4]

Vickers (1978) surveyed all women candidates for federal and provincial elections from 1945 to 1975. One-seventh of the women in her sample were Communist Party candidates; one-third were Liberal or Conservatives. Sixty-three per cent of Vicker's sample ran in ridings where the party had not won in the previous five elections! Of the eighty-two women candidates running for one of the three major parties in the 1979, only one-quarter were considered to have a good chance of being elected. (Gray, 1979: 63) Women candidates are often consigned to areas where the party finds its weakest support. The Conservatives have run women in Quebec; the Liberals have done the same thing in the West. The Conservatives ran a woman against Trudeau in 1968; the Liberals ran a woman against Diefenbaker in 1965. (RCSW, 1970: 339) From the party's point of view, ridings may be categorized as safe, unsafe, or marginal. "Safe" means that the party has a high probability of success. According to Langevin (1977: 24), between 1921 and 1974 only six ridings were safe victories for women candidates.[5] It is not surprising that the success rate for women candidates is about one in ten, compared to about one in five for men. (Brodie and Vickers, 1982: 35)

Why do we have so few women political representatives in Canada? On other measures of political participation—voting for example—women are as active as men. Some optimists feel it is simply a matter of time until women assume a more active role in government. McCormack (1975), on the other hand, suggests turning the question on its head. When women have been so thoroughly excluded from politics, it is a wonder

---

[4] 1974 and 1979 figures, Brodie & Vickers, 1982; 1980 figures, Doerr, 1984; 1984 figures, Stewart, 1984; 1988 figures, Information Services, Elections Canada.

[5] There are some interesting exceptions. For example, Ursula Appolloni unseated David Lewis, former NDP leader, in 1974. Her husband had tried—unsuccessfully—to unseat Mr. Lewis in 1972.

they vote at all! That women vote in the face of political exclusion indicates that women "must have a stronger sense of political efficacy than men." (*Ibid.:* 20) According to McCormack, women and men belong to different political cultures and are defined by differences in socialization, political opportunity structures, and the ways these are defined by the media. Party organizers prefer to repeat that it is difficult to find women to run for public office.

The Report of the Royal Commission on the Status of Women cited three reasons for the paucity of women candidates in federal elections. The first barrier is prejudice of the constituency associations; the second is lack of financial resources; and the third is women's limited geographical mobility. Women candidates interviewed by the Commission confirmed that winning the nomination was a more formidable hurdle than winning the election. (*Ibid.:* 349) According to Vickers (1978: 49), it is probable that party control of the recruitment process at the federal and provincial levels "is the single structural factor most likely to deter (or accelerate) the integration of Canadian women into the political elite."

Women's auxiliaries in the Liberal and Conservative parties were originally established to educate women politically. Some were formed before women had voting rights. These groups were organizationally separate from the party structure. Over time, their role became largely one of fundraising and support. By the 1960s, such a role was being openly criticized. According to the Royal Commission on the Status of Women, the auxiliaries "hinder rather than help the participation of women at policy-making levels.... The women's associations have not accepted as part of their function the task of supporting women contestants for election to top policy-making positions in the party, or of supporting women candidates." (RCSW, 1970: 346)

In 1973, the Liberal party dissolved its women's auxiliaries, replacing them with the Women's Liberal Commission. The Conservative party made a similar move in 1981 with the formation of the National Progressive Women's Caucus. Both of these groups are formally committed to improving the "numerical and substantive representation" of women within the parties. (Bashevkin, 1985: 99–100) To this end they organize conferences and training sessions and draw attention to women's issues regarding employment, child care, and so on. CCF/NDP women's committees have always been organizationally integrated within the party structure, although their role has been the subject of much internal debate. (*Ibid.:* 106–113) This structural integration combined with the egalitarian ideology of the party helps to account for the higher representation of women in decision-making positions in the NDP and its long-term concern with issues such as equal pay. In 1982, the women's committee of the Ontario NDP successfully achieved the first formalized affirmative action initiative within the party. (*Ibid.:* 85–89) But, as Bashevkin has pointed out, these changes are recent and their success is difficult to measure.

Cost is a problem for all political candidates. "Constituency nominations in winnable seats, as well as contests for party executive and leadership have become increasingly expensive pursuits, which effectively discourage all but the most well-heeled competitors." (Bashevkin, 1985: 158) Women typically have less earning power than men and more trouble gaining access to funding sources. Brodie (1977) found that women in her sample of provincial legislators were well educated and held prestigious jobs. But, she noted that the proportion of women candidates had not increased, although the number of qualified women in the population had. Because they do not share the legal and business occupational backgrounds of their male counterparts, women have not developed the networks upon which election depends.

Women political candidates face the same dilemmas of working mothers everywhere in juggling family and work responsibilities. It is no surprise that federal politicians have usually been recruited from the ranks of independent women or married women without young children. Although four of the women federal MPs elected in 1979 had young children at home (Gray, 1979), none of the fourteen winning candidates in the 1980 election did. The high costs of political campaigning and the difficulties of managing family responsibilities mean that our few women politicians are a self-selected group. More often than not they are single, middle-aged, or older career women of middle to upper social class background.

The political representation of women is higher at the municipal than at the provincial or federal level. About one-fifth of municipal politicians are women, although there is considerable regional variation. (In an unprecedented electoral decision, the community of Tweed, Ontario, elected an all-woman council in 1967.) This pyramid structure seems to be a universal pattern. "The higher the political position, the greater the power it controls, the smaller the percentage of women occupying such positions." (Vickers, 1978: 46) One reason is that the barriers are less restrictive at the local level. Municipal politics is, on the surface, divorced from party politics. Municipal nominations do not come from party associations, nor are candidates constrained by the "party line." Yet, as Vickers (1978) points out, the level of power and influence is also much less. "In general, therefore, the municipal level is more open to participation by women in Canada because it is a less desirable arena for participation by men." (*Ibid.*: 46)

Although few women candidates have run on an explicitly feminist platform, the women's movement has increasingly brought concerns such as abortion, day care, equal pay, and the feminization of poverty into public debate. The Feminist Party of Canada, active from 1979 to 1982, was organized by women who felt that the established parties had ignored their concern for peace and environmental protection. (Zaborszky, 1987) Although this particular initiative did not gain the wide following it hoped for, there are signs that "women's issues" are increasingly defined as "election issues." The fact that women's rights are now ensured by the

Charter of Rights attests to the effectiveness of persistent lobbying by women. In the 1984 election in Canada, the National Action Committee on the Status of Women, an umbrella organization of Canadian women's groups, was responsible for bringing together the leaders of Canada's three main parties to formally debate their party's position on women. The debate, which attracted widespread media and public interest, served to formally locate women's concerns within the structure of mainstream partisan politics in Canada.

Much of women's political involvement has been in what Black (1980) refers to as "invisible politics." The issues that have become identified with the women's movement rarely lend themselves to partisan political debates. They are either "social" issues like education or health, or issues such as nuclear disarmament and the environment—"so large as to transcend politics." (*Ibid.:* 63) In the following section we will describe the involvement of women in the "invisible politics" of the women's movement.

THE CONTEMPORARY WOMEN'S MOVEMENT

In the late nineteenth century, women's groups were drawn together in an effort to gain voting rights. On the surface the movement seemed to lose momentum after the vote. But although women's groups were no longer held together by a single goal, they continued to press for women's rights on several fronts. They worked to achieve equal pay legislation and continued to petition to secure the economic well-being of women and children. However, it wasn't until the 1960s that the movement regained its previous strength. This movement, sometimes called the Second Wave of feminism, was widespread enough to be called a universal event.

Why did the revival of feminism occur at the time it did? In one sense, it was part of the growing awareness of the contradictions of an affluent society combined with a general radicalism of the 1960s. Postwar optimism turned to skepticism in the 1960s. Canadians were divided by Quebec nationalism, threatened by the possibility of nuclear war, and critical of American imperialism and the industrial-military complex that drove it. (Kostash, 1980) Economic and demographic changes in the early postwar years created opportunities for women in education and employment. But women faced blatant discrimination at work and received low pay relative to equally qualified and experienced men. There were few social supports for employed mothers, and, at home, women continued to do the bulk of the housework and child care. These contradictions had existed for some time but came to a head in the 1960s when women in all Western countries became increasingly vocal in their criticisms.

Although there were some key differences, the American experience was an important factor in the growth of Canadian feminism in the late 1960s. In both countries the movement developed along two paths. (Freeman, 1984, Adamson *et al.,* 1988) For the sake of argument we can call these institutional feminism and grass-roots feminism. "Institutionalized feminism operates within traditional institutions—inside political parties and government ministries, for example—while grass-roots feminism is more community-based, emphasizing collective organizing, consciousness-raising, and reaching out to women 'on the street'." (Adamson et al., 1988: 12) These labels are applied cautiously. It is only in retrospect that their distinctions appear, and the differences are not always as clear as the labels infer. Although some women were active in both kinds of groups, the groups generally differed in origins, membership, and organizational structure.

INSTITUTIONAL FEMINISM

The National Organization of Women, started by Betty Friedan in 1966, is the backbone of institutionalized feminism in the United States. Using organizational networks put in place by the 1961 President's Commission on the Status of Women and the later appointment of State Commissions, Friedan was able to create a national organization in a short period of time. She was also able to use her extensive media contacts to enhance the impression of the movement's strength and size. NOW sought change within the existing structure and concentrated on legal and economic barriers to equality. Later, NOW members turned their attention to ratifying the Equal Rights Amendment. In the wake of the defeat of the ERA NOW's membership declined, but it jumped again in 1989 when NOW rallied to forestall erosion of abortion rights.

Finding a rallying point was perhaps more difficult in Canada because of our size, sparse population, and the regional, ethnic, racial, and language differences that exist. Until the 1960s, organizations like the Canadian Federation of University Women, the YWCA, the Canadian Business and Professional Women, and the National Council of Jewish Women, while actively supporting women's issues, lacked a unifying issue. The Royal Commission on the Status of Women was the vehicle that drew these groups together.

In 1966, Laura Sabia, then president of the Canadian Federation of University Women, called together other women's groups to form the Committee for Equality for Women. The primary goal of CEW was to initiate a Royal Commission to study sexual inequality in Canada. In July 1966, the editorial column in *Chatelaine* reinforced the need for such a Commission. *Chatelaine*, under Doris Anderson's editorship, had been particularly vocal about women's issues and so must receive part of the credit for the extent to which Canadian women rallied behind this issue. (Adamson, et al., 1988: 51) Sabia, when pressed by a *Globe and Mail* reporter, threatened to march on Parliament if the need for a Royal Commission was ignored. The following day, (January 5, 1967) "Women's March May Back Call for Rights Probe" was front page news in the *Globe*. The Commission was appointed twenty-nine days later. (Morris, 1980; Kome, 1985; 79–82)

When appointed in 1967, the Royal Commission on the Status of Women strengthened the network of women's organizations across Canada as many worked to prepare briefs for the public hearings held in fourteen cities across the country. When the report was published in 1970, it provided a thorough documentation of sexual inequalities in Canada and 167 recommendations for alleviating them. These recommendations set the agenda for the 1970s.

Women from various groups were invited to attend a follow-up conference, "Strategy for Change," in April 1972. This conference gave birth to the National Action Committee on the Status of Women (NAC), an umbrella organization that continues to provide a formal network for Canadian women. With the goal to "unite women and women's groups from across the country in the struggle for equality," NAC's size makes it an important pressure group. It speaks for almost 600 women's organizations and three million Canadian women.

In the period from 1980 to 1982, women's groups in Canada again proved their effectiveness in rallying around a single issue. In this case it was to entrench women's rights in the Canadian Constitution. Women formed a new coalition, the Ad Hoc Committee of Canadian Women, to ensure the inclusion of an equal rights clause. On November 24, 1981, section 28 of the Constitution was reinstated to read "Notwithstanding anything in this charter, all the rights and freedoms in it are guaranteed equally to male and female persons." (Kome, 1983)

GRASS-ROOTS FEMINISM

Grass-roots feminism grew out of women's involvement in student, peace, and New Left movements. Consciousness-raising groups provided a vehicle for women to talk about their experiences of sexism and to express their frustrations. These shared experiences lead to an understanding of the systemic nature of women's oppression and influenced the development of feminist theory and feminist practice. (Adamson, 1988: 198–217) Some women were drawn to activism through this involvement. Others had long been active in their communities, providing services for women and children.

It is difficult to succinctly describe grass-roots feminism. There are few national organizations, and no individuals to speak about general strategies or tactics. By definition, grass-roots groups are loosely organized. They avoid traditional hierarchical organizational structures and resist the idea that any individual speaks for the group.[6]

---

[6] The first major organization of the Second Wave in Canada, the Voice of Women, was established by women who shared some of the ideas of maternal feminism: that women as mothers were instinctively committed to humanistic values. VOW was formed in 1960 by a group consisting primarily of married

There are two currents in what Adamson *et al.* (1988) call grass-roots feminism in Canada: radical feminism and socialist feminism. Both are committed to involving large numbers of women in the struggle for change (*Ibid.:* 64), but there are important ideological and strategic differences between them. Although academics have written about theoretical differences, there has been little record of the practices of either group. (Adamson *et al.*, 1988 and Egan, 1987 are exceptions.) In a sense, there has developed a division of labour within the Canadian women's movement. Socialist feminists focus on class issues and coalition politics, radical feminists on violence against women and women's culture. (Weir, 1987) Both viewpoints find expression in community and workplace organizing, typically around particular issues.

One issue that brought radical feminists together was the abortion caravan in 1970.[7] Started by the Vancouver Women's Caucus to protest the discriminatory basis of the new legislation, the caravan drew support from women across the country as they travelled to Ottawa to present their demands to the House of Commons. Socialist feminists were drawn together in the Toronto International Women's Day Committee (IWDC). (Egan, 1987) This group started in 1977 to plan an International Women's Day march, but has, over the years, broadened its focus to bring together working-class women from trade unions and immigrant and other minority women's groups. A rallying point of socialist feminism has been the support of women's union activity. One of the main contributions of the IWDC has been to bring women's committees from various unions together. The movement as a whole has been slower to encompass women of colour or lesbian women. (Wall, 1982: 25)

Grass-roots feminism is a response to the ambiguity women feel about formal politics. Given the small number of women elected representatives and the general lack of sensitivity to the issues women define as central, grass-roots organizing is a more appropriate political strategy. Women have a long history of community-based reform. Grass-roots organizations "have provided the context for the empowerment of women other-

---

women and mothers. Their main concern was the threat of nuclear war. Gradually this group broadened their focus to include environmental protection and other feminist concerns, including reproductive choice.

[7] Because their tactics and their arguments provided much more drama than the plodding work of the liberals, the radical feminists received much more media attention in the early years. For example, the founding of the National Organization of Women (NOW) in the U.S. in 1964 was treated cursorily by the *New York Times*. It was reported several days after the event and placed between a recipe for turkey stuffing and a fashion bulletin. (Tuchman, 1978: 201–202) However, when radical feminists disrupted the Miss America Pageant in 1969, throwing dish towels and, yes, bras in the garbage, it was a media event *par excellence*. The person who erroneously reported that women were burning their bras created a media myth that persisted for a decade.

wise politically marginalized because of poverty, physical location and lack of resources." (Vickers, 1988: 49) The flexible structure of these groups and their sensitivity to financial and child-care needs of participants encourage the participation of those most affected by barriers to conventional political involvement.

It is difficult to know how many women have participated in grass-roots feminism in Canada. Some groups and organizations have become "institutionalized" over time; others come together and disband as needs change. The following description of women's groups in Quebec shows how extensive these grass-roots networks are.

> In Québec, in 1985, within the women's movement broadly defined, there were 755 women's groups and 618 regional and local circles of the Association féminine d'éducation et d'action sociale (A.F.E.A.S.). The membership of these groups and associations varies considerably. Some consist of just a handful of women (such as the Collectif des femmes immigrantes). Others, such as A.F.E.A.S. which has 33,000 members, have branches in every region of Québec. The Circles des fermières have a membership of 75,000 women and the 52 associations of the Fédération des femmes du Québec (F.F.Q.) have a total of 40,000 members. Roughly 1,400 groups and associations of women exist in Québec alone. Obviously the activities, objectives, struggles, and approaches of these 1,400 groups and associations are extremely varied. (Vickers, 1988: 35-36)

Even with differences in strategy, grass-roots and institutional feminists agree about major issues. In many cases issues first exposed by grass-roots feminists at the community level have been later addressed by institutional feminists at the national level. Their combined efforts have created a host of organizations and services to meet the needs of Canadian women.

Grass-roots feminists have established a network of shelters, crisis centres, and counselling centres for women. Women in trade unions have worked hard to ensure that maternity benefits, equal pay for work of equal value, child care, and sexual harassment are part of union policy statements and contracts. NAC has proved to be an effective lobby group monitoring legislative progress and assessing the impact of legislative and policy changes on women. Working within established political parties, women have pressed for equitable substantive and numerical representation of women. Magazines, newsletters, journals, women's publishing houses, and bookstores provide a forum of information and debate.[8]

---

[8] All "alternate" services provided by women (hostels, clinics, and women's communication media) suffer constant financial and funding crises. The financial dependence of women's groups on state funding mirrors women's privately experienced financial dependence and creates a similar dilemma. On both the interpersonal and institutional levels, women are tied in a web of contradiction: they are critical and distrustful of the very system on which their financial viability depends.

The overriding challenge for all women's organizations and services is to meet the needs of all women, whatever their race, social class, sexual orientation, or age. In the last decade, the women's movement has faced a different kind of challenge—the increased organizational activity and visibility of antifeminism.

ANTIFEMINISM

In February 1980, a bold-typed ad appeared in a small Ontario weekly:

FOR WOMEN ONLY
Seven Basic Needs of a Husband
How can you become more of the wife
of your husband's dreams?

Clearly feminism has not appealed to all Canadian women. In the last two decades antifeminism spawned several best-selling books[9] and many training sessions, like the one advertised in the newspaper. Fuelled by political and economic conservatism, the rise of religious fundamentalism, and the growth of the anti-abortion movement, antifeminism grew in organizational strength in the 1980s. Much of the strength of the New Right lies in its ability to link economic and sexual conservatism in a defense of the traditional, patriarchal family. (Dubinsky, 1985: 33) Although these institutional linkages are less well established in Canada than in the United States, here, too, New Right groups have gained in organizational strength and visibility.

Although there are differences in basic philosophies, antifeminists generally believe that sex differences and a sexual division of labour are biological givens. Many believe differences between women and men are divinely ordained, and quotations from the Bible are used to support this assumption. The authority of the church is reinforced physically: church buildings are customarily used as meeting places. Antifeminists are concerned about the breakdown of the family and the deterioration of values on which traditional family life is based. "They have an ideal image of woman as mother and helpmate to man, an ideal that has little room for lesbians, single mothers or independent women." (Adamson *et al.*, 1988: 85)

In the United States, antifeminist sentiment found a focus in the campaign to halt state ratification of the Equal Rights Amendment. Stop-ERA

---

[9] *The Total Woman* (Morgan, M., New York: Simon and Schuster, 1975) and *Fascinating Womanhood* (Andelin, H. B., New York: Basic Books, 1973) are perhaps the best known.

was started by Phyllis Schlafly in 1972. "Drawing on a network composed of readers of her newsletter, *Eagle Forum*, Republican women's clubs, and fundamentalist churches, she was able to bring to the anti-ERA campaign a political expertise the feminist organizations did not yet have." (Freeman, 1984: 548) They, like Canadian antifeminist groups opposed to entrenching women's rights in the Constitution, object fundamentally to official denials of inherent sex differences. Fuelled by a general conservative sentiment and aligned with other New Right organizations, the Stop-ERA campaign can only be defined as a success. Since 1977, no additional states have ratified the ERA and several have voted to rescind earlier ratification. (Marshall, 1984)

REAL Women (Realistic, Equal, Active for Life) is in many ways the Canadian counterpart to Stop-ERA. REAL Women was started in 1984 in response to two events. One was the inclusion of women's rights in the Charter of Rights, a move that REAL Women fear may have adverse effects on traditional family values. Their motto is "Women's Rights but Not at the Expense of Human Rights." The second event was Judy Erola's suggestion that the tax exemption for dependent spouses be discontinued. The founders of REAL Women interpret this as a denial of the social importance of mothering. REAL Women claimed a membership of 20 000 following its first national conference in 1985.

REAL Women identify themselves as explicitly pro-family, but as Eichler (1986: 27) argues, this is an inappropriate label. "The pro-family movement is in fact advocating one type of family, namely the patriarchal family who can subsist on one income." This view of the family is the crux of antifeminist objections to feminism and the basis of their arguments against women's employment. REAL Women oppose nonmarital, nonprocreative sexuality (Eichler, 1986) homosexuality, abortion, no-fault divorce, and measures to ensure employment equity.

REAL Women objects strongly to the media's apparent assumption that NAC speaks for all Canadian women.[10] They have criticized the NAC for failing women, especially housewives. Yet as Eichler (1986) has shown, these criticisms are erroneous. Indeed there are many issues about which the NAC and REAL Women share concern, including pornography and the status of women as housewives. Both have argued for increased recognition of domestic work and financial protection for full-time mothers in Canadian pension plans. (Eichler, 1986)

According to Erwin's (1988) survey of members of antifeminist groups in Canada, members are largely middle-class, middle-aged people "whose

---

10 REAL Women has been very critical of the NAC in its publications and media releases. Gwen Landolt, one of the founders, was quoted in the press as saying that feminists tried to capitalize on the 1989 Montreal killings to push for more funding for their cause. (*Kitchener-Waterloo Record*, December 12, 1989. p. A2)

lives exemplify the conservative values of the post-World War I period." (*Ibid.:* 276) They are also an extremely religious group—mostly Roman Catholic and Protestant fundamentalist. More than three-quarters send their children to religious schools and 63 per cent attend church at least twice a week. (*Ibid.:* 270) Church involvement was a key to recruitment. "Because the movement's recruitment network is largely located in the conservative churches, it has succeeded in mobilizing a specific type of homemaker—the deeply religious one." (*Ibid.:* 275) In more general terms, antifeminism is a response to the same economic and political shifts that gave rise to the Second Wave of feminism. As Dubinsky (1985: 40) argues, when we recognize that the economic and social conditions of most women's lives have changed little, "we can begin to understand why feminism is losing ground to the right on issues such as sexuality and the desirability of the patriarchal family."

In her book *The Second Stage* (1982), Betty Friedan held radical feminists responsible for the strength of the antifeminist backlash. Eisenstein (1984: 137–138) disagrees. In her opinion, the radical views of some feminists paved the way for less radical reforms. "Precisely because women were raising such a wide range of issues, across such a broad spectrum of sexual, social, economic and political demands, certain of the less threatening of these were able to find their way into legislative and judicial decisions benefiting women." Clearly, coming to terms with the New Right is one of the most important challenges feminism currently faces.

CONCLUSION

The women's movement has done a great deal to alter the structures that maintain sexual inequality and the attitudes that reinforce these structures. Attempts to reduce restrictions limiting women's access to education, to employment, to political participation, and to ensure equality before the law have all met with resistance. And with each new change a new set of loopholes is uncovered. The inability to legislate desired changes in these areas supports the conclusion that much of the problem lies beyond the influence of formal control. The final chapter will consider subtle ways male dominance is maintained.

8 CIRCLES OF SOCIAL CONTROL

Berger's (1963: 68–78) metaphor of circles of social control is a useful one.[1] He invites us to imagine that an individual is situated at the centre of a set of concentric circles. The outermost circles are explicit, formally defined, legal, political, and economic controls. The inner circles are the more subtle and implicit controls that operate in the context of interpersonal relationships: persuasion, ridicule, gossip, and so on. Earlier chapters focused on the outer circles: family law reform, reproductive control, political representation, anti-discrimination legislation, equal pay, and so on. Creating change in these areas has been plodding work. Each step has uncovered another loophole and each advance has met strong resistance. Yet, regardless of voting rights, women are underrepresented in political power structures; regardless of pay equity laws, women are consistently paid less. Equality of access to education has done little to change the number of women seeking nontraditional, professional, or managerial training. Efforts to legislate against sexual harassment and wife battering have not eliminated these as problems. That such inequities persist in areas covered by legislation suggests the complexity of the situation. It also suggests that many obstacles and barriers lie beyond the realm of public policy.

This chapter discusses some ways definitions of masculinity and femininity recreate sexual inequality. Gender norms are neither formally stated nor legally sanctioned. They nonetheless have a powerful, if subtle, influence on behaviour.

We are born into a society structured on male privilege. Our own observations and experiences, the reactions of others, and the language we learn to categorize experience all reinforce cultural definitions of masculinity and femininity. These cultural definitions, coupled with a tradition of male authority, interact with economic controls to maintain gender distinctions. Gender distinctions are established at the institutional level and reinforced through socialization, custom, and where these fail, intimidation and (occasionally) force.

NORMATIVE RESTRICTION

Western societies typically use what Fox (1977) calls normative restriction to regulate the behaviour of women. Normative restriction gives the illusion that women are independent because behaviour is rarely formally sanctioned. Instead, normative restriction operates through internalized

---

[1] Unfortunately this discussion is found in a chapter subtitled "Man in Society."

norms and values—through value constructs like "nice girl" or "lady." As such, normative control can be extended to cover a wide range of behaviour. "There seems to be little that a woman does that cannot be used as a test of her niceness and therefore as an opportunity for control." (*Ibid.*: 811)

According to Fox, to be publicly labelled unchaste is the surest way to lose one's "nice-girl" status. Young women may therefore be encouraged to "withdraw early to the moral safety of marriage." (*Ibid.*: 815) Limited alternatives for working-class girls increases the attractiveness of marriage. According to a British study (McRobbie, 1978: 106), a girl who has no opportunity to leave her parents' home for education or a job, who is closely closeted in a culture of femininity that restricts expressions of sexuality, will automatically think of marriage. As one fifteen-year-old said, "I worry a lot about not getting married. I mean what if no one wants me and I had to stay with me Mum and Dad." A Canadian teenager interviewed by journalist Ann Pappert (1980) felt the same way. "I can't imagine myself not married within five years. I'd consider myself a failure if I wasn't." Pappert found the world view held by the female students she talked to more influenced by the television image of women than by the women's movement.

The media have been strongly criticized by feminists for contributing to the inculcation of gender stereotypes. Without exception, studies investigating the image of women and children in advertising, literature, textbooks, movies, and television all support the same conclusion: women are underrepresented in the media. When they appear, it is usually in a stereotyped way. By portraying women in stereotypically female roles and postures, the media contribute to cultural assumptions of heterosexism, supporting the notion that women are economically and socially dependent. Idealizations of romantic love, marriage, and motherhood encourage young women to see these as desirable and expected for them, and encourage young men to see women in these terms.

Gerbner (1978) is very pessimistic about (what he sees as) the increasingly repressive image of women in television. He argues that this image is indicative of the part played by the media in cultivating resistance to change. In Gerbner's view, television is unique among the media because it is so pervasive. He feels television has assumed a role similar to that occupied by religion in pre-industrial society—one is born into its symbolic environment, and one rarely challenges its cultural assumptions. In a series of studies that began in 1967, Gerbner and his associates have regularly monitored television content and compared these trends to trends in audience perceptions. His findings confirm that frequent viewers have internalized a world view and a value system congruent with the world of television. In this way, television acts as an effective means of social control.

Media stereotypes of women extend beyond the portrayal of women in stereotypically female roles. Goffman (1979:1) used the term "gender display" to describe conventionalized portrayals of "culturally established correlates of sex." Once gender displays become established, they can be used by advertisers as idealizations of masculinity and femininity. Goffman described (and provided countless examples of) gender displays used by print advertisers to portray male dominance. By objectifying and depicting women as fearful and submissive, high fashion advertising reinforces the notion of woman as other, as different, as separate.

Norms governing women's appearance "constitute a central element in the objectification and devaluation of females." (Schur, 1983: 66) The image of women created by the advertising, fashion, and cosmetic industries is a narrow, superficial, and largely unattainable picture of female beauty. The pervasiveness of this flawless image affects both men and women. Women will inevitably fall short of the ideal in their own eyes and in the eyes of men. "Widespread imagery of this sort encourages and in a sense 'trains' men to visually objectify women. It also provides physical criteria of assessment, according to which men are likely to find real women deficient." (Schur, 1983: 69) Women who violate presentation norms by giving insufficient attention to their appearance may be strongly sanctioned, as Millman's (1980) study of overweight women makes clear. On the other hand, much to the detriment of her health, a woman can never be too thin. (Szekely, 1988)

The following paragraphs show how patterns of interaction reflect, construct, and maintain the subordination of women. Mechanisms of control form a continuum from sexist language to sexual harassment to overt acts of violence linked by an assumption of male privilege. The subtle ways men dominate social interaction may seem innocuous in isolation. But as Schur (1982) argues, tolerating these everyday expressions of sexism opens the door to more overt and intolerable expressions such as sexual harassment or sexual assault.

PATTERNS OF INTERACTION

Social interaction is the battlefield on which the daily war between the sexes is fought. It is here that women are constantly reminded what their "place" is and here that they are put back in their place should they venture out. Thus social interaction serves as the locus of the most common means of social control employed against women. By being continually reminded of their inferior status in their interactions with others, and continually compelled to acknowledge that status in their own patterns of behaviour, women may internalize society's definition of them as inferior so thoroughly that they are often unaware of what their status is. Inferiority becomes habitual, and the inferior place assumes the familiarity—and eventual desirability—of home. (Henley and Freeman, 1984: 465)

The study of language use and interaction patterns tells us a great deal about the exercise of power in everyday life. According to Fishman (1978:

397), "power is the ability to impose one's definition of what is possible, what is right, what is rational, what is real." How do tactics used by men and women in conversation reflect this? Considerable research supports the observation that men and women structure conversation differently. But are these sex differences or are they power differences? Can the two be disentangled?

"There are two major elements to the division of labor within verbal interaction: conversational dominance and conversational support." (Kollock et al., 1985: 35) Conversational dominance is established in a number of ways, all of which involve a measure of compliance by the other party. Two common ways of controlling conversations are to monopolize conversational time or to interrupt. Conversational support is accomplished by asking questions, using tag questions, or by using minimal responses like "um-mum." Women more often than men use these kinds of supports; men more typically use control devices. The myth that women are more talkative than men is simply not supported by research evidence. On the contrary, men establish conversational dominance by taking longer "turns" when talking. Men also interrupt women more frequently than women interrupt men. This lack of symmetry is also found in conversations between adults and children (adults interrupt more), supporting the assumption that these differences are tied to status.

Women initiate conversations by asking questions more often than men do. (Fishman, 1978) This tendency has been interpreted by some as a reflection of insecurity and a hesitancy to state an opinion. Lakoff (1975), for example argues that women commonly use devices like "tag questions" in their conversations. A "tag question" is a conversational gambit that is half statement, half question. For example: "This is an interesting idea, isn't it?" Another mechanism women use is the qualifying adjective—"This idea is *rather* interesting." Women also inflect a statement as though it were a question, using a technique called a "high-rise." (McConnell-Ginet, 1978) Women also use what Lakoff refers to as "prefacing declarations": "I guess..." or "I wonder...." Or they might disparage their own opinions: "I don't know anything about it but it sounds interesting to me." (Henley, 1975: 188) In each of these examples, the speaker avoids having to directly state an opinion. Should someone disagree, the speaker can easily change her opinion.

Why do women use these devices? Fishman (1978) is not convinced that women are unsure of their opinions. But their attempts to converse as men do have not been successful. Men typically initiate a conversation with a statement; they expect a response and usually receive one. But women's statements are often ignored. By asking a question women can usually count on some sort of reaction.

Conversation is "work" for women in a way that it is not for men. (Fishman, 1978) Women must engage in tactics to ensure ongoing interaction. And this work "is not seen as what women do, but as part of what they are." (*Ibid.*: 405) Women are submissive in conversation; they hesitate more, and apologize more than men do. And they take more responsibility for conversation flow by encouraging other speakers. In other words, the way conversation is structured is another of the enveloping circles of social control.

Language is more than a means of communication. The words we use to identify the social world and define our experience orient us to particular aspects of the social environment. Thus when we acquire language, we acquire at the same time a way of organizing our experience. It is not, therefore, an accident that there are far more English words to describe women than men and that many of these have negative connotations.[2] The use of sexist language is a way of making women's experience invisible or different. For example, we sometimes use different words to describe men's and women's work (chef versus cook)—even when the work is the same. (Epstein, 1988: 215) The use of terms like "family violence" obscures the fact that the overwhelming majority of victims are women. (Eichler, 1984) Describing independent women as *un*married, children born to single women as *illegitimate*, or women who are not mothers as child*less* reinforces the social expectation of marriage and motherhood. Stigmatizing lesbians similarly reinforces heterosexism.

A number of studies investigating the implicit meaning of generic terms such as "man" and "he" support the conclusion that people envision a male when they see or hear generic terms. When students are asked to respond to cues using singular generic pronouns, they more frequently identify male referents than when plural pronouns are used. Similarly, when asked to interpret the generic "he," most students assumed it referred to men only. (Pearson, 1985) Of course, sometimes it does. Adams and Ware (1984: 481) report that at the end of one of the segments of the acclaimed television series "The Ascent of Man," the host chatted with a guest anthropologist for a few minutes about women!

In the past two decades there have been some important shifts in language use. Changing traditional designations such as policeman, chairman, or salesman to police officer, chairperson (or simply chair), and sales representative are relatively easily accomplished. Some changes have been occasioned by the movement of women into what were once male-only occupations. For example, the U.S. Supreme Court changed the form of address from Mr. Justice to Justice after Sandra Day O'Connor's appointment. (Epstein, 1988: 228) One can avoid generic pronouns by using plural forms, or by alternating singular masculine and feminine forms. These adaptations seem more readily acceptable than the idea that we create a nonsexist singular pronoun such as "tey." A number of government agencies, educational institutions, publishing houses, and professional

---

[2] There are over 500 synonyms for prostitute in English and approximately 1000 terms to describe women in derogatory ways.

associations have endorsed language change and issued guidelines for nonsexist usage. Some continue to trivialize the concern ("Never before in the herstory of personkind have such serious assaults been mounted on the Queen's English"),[3] but such complaints receive less attention than they did in the past.

As more women move into decision-making positions in the labour force, we will no doubt see continued erosion of patterns of sexist language and begin to see more gender similarity in interpersonal interaction. On the other hand, there is no evidence that more overt acts of sexism like sexual harassment are on the wane.

SEXUAL COERCION, VIOLENCE, AND THE THREAT OF VIOLENCE

In uncovering the systemic nature of sexual coercion and its pervasiveness, feminists have shown how sexual intimidation is integral to the maintenance of dominance. "Everyday" occurrences of sexual harassment, obscene telephone calls, sexual humour that plays on exploitation and violence all remind women that they are at risk and vulnerable just because they are female. (Sheffield, 1989) "Fear of rape and attack, of which low-level aggravation is a reminder, plays a part in keeping women from claiming public space as their own. We are brought up to be wary— of strange men, of dark streets, of underpopulated subway cars." (Pollitt, quoted in Epstein, 1988: 134–135) Intimidation and fear are important components in maintaining dominance. They are so often backed by acts of violence, which impresses their coercive impact. Fifty-six per cent of women who live in Canadian cities are afraid to be alone on city streets at night. (Smith, 1990: 8)

North Americans are ambivalent in their reactions to violence. We seemingly have a high tolerance for media violence, including sexual violence. Although we publicly condemn overt acts of violence, enforcement agencies have turned a blind eye to family violence. (Propper, 1990) Far from being rare occurrences, battery, sexual coercion, acts of or threats of sexual violence are appallingly commonplace. *Most* women report experience of sexual harassment. (Kadar, 1982) Each year an estimated one million Canadian women are beaten by their husbands. (MacLeod, 1987) Twenty-three per cent of Canadians said they were personally aware of serious incidences of physical abuse of wives by their husbands. (Canadian Gallup Poll, November, 1988) One in four Canadian women will be sexually assaulted in their lifetime. (Smith, 1990) In 1988, half of the 143 homicides in Canada committed by an immediate family member were women killed by their husbands. (Women in Canada, 1990: 155)

---

[3] Quoted in Kramer, Thorne and Henley, 1978, page 648.

The following paragraphs describe the systemic nature of sexual harassment and wife battering. Historically, cultural definitions of masculine authority, particularly in the family, have amounted to a tacit acceptance of sexually aggressive male behaviour. Whether at work or among intimates, the line between what is socially defined as acceptable and what is personally intolerable is a fine one. (MacLeod, 1987: 41–42) By focusing on systemic patterns, the women's movement has dispelled myths that these are rare occurrences, that women precipitate the reaction, or that men who harass or batter are psychologically disturbed.

Radical, socialist, and liberal feminists have approached these issues from different vantage points. Radical feminists were instrumental in initiatives to establish the network of shelters and centres across the country to house and support women victims of rape or physical abuse. Socialist feminists have worked with unions to draw attention to the issue of sexual harassment at work and to institute ways of dealing with it. Lobbying and public education on the part of liberal feminists has lead to increased public awareness and legislative changes, including improved procedures for handling calls for assistance from abused women. These are recognized as interim solutions. Eliminating unwanted sexual aggression and violence against women depends on eliminating the conditions that give rise to these behaviours in the first place: structured inequality and social tolerance.

SEXUAL HARASSMENT

The Canadian Labour Code defines sexual harassment as

> any conduct, comment, gesture, or contact of a sexual nature that is likely to cause offense or humiliation to any employee or that might, on reasonable grounds, be perceived by that employee as placing a sexual condition on employment or on any opportunity for training or promotion. (Labour Canada Factsheet *Sexual Harassment at Work*)

"Sexual harassment is one of those levers those in power use to control those who are not." (Kadar, 1982: 169) Because women typically work in jobs where supervisors or bosses are male, the structural conditions of women's work create an environment conducive to sexual harassment. Women in "display jobs," like actresses or waitresses, or women in nontraditional work where male culture is strong may seem to be particularly at risk. Yet as Field (1983) says, women in nontraditional jobs are no more subject to sexual harassment than women in high status professional or managerial jobs, because their job security is protected by unions. However the assumption that nontraditional jobs are worse may serve as an effective gatekeeping function keeping women from considering this kind of work.

Field (who was among the first women to be employed in the mill at Stelco in Hamilton, Ontario) says we should distinguish between employer initiated and co-worker harassment. "The more intense forms—physical violence, sexual ultimatums and threats—are primarily perpetuated by men who have direct authority to hire and fire, promote and demote." (Field, 1983: 145) Co-worker harassment is not usually geared to eliciting sexual favours. Because co-workers do not have the leverage that bosses have, co-worker harassment is unlikely to be coercive. In certain work environments, men use sexually explicit language, make sexual remarks, and tell sexist jokes whether or not women are present. (*Ibid.:* 146) This behaviour reflects a particular work culture where such bantering is encouraged. "Co-workers harassment occurs daily in thousands of different ways as men, consciously or not, turn women into sexual objects, put us down, joke about our bodies and our brains." (Field, 1983: 146)

Eliminating these two kinds of harassment require different tactics. Many unions have taken stands against employer-initiated sexual harassment to ensure the protection of women's jobs (although these initiatives have not been taken without resistance). The Canadian Labour Code requires employers to issue policy statements regarding sexual harassment, explaining the law, and outlining the complaint mechanism. Long-term strategies must focus on both structured inequality in the labour force and cultural definitions of masculinity as they are played out at work. "Eliminating workplace sexual harassment requires an attitudinal change on the part of men. As such it cannot be legislated but must come about through pressure on men and our ability to force them to change." (Field, 1983: 151)

WIFE BATTERY

Wife battery, like sexual harassment, reflects economic dependence and cultural assumptions of male authority and female passivity. Understanding the extent of such abuse of power is complicated by the fact that its exercise has long been tolerated. (MacLeod, 1980) "The absence of clear-cut legal prohibitions and penalties for intrafamily violence throughout our society's history is a major reason for our present attitudes and relative lack of interest in punishing wife beaters." (Propper, 1990: 281) "Attitudes that tolerated and perpetuated the abuse of women remained long after the laws permitting assault were repealed." (*Ibid.:* 282) As MacLeod (1980: 66) explains, "wife battering is much more than individual cases of physical violence. It is the licence society gives a man to use violence against his wife without fear of retribution—he may never take this licence, but he possesses it nonetheless."

Battering can be psychological, sexual, verbal, or economic abuse, as well as physical abuse. (MacLeod, 1987: 16) To live under the constant threat of violence is extremely stressful, as a respondent in MacLeod's (1987: 14) study made clear. "It's probably hard to imagine, but I used to pray that my husband would hit me, or do whatever he was going to do to me. I figured the pain couldn't be worse than living in constant fear."

Neither batterers, nor their victims fit a psychological or socio-emotional profile (MacLeod, 1987: 38–40), although women who have lived with abuse suffer low-self esteem, isolation, and guilt. Women are held in abusive relationships by their lack of alternatives. They may quite literally have nowhere to go. Most of the 15 730 women who stayed in transition houses in 1985 were poor. (*Ibid.:* 21) But controls are more complex than this. Many women have been conditioned to accept responsibility for the success of their relationship. Battering often begins with behaviour that seems a "normal" expression of jealousy, possessiveness, or rough sexual play. Initially it is interpreted as a sign of love; of the intensity of the relationship. It is not until minor incidences become major that the pattern is recognized, and this may take months or even years. (*Ibid.:* 43)

Legislators now take wife battering much more seriously than they did in 1982 when its mention in the House of Commons was greeted with unveiled amusement. (MacLeod, 1987: 3) Many communities now have provisions for interim interventions: shelters for battered women, public education, training of law enforcement people to be more sensitive to the needs of battered women, and counselling for abusive partners. As with other mechanisms of sexual coercion, the long-term goal of prevention requires restructuring the institutional props that perpetuate gender inequality.

Canadians were grimly reminded of the depth of misogynist feeling and its potentially horrifying consequences in the fall of 1989 when Marc Lepine murdered fourteen women students at the University of Montreal. Lepine left no doubt that this extreme act of violence was specifically directed at women. He literally stalked the engineering building, shooting women with a semi-automatic rifle. After ordering the men to leave a classroom he shouted at the women: "You're all a bunch of feminists, I hate feminists." His three page suicide letter blamed feminists for ruining his life and preventing him from being accepted to the engineering school. Although Lepine had openly expressed his anger and resentment towards women before, his behaviour was otherwise not unusual enough to warn of this extreme act of violence. Two aspects of this man's history seem common to sex offenders: he had been physically abused by his father as a young child, and he had a strong interest in violent movies—but neither of these made him unique.

CONCLUSION

"The social control of women assumes many forms, it may be internal or external, implicit or explicit, private or public, ideological or repressive." (Smart and Smart, 1978: 2) Women's subordination is reflected and recreated in our institutional exclusion, in the social myths that define appropriate behaviour, and in patterns of everyday interaction. Women are rewarded for conforming to social expectations and sanctioned for deviating. In consequence, patterns of speech, demeanor, and sexual behaviour are characteristically those of subordinates. The circles of social control enclose and encapsulate women. Goffman (1979: 6) makes the point with poetic flair:

> The expression of subordination and domination through this swarm of situational means is more than a mere tracing of symbol or ritualistic affirmation of the social hierarchy. These expressions considerably constitute the hierarchy; they are the shadow and the substance.

While we may despair at the pervasiveness of sexism and become frustrated that so little seems to change, there are reasons to be optimistic about the future. First, it is important to recognize that the efforts of countless women—housewives and community workers, union activists and lobbyists, teachers and volunteer counsellors—have indeed created significant change in one generation. Canadians are much more aware of, and sympathetic to, issues of structured inequality than two decades ago. There is now general support for policy provisions regarding reproductive control, child care, equal pay for work of equal value, employment equity, and freedom from sexual coercion and physical abuse. Feminists have developed coalitions between women's groups and within unions and community groups. In unions, in community groups, and in private households, men have taken up issues of pay equity, child care, violence against women, and reproductive choice. Urban environmental protection agencies are beginning to question the rigidity of assumptions about the structure of work patterns. Men and women with nonwork interests or responsibilities will benefit as companies are required to enable flexible work schedules and periodic telecommuting. The following two examples illustrate the potential of coalitions generally to improve the conditions of women's lives—to the ultimate benefit of all.

In the past two decades women have been increasingly visible in the union movement. Women's increased membership and their solidarity through women's committees and caucuses has challenged unions to better represent their interests. An important transition has been the increased recognition within unions that workplace issues and private, family issues are interrelated. For example "Day care is a workplace issue, a family issue, an issue of women's rights and most certainly a union issue." (Briskin, 1983: 262.) Consequently, unions have begun to take up issues of sexual harassment, maternity leave, sexual orientation, and reproductive control, as well as the more traditional concerns of pay equity. (Egan and Yanz, 1983)

Recognizing their communality of interest has led to increased mutual support among union and nonunion feminists. Union activists have made sexual orientation and reproductive rights union issues, and nonunion feminists have made wage control and the right to organize and strike part of their agenda. These developing alliances, between women and men in the union movement and between unionized and nonunionized women, provide a solid base of support for the future.

Another example of an alliance that cuts across age, sex, and potentially racial barriers is the increased social activism of older people. (Wilson, 1989) Older people form a sizable lobby group. Their political voice is strengthened by the fact that they are more inclined to vote than younger people. Seniors have created an impressive array of organizations to increase their economic security, to correct misconceptions about aging and the aged, and to foster an image of older people as vital and productive. For example the American Association of Retired People (AARP) has 28 million members and 35 000 active volunteers. (DeVoss, 1989) As a national organization it is second in size only to the American Automobile Association, and its monthly publication, *Modern Maturity*, recently surpassed *TV Guide* as the widest circulating magazine in America. There are a number of senior citizen and pension organizations in Canada, as well as several chapters of American-based groups. There is also a network of federal and provincial Advisory Councils on Aging and a Ministry of State for Senior Citizens. While the Canadian groups are relatively small and less vocal than the American groups, the same potential exists. Predictably, Canadian seniors will become increasingly vocal in future.

The fact that older women outnumber older men suggests a potential power base for protecting and enhancing women's options. Many of the issues of concern to older women (money, housing, health care, support systems) are also of concern to older men. In a sense age *is* an equalizer. As Rossi (1986: 141) argues, "in an aging society, a female majority, combined with dramatic blurring of sex and gender differences in the second half of life, may well effect a change in the structure of social institutions, and in the values that become dominant in the society."

The challenge of social and economic equality is a monumental one. But, as we become aware of women's history, women's culture, and the nature of women's social contribution, it is clear that there is a strong tradition on which to draw. In this tradition, it is possible to envision and to continue to struggle for a different kind of future.

REFERENCES

Abella, Rosalie, 1984. *Report of the Commission on Equality in Employment*. Ottawa: Minister of Supply and Services.

Achilles, Rona, 1988. "Artificial Reproduction: Hope Chest or Pandora's Box?" In Burnet, Jean, ed., *Looking into my Sister's Eyes: An Exploration in Women's History*, pp. 291-312. Toronto: The Multicultural Society of Ontario.

Acker, Joan, 1989. "Making Gender Visible." In Ruth Wallace, ed., *Feminism and Sociological Theory*, pp. 65-81. Newbury Park: Sage.

Acton, Janice, Penny Goldsmith and Bonnie Shepard, eds., 1974. *Women at Work: Ontario, 1850-1930*. Toronto: Canadian Women's Educational Press.

Adams, K.L., and N.C. Ware, 1984. "Sexism and the English Language: The linguistic implications of being woman." In Jo Freeman, ed., *Women: A Feminist Perspective*. Third Edition, pp. 478-491. Palo Alto: Mayfield Publishing.

Adamson, Nancy, Linda Briskin and Margaret McPhail, 1988. *Feminists Organizing for Change*. Toronto: Oxford.

Akyeampong, Ernest, 1987. "Involuntary Part-Time Employment in Canada, 1975-1986." *Canadian Social Trends*, Autumn: 26-29.

Alcoff, Linda, 1988. "Cultural Feminism versus Post-Structuralism." *Signs*, 13: 405-436.

Anderson, Bonnie, and Judith Zinsser, 1988. *A History of Their Own*, Vol II. New York: Harper and Row.

Anisef, P., J. Paasche and A. Turritten, 1980. *Is the Die Cast? Educational Achievements and Work Designations of Ontario Youth*. Toronto: Ministry of Colleges and Universities.

Archibald, Kathleen, 1970. *Sex and the Public Service*. Ottawa: Information Canada.

Armstrong, Pat, and Hugh Armstrong, 1985. "Beyond Sexless Class and Classless Sex: Toward Feminist Marxism." In Pat Armstrong, Hugh Armstrong, Pat Connelly and Angela Miles, eds., *Feminist Marxism or Marxist Feminism: A Debate*, pp. 1-38. Toronto: Garamond Press.

Armstrong, Pat, 1984. *Labour Pains: Women's Work in Crisis*. Toronto: The Women's Press.

Armstrong, Pat, and Hugh Armstrong, 1984. *The Double Ghetto*. Revised Edition. Toronto: McClelland and Stewart.

Arnopoulos, S. M., 1979. *Problems of Immigrant Women in the Canadian Labour Force*. Ottawa: The Canadian Advisory Council on the Status of Women.

Baker, Maureen, 1988. *Aging in Canadian Society*. Toronto: McGraw-Hill Ryerson.

Baker, Maureen, 1985. *What Will Tomorrow Bring...?* Ottawa: The Canadian Advisory Council on the Status of Women.

Barber, Marilyn, 1986. "Sunny Ontario for British Girls, 1900–1930." In Burnet, Jean, ed., 1986. *Looking into my Sister's Eyes: An Exploration in Women's History*, pp. 55-73. Toronto: The Multicultural Society of Ontario.

Barron, R. D., and G.M. Norris, 1976. "Sexual Divisions and the Dual Labour Market." In S. Allen and D. Barker eds., *Dependence and Exploitation in Work and Marriage*, pp. 47-69. London: Longman.

Bart, Pauline, 1971. "Sexism and Social Science: From the Guilded Cage to the Iron Cage, or the Perils of Pauline." *Journal of Marriage and the Family*, 33: 734-735.

Bashevkin, Sylvia, 1985. *Toeing the Lines: Women and Party Politics in English Canada*. Toronto: University of Toronto Press.

Becker, Gary, 1971. *The Economics of Discrimination*. Second Edition. Chicago: University of Chicago Press.

Becker, Gary, 1964. *Human Capital*. New York: National Bureau of Economic Research.

Benston, Margaret, 1969. "The Political Economy of Women's Liberation." *Monthly Review*, 21: 13-27.

Berger, Peter, 1963. *Invitation to Sociology*. Garden City, New York: Doubleday.

Bergmann, Barbara, 1987. *The Economic Emergence of Women*. New York: Basic Books Inc.

Bergmann, Barbara, 1974. "Occupational segregation, wages, and profits when employers discriminate by race or sex." *Eastern Economic Journal*, 1: 103-110.

Bernard, Jesse, 1989. "The Dissemination of Feminist Thought: 1960 to 1988." In Ruth Wallace, ed., *Feminism and Sociological Theory*, pp. 23-33. Newbury Park: Sage.

Black, Naomi, 1980. "Of Lions and Mice: Making Women's Politics Effective." *Canadian Women's Studies*, 2: 62-64.

Blumstein, Philip, and Pepper Schwartz, 1983. *American Couples*. New York: William Morris.

Bose, Christine, 1987. "Dual Spheres." In Beth Hess and Myra Marx Ferree, eds., *Analyzing Gender: A Handbook of Social Science Research*, pp. 267-285. Newbury Park: Sage.

Bose, Christine, 1980. "Social Status of the Homemaker." In S.F. Berk, ed., *Women and Household Labour*, pp. 69-88. Beverly Hills: Sage.

Boyd, Monica, 1988. "Immigrant Women in Canada." In Arlene McLaren, ed., *Gender and Society*, pp. 316-336. Toronto: Copp Clark Pitman.

Boyd, Monica, 1984. *Canadian Attitudes Toward Women: Thirty Years of Change*. Ottawa. The Women's Bureau, Labour Canada.

Breines, Wini, 1985. "Domineering Mothers in the 1950's: Image and Reality." *Women's Studies International Forum*, 8: 601-608.

Briskin, Linda, 1983. "Women's Challenge to Organized Labour." In Linda Briskin and Lynda Yanz, eds., *Union Sisters: Women in the Labour Movement*, pp. 259-271. Toronto: The Women's Press.

Briskin, Linda, and Lynda Yanz, eds., 1983. *Union Sisters: Women in the Labour Movement*. Toronto: The Women's Press.

Brodie, Janine, 1985. *Women and Politics in Canada*. Toronto: McGraw-Hill Ryerson.

Brodie, Janine, and Jill Vickers, 1982. *Canadian Women in Politics: An Overview*. Ottawa: CRIAW/ICREF.

Brodie, Janine, 1977. "The Recruitment of Canadian Women Provincial Legislators, 1950-1975." *Atlantis*, 2: 6-17.

Brown, Scott, Melissa Ludtke and Martha Smilgis, 1989. "Onward Women." *Time*, (December, 4) pp. 82-89.

Bruce, Mary, 1985. "Equal Opportunity, Affirmative Action, Employment Equity." *Canadian Women's Studies*, 6: 52-55.

Burke, Mary Ann, 1986. "The Growth of Part-Time Work." *Canadian Social Trends*, Autumn: 9-14.

Burnet, Jean, ed., 1986. *Looking into my Sister's Eyes: An Exploration in Women's History*. Toronto: The Multicultural Society of Ontario.

Burt, Sandra, Lorraine Code and Lindsay Dorney, eds., 1988. *Changing Patterns: Women in Canada*. Toronto: McClelland and Stewart.

Burt, Sandra, 1988. "Legislators, Women and Public Policy." In Sandra Burt, Lorraine Code and Lindsay Dorney, eds., *Changing Patterns: Women in Canada*, pp. 129-183. Toronto: McClelland and Stewart.

Chafetz, Janet S., and Anthony G. Dworkin, 1987. "In the Face of Threat: Organized Antifeminism in Comparative Perspective." *Gender and Society*, 1: 33-60.

Chodorow, Nancy, 1978. *The Reproduction of Mothering: Psychoanalysis and the Sociology of Gender*. Berkeley: University of California Press.

Clemenson, Heather, 1987. "Unemployment Rates for the Full-Time and Part-Time Labour Forces." *Canadian Social Trends*, Autumn: 30-33.

Cleverdon, Catherine, 1974. *The Woman Suffrage Movement in Canada*. Toronto: University of Toronto Press.

Coburn, Judi, 1974. "I See and Am Silent: A Short History of Nursing in Ontario." In Janice Acton, Penny Goldsmith and Bonnie Shepard, eds., *Women at Work: Ontario, 1850-1930*, pp. 127-163. Toronto: Canadian Women's Educational Press.

Cochrane, Jean, 1977. *Women in Canadian Life: Politics*. Toronto: Fitzhenry and Whiteside.

Cohen, Marjorie, 1985. "Employment Equity is Not Affirmative Action." *Canadian Women's Studies*, 6: 23-25.

Cohen, Marjorie, 1983. "The Problem of Studying 'Economic Man'." In Geraldine Finn and Angela Miles, eds., *Feminism in Canada: From Pressure To Politics,* pp. 89-102. Montreal: Black Rose Books.

Connelly, Patricia, and Martha MacDonald, 1990. *Women and the Labour Force.* Catalogue 98-125. Ottawa: Statistics Canada.

Connelly, Patricia, 1978. *Last Hired: First Fired.* Toronto: The Women's Press.

Cooke, Katie, 1986. *Report of the Task Force on Childcare.* Ottawa: Status of Women Canada.

Copp, Terry, 1974. *Anatomy of Poverty.* Toronto: McClelland and Stewart.

Cowan, Ruth Schwartz, 1987. "Women's Work, Housework and History: The Historical Roots of Inequality in Work-Force Participation." In Naomi Gerstel and Harriet Gross, eds., *Families and Work,* pp. 164-177. Philadelphia: Temple University Press.

Cowan, Ruth Schwartz, 1983. *More Work for Mother.* New York: Basic Books.

Cronan, Sheila, 1984. "Marriage." In Alison Jaggar and Paula Rothenberg, eds., *Feminist Frameworks,* Second Edition, pp. 329-333. New York: McGraw Hill.

Cross, Suzanne, 1977. "The Neglected Majority: The Changing Role of Women in Nineteenth Century Montreal." In Susan Trofimenkoff and Alison Prentice, eds., *The Neglected Majority,* pp. 66-86. Toronto: McClelland and Stewart.

Dahlerup, Drude, ed., 1986. *The New Women's Movement.* Beverly Hills: Sage.

Daly, Mary, 1978. *Gyn/Ecology: The Metaphysics of Radical Feminism.* Boston: Beacon Press.

Daniels, Arlene, 1987. "Invisible Work" *Social Problems,* 34: 403-415

Danylewycz, Marta, 1987. *Taking the Veil: An Alternative to Marriage, Motherhood, and Spinsterhood in Quebec,* 1840-1920. Toronto: McClelland and Stewart.

Davis, Kingsley, and Pietronella Van den Oever, 1982. "Demographic Foundations of New Sex Roles." *Population and Development Review,* 8: 495-511.

Davitt, Patricia, Colette French, Marge Hollibaugh, Andrea Lebowitz and Barbara Todd, 1974. *Never Done: Three Centuries of Women's Work in Canada.* Toronto: Canadian Women's Educational Press.

Department of Labour, 1964. *Women at Work in Canada,* 1964. Ottawa: Information Canada.

DeVault, Marjorie, 1987. "Doing Housework: Feeding and Family Life." In Naomi Gerstel and Harriet Gross, eds., *Families and Work,* pp. 178-191. Philadelphia: Temple University Press.

Devereaux, Mary Sue, 1987. "Aging of the Canadian Population." *Canadian Social Trends,* Winter: 37-38.

DeVoss, David, 1989. "Empire of the Old." *Los Angeles Times Magazine,* February 12.

Doerr, A., 1984. "Women's Rights in Canada: Social and Economic Realities." *Atlantis,* 9, 2: 35-47.

Dubinsky, Karen, 1985. "Lament for a 'Patriarchy Lost'? Anti-feminism, Anti-abortion, and R.E.A.L. Women in Canada." Ottawa: CRIAW/ICREF.

Duffy, Ann, 1988. "Struggling with Power: Feminist Critiques of Family Inequality." In Nancy Mandel and Ann Duffy, eds., *Reconstructing the Canadian Family: Feminist Perspectives*, pp. 111-139. Toronto: Butterworths.

Duffy, Ann, Nancy Mandell and Norene Pupo, 1989. *Few Choices: Women, Work and Family*. Toronto: Garamond.

Egan, Carolyn, 1987. "Toronto's International Women's Day Committee: Socialist Feminist Politics." In Heather Maroney and Meg Luxton, eds., *Feminism and Political Economy: Women's Work, Women's Struggles*, pp. 109-118. Toronto: Methuen.

Egan, Carolyn, and Lynda Yanz, 1983. "Building Links: Labour and the Women's Movement." In Linda Briskin and Lynda Yanz, eds., *Union Sisters: Women in the Labour Movement*, pp. 361-375, Toronto: The Women's Press.

Ehrenreich, Barbara, and Deirdre English, 1978. *For Her Own Good*. New York: Anchor Press.

Ehrich, C., 1971. "The Male Sociologist's Burden: The Place of Women in Marriage and Family Texts." *Journal of Marriage and the Family*, 33, 3: 421-430.

Eichler, Margrit, 1988. *Families in Canada Today*, Second Edition Toronto: Gage.

Eichler, Margrit, 1986. *The Pro-Family Movement in Canada: Are They For or Against Families?* Ottawa: CRIAW/ICREF.

Eichler, Margrit, 1984. "Sexism in Research and Its Policy Implications." In Jill Vickers ed., *Taking Sex into Account*, pp. 17-39. Don Mills: Oxford University Press.

Eichler, Margrit, 1977a. "Sociology of Feminist Research in Canada." *Signs*, 3: 409-422.

Eichler, Margrit, 1977b. "The Prestige of the Occupation Housewife." In Pat Marchak ed., *The Working Sexes*, pp. 151-175. British Columbia: Institute of Industrial Relations.

Eisenstein, Hester, 1984. *Contemporary Feminist Thought*. London: Unwin.

Eisenstein, Zillah, 1984. *Feminism and Sexual Equality*. New York: Monthly Review Press.

Ellis, Dormer, and Lyz Sayer, 1986. *When I Grow Up...Career Expectations and Aspirations of Canadian Schoolchildren*. Ottawa: Women's Bureau, Labour Canada.

England, Paula, 1982. "The Failure of Human Capital Theory to Explain Occupational Sex Segregation." *The Journal of Human Resources*, 17: 358-370.

Epstein, Cynthia, 1988. *Deceptive Distinctions: Sex, Gender and the Social Order*. New York: Yale University Press.

Epstein, Cynthia, 1984. "Ideal Images and Real Roles." *Dissent*, 31: 441-447.

Epstein, Cynthia, 1974. "A Different Angle of Vision: Notes on the Selective Eye of Sociology." *Social Science Quarterly*, 55: 645-656.

Errington, Jane, 1988. "Pioneers and Suffragists." In Sandra Burt, Lorraine Code and Lindsay Dorney, eds., *Changing Patterns: Women in Canada*, pp. 51-79. Toronto: McClelland and Stewart.

Erwin, Lorna, 1988. "What Feminists Should Know About the Pro-Family Movement in Canada: A Report on a Recent Survey of Rank-and-File Members." In Peta Tancred-Sheriff, ed., *Feminist Research: Prospect and Retrospect*. Montreal: McGill-Queen's University Press.

Ferree, Myra, 1987. "The Superwoman Syndrome" In Christine Bose, Roslyn Feldberg and Natalie Sokoloff, eds., *Hidden Aspects of Women's Work*, pp. 161-180. New York: Praeger.

Ferree, Myra, 1980. "Satisfaction with Housework: The Social Context." In Sarah Berk, ed., *Women and Household Labor*, pp. 89-112. Beverly Hills: Sage.

Field, Debbie, 1983. "Coercion or Male Culture: A New Look at Co-worker Harassment." In Linda Briskin and Lynda Yanz, eds., *Union Sisters: Women in the Labour movement*, pp. 144-160, Toronto: The Women's Press.

Finn, Geraldine, and Angela Miles, eds., 1982. *Feminism in Canada: From Pressure to Politics*. Montreal: Black Rose Books.

Firestone, Shulamith, 1970. *The Dialectic of Sex*. New York: Bantam Books.

Fischer, Linda, and J.A. Cheyne, 1977. *Sex Roles*. Ontario, Ministry of Education.

Fishman, P., 1978. "Interaction: The Work Women Do." *Social Problems*, 25: 397-406.

Fitzgerald, Maureen, Connie Guberman and Margie Wolfe, eds., 1982. *Still Ain't Satisfied: Canadian Feminism Today*. Toronto: The Women's Press.

Fox, Bonnie, 1990. "Selling the Mechanized Household: 70 Years of Ads in *Ladies Home Journal*." *Gender and Society*, 4: 25-40.

Fox, Bonnie, 1988. "Conceptualizing 'Patriarchy'." *Canadian Review of Sociology and Anthropology*, 25: 163-182.

Fox, Bonnie, and John Fox, 1987. "Occupational Gender Segregation in the Canadian Labour Force, 1931-1981." *Canadian Review of Sociology and Anthropology*, 24: 374-397.

Fox, Bonnie, ed., 1980. *Hidden in the Household*. Toronto: The Women's Press.

Fox, Greer, 1977. " 'Nice Girls': Social Control of Women Through a Value Construct." *Signs*, 2: 805-817.

Frager, Ruth, 1983. "Women Workers and the Canadian Labour Movement, 1870-1940." In Linda Briskin and Lynda Yanz, eds., *Union Sisters: Women in the Labour Movement*, pp. 44-64, Toronto: The Women's Press.

Freeman, Jo, 1984. "The Women's Liberation Movement: Its Origins, Structure, Activities and Ideas." In Jo Freeman, ed., *Women: A Feminist Perspective*. Third Edition, pp. 543-556. Palo Alto: Mayfield Publishing.

Frenken, Hubert, 1986. "Retirement Income Programs in Canada" *Canadian Social Trends*, Winter: 21-26.

Friedan, Betty, 1982. *The Second Stage*. New York: Summit Books.

Friedan, Betty, 1963. *The Feminine Mystique*. New York: Dell Publishing.

Fuchs, Victor, 1988. *Women's Quest for Economic Equality*. Cambridge, Mass.: Harvard University Press.

Gannage, Charlene, 1986. *Double Day, Double Bind: Women Garment Workers*. Toronto: The Women's Press.

Galbraith, John, 1974. *Economics and the Public Purpose*. London: Andre Deutsch.

Gaskell, Jane, 1986. "Conceptions of Skill and the Work of Women: Some Historical and Political Issues." In Roberta Hamilton and Michele Barrett, eds., *The Politics of Diversity*, pp. 361- 380. London: Verso.

Gerbner, George, 1978. "The Dynamics of Cultural Resistance." In Gaye Tuchman, Arlene Daniels and J. Benet, eds., *Hearth and Home*, pp. 46-50. New York: Oxford University Press.

Gerson, Kathleen, 1987. "How Women Choose Between Employment and Family: A Developmental Perspective." In Naomi Gerstel and Harriet Gross, eds., *Families and Work*, pp. 270-288. Philadelphia: Temple University Press.

Gerson, Kathleen, 1985. *Hard Choices: How Women Decide About Work, Career and Motherhood*. Berkeley: University of California Press.

Gerstel, Naomi, and Harriet Gross, eds., 1987. *Families and Work*. Philadelphia: Temple University Press.

Gibbons, R., J.R. Ponting and G. Symons, 1978. "Attitudes and Ideology: Correlates of Liberal Attitudes Towards the Role of Women." *Journal of Comparative Family Studies*, 9,1: 19-40.

Gilman, Charlotte Perkins, 1898. *Women and Economics*. Boston: Small, Maynard.

Glazer, Nona, 1987. "Servants to Capital: Unpaid Domestic Labor and Paid Work." In Naomi Gerstel and Harriet Gross, eds., *Families and Work*, pp. 236-255. Philadelphia: Temple University Press.

Glazer, Nona, 1980a. "Everyone Needs Three Hands: Doing Unpaid and Paid Work." In Sarah Berk, ed., *Women and Household Labor*, pp. 249-274. Beverly Hills: Sage.

Glazer, Nona, 1980b. "The Double Day in a Mass Magazine." *Women's Studies International Quarterly*, 3: 69-73.

Glenn, Evelyn, 1987. "Gender and the Family." In Beth Hess and Myra Marx Ferree, eds., *Analyzing Gender: A Handbook of Social Science Research*, pp. 348-380. Newbury Park: Sage.

Glenn, E., and R. Feldberg, 1984. "Clerical Work: The Female Occupation." In Jo Freeman, ed., *Women: A Feminist Perspective*. Third edition, pp. 316-336. Palo Alto: Mayfield Publishing.

Glick, Paul, 1984. "How American Families are Changing." *American Demographics*, January: 21-25.

Goffman, Erving, 1979. *Gender Advertisements*. New York: Harper and Row.

Gower, David, 1988. "Annual Update on the Labour Force Trends." *Canadian Social Trends*, Summer: 17-20.

Gray, Charlotte, 1980. "The New Backroom Girls." *Chatelaine*, July: 25-26.

Gray, Charlotte, 1979. "Ten Women MP's: A New Breed." *Chatelaine*, October: 62-63.

Gunderson, Morley, 1985. "Labour Market Aspects of Inequality in Employment and their Application to Crown Corporations." In *Research Studies of the Commission on Equality in Employment*, pp. 1-48. Ottawa: Minister of Supply and Services.

Gunderson, Morley, 1981. *Sex Discrimination in the Canadian Labour Market: Theories, Data and Evidence*. Ottawa: Women's Bureau, Labour Canada.

Gunderson, Morley, 1977. "Logit Estimates of Labour Force Participation Based on Census Cross-Tabulations." *Canadian Journal of Economics*, 10: 453-462.

Hamilton, Roberta, 1988. "Women, Wives and Mothers." In Nancy Mandel and Ann Duffy, eds., *Reconstructing the Canadian Family: Feminist Perspectives*, pp. 3-26. Toronto: Butterworths.

Harevan, Tamara, 1984. "Themes in the Historical Development of the Family." In R. Parke, ed., *Review of Child Development Research, Vol. 7, The Family*, pp. 137-178. Chicago: The University of Chicago Press.

Hartmann, Heidi, 1981. "The Family as the Locus of Gender, Class and Political Struggle: The Example of Housework." *Signs*, 6: 366-394.

Hawrylshyn, O., 1978. "Estimating the Value of Household Work in Canada, 1971." Ottawa: Statistics Canada, Catalogue 13-566.

Hayden, Dolores, 1981. *The Grand Domestic Revolution: A History of Feminist Designs for American Homes, Neighborhoods and Cities*. Cambridge, Mass.: MIT Press.

Henley, Nancy, 1975. "Power, Sex and Nonverbal Communication." In Barrie Thorne and Nancy Henley, eds., *Language and Sex: Difference and Dominance*, pp. 184-203. Massachusetts: Newbury House Publishers.

Henley, Nancy, and Jo Freeman, 1984. "The Sexual Politics of Interpersonal Behavior." In Jo Freeman, ed., *Women: A Feminist Perspective*. Third Edition, pp. 465-477. Palo Alto: Mayfield Publishing.

Hess, Beth, and Myra Marx Ferree, 1987. *Analyzing Gender: A Handbook of Social Science Research*. Newbury Park: Sage.

Hewlett, Sylvia, 1986. *A Lesser Life: The Myth of Women's Liberation in America*. New York: William Morrow.

Hickl-Szabo, R., 1983. "Working Women Feel the Brunt of Technology." *Globe and Mail*, January 4, pp. 1,2.

Hochschild, Arlie, 1989. *The Second Shift: Working Parents and the Revolution at Home*. New York: Viking.

Hollands, Judith, 1988. "Women Teaching at Canadian Universities." *Canadian Social Trends*, Summer: 5-7.

Hooyman, N., and S. Johnson, 1977. "Sociology's Portrayal of Women: Sociopolitical Implications." *Soundings*, 60: 449-465.

Hunt, Janet, and Larry Hunt, 1987. "Male Resistance to Role Symmetry in Dual-Earner Households: Three Alternative Explanations." In Naomi Gerstel and Harriet Gross, eds. *Families and Work*, pp. 192-203. Philadelphia: Temple University Press,

Hunt, Janet, and Larry Hunt, 1982. "The Dualities of Careers and Families: New Integrations or New Polarizations?" *Social Problems*, 29: 499-519.

Jaggar, Alison, and Paula Rothenberg, 1984. *Feminist Frameworks*. Second Edition. New York: McGraw Hill.

Jaggar, Alison, 1983. *Feminist Politics and Human Nature*. Sussex: The Harvester Press.

Johnson, Laura, (with R. Johnson), 1982. *The Seam Allowance*. Toronto: The Women's Press.

Kadar, Marlene, 1982. "Sexual Harassment as a Form of Social Control." In Maureen Fitzgerald, Connie Guberman and Margie Wolfe, eds., *Still Ain't Satisfied: Canadian Feminism Today*. pp. 168-180. Toronto: The Women's Press.

Kamerman, Sheila, and Alfred Kahn, 1987. *The Responsive Workplace: Employers and a Changing Labor Force*. New York: Columbia University Press.

Kanter, Rosabeth, 1977. *Men and Women of the Corporation*. New York: Basic Books.

Katz, Michael, and Ian Davey, 1978. "Youth and Early Industrialization in a Canadian City." *American Journal of Sociology*, 84 (Supplement): 81-119.

Kealey, George, ed. 1973. *Canada Investigates Industrialism, The Royal Commission on the Relations of Labour and Capital*. Toronto: The University of Toronto Press.

Kealey, Linda, ed., 1979. *A Not Unreasonable Claim: Women and Reform in Canada, 1880-1920*. Toronto: The Women's Press.

Kelly, Joan, 1984. *Women, History and Theory*. Chicago: University of Chicago Press.

Kessler-Harris, Alice, 1987. "The Debate Over Equality for Women in the Workplace: Recognizing Differences." In Naomi Gerstel and Harriet Gross, eds., *Families and Work*, pp. 520-539. Philadelphia: Temple University Press.

Kirschner, B., 1973. "Introducing Students to Women's Place in Society." *American Journal of Sociology*, 78: 289-92.

Klein, Ethel, 1984. *Gender Politics*. Cambridge, Mass.: Harvard University Press.

Kollock, P., P. Blumstein and P. Schwartz, 1985. "Sex and Power in Interaction: Conversational Privileges and Duties." *American Sociological Review*, 50: 34-46.

Kome, Penney, 1985. *Women of Influence*. Toronto: Doubleday Canada.

Kome, Penney, 1983. *The Taking of the Twenty-Eight: Women Challenge the Constitution*. Toronto: The Women's Press.

Kome, Penney, 1982. *Somebody Has To Do It*. Toronto: McClelland and Stewart.

Kome, Penney, 1978. "How Canadian Women Really Feel About Housework." *Homemakers Digest*, October: 27-60.

Kopinak, Kathryn, 1980. "Polity." In Richard Hagedorn, ed., *Sociology*, pp. 429-473. Toronto: Holt, Rinehart and Winston of Canada.

Kostash, Myrna, 1980. *Long Way from Home*. Toronto: James Lorimer and Company.

Kramer, Cheris, Barrie Thorne and Nancy Henley, 1978. "Perspectives on Language and Communication." *Signs*, 3: 638-651.

Labour Canada, Women's Bureau, 1987. *Women in the Labour Force: 1986-1987 edition*. Ottawa: Minister of Supply and Services.

Labour Canada, Women's Bureau, 1986a. *Equal Pay for Work of Equal Value*. Ottawa: Minister of Supply and Services.

Labour Canada, Women's Bureau, 1986b. *Equal Pay: Collective Bargaining and the Law*. Ottawa: Minister of Supply and Services.

Lakoff, Robin, 1975. *Language and Women's Place*. New York: Harper and Row.

Langevin, L., 1977. *Missing Persons: Women in Canadian Federal Politics*. Ottawa: The Canadian Advisory Council on the Status of Women.

Laslett, Peter, 1977. "Characteristics of the Western Family Considered Over Time." *Journal of Family History*, 2: 89-115.

Lavigne, M., and J. Stoddart, 1977. "Women's Work in Montreal at the Beginning of the Century." In Marylee Stephenson, ed., *Women in Canada*, pp. 129-147. Don Mills: General Publishing.

Lenskyj, Helen, 1987. "From Prejudice to Policy." *Broadside*, 8: 4-6.

Leslie, Genevieve, 1974. "Domestic Service in Canada, 1880-1920." In Janice Acton, Penny Goldsmith and Bonnie Shepard, eds., *Women at Work: Ontario, 1850-1930*, pp. 71-125. Toronto: Canadian Women's Educational Press.

Levine, Helen, 1983. "The Power Politics of Motherhood." In Joan Turner and Lois Emery, eds., *Perspectives on Women in the 1980's*, pp. 28-40. Winnipeg: University of Manitoba Press.

Light, Beth, and Alison Prentice, eds., 1980. *Pioneer and Gentlewomen of British North America, 1713–1867*. Toronto: New Hogtown Press.

Lindstrom-Best, Varpu, 1986. " 'I Won't be a Slave!'—Finnish Domestics in Canada, 1911-1930." In Jean Burnet, ed., *Looking into my Sister's Eyes: An Exploration in Women's History*, pp. 33-53. Toronto: The Multicultural Society of Ontario.

Lopate, C. 1974. "Women and Pay for Housework." *Liberation Magazine*, June: 8-11.

Lowe, Graham, 1980. "Women, Work and the Office: The Feminization of Clerical Occupations in Canada, 1901-1931." *The Canadian Journal of Sociology*, 5: 361-381.

Luxton, Meg, 1986a. "Two Hands on the Clock." In Meg Luxton and Harriet Rosenberg, eds., *Through the Kitchen Window: The Politics of Home and Family*, pp. 17-36. Toronto: Garamond Press.

Luxton, Meg, 1986b. "From Ladies Auxiliaries to Wives' Committees: Housewives and the Unions." In Meg Luxton and Harriet Rosenberg, eds., *Through the Kitchen Window: The Politics of Home and Family*, pp. 63-82. Toronto: Garamond Press.

Luxton, Meg, 1985. "Introduction." In Pat Armstrong, Hugh Armstrong, Pat Connelly and Angela Miles, eds., *Feminist Marxism or Marxist Feminism: A Debate*, pp. i-ii. Toronto: Garamond Press.

Luxton, Meg, 1980. *More Than a Labour of Love*. Toronto: The Women's Press.

Maccoby, Eleanor, and Carol Jacklin, 1974. *The Psychology of Sex Differences*. Stanford, Calif.: Stanford University Press.

Mackie, Marlene, 1986. "Women in the Professions: Status and Productivity." *Society*, 10: 3-8.

MacLellan, M., 1972. *History of Women's Rights in Canada, Study No. 8, Report of the Royal Commission on the Status of Women in Canada*. Ottawa: Information Canada.

Macleod, Catherine, 1974. "Women in Production: The Toronto Dressmakers' Strike of 1931." In Janice Acton, Penny Goldsmith and Bonnie Shepard, eds., *Women at Work: Ontario, 1850-1930*, pp. 309-329. Toronto: Canadian Women's Educational Press.

MacLeod, Linda, 1987. *Battered But Not Beaten... Preventing Wife Battering in Canada*. Ottawa: Canadian Advisory Council on the Status of Women.

MacLeod, Linda, 1980. *Wife Battering in Canada: The Vicious Circle*. Ottawa: Canadian Advisory Council on the Status of Women.

Mandel, Nancy, and Ann Duffy. 1988. *Reconstructing the Canadian Family: Feminist Perspectives*. Toronto: Butterworths.

Manpower Review, 1975. "Women's Employment in Canada: A Look at the Past," pp. 1-8. "Women in the Labour Force: Recent Trends," pp. 15-24. Vol. 8,1.

Margolis, Maxine, 1984. *Mothers and Such*. Berkeley: University of California Press.

Maroney, Heather, 1987. "Feminism at Work." In Heather Maroney and Meg Luxton, eds., *Feminism and Political Economy: Women's Work, Women's Struggles*, pp. 85-108. Toronto: Methuen.

Maroney, Heather, 1986. "Embracing Motherhood: New Feminist Theory." In Roberta Hamilton and Michele Barrett, eds., *The Politics of Diversity*, pp. 398-423. Norfolk: Verso.

Maroney, Heather, and Meg Luxton, eds., 1987. *Feminism and Political Economy: Women's Work, Women's Struggles*. Toronto: Methuen.

Marsden, Lorna, and Joan Bushy, 1989. "Feminist Influence Through the Senate: The Case of Divorce, 1967." *Atlantis*, 14, 2: 72-80.

Marshall, Katherine, 1987. "Women in Male Dominated Professions." *Canadian Social Trends*, Winter: 7-11.

Marshall, S. E., 1984. "Keep us on the Pedestal: Women Against Feminism in Twentieth Century America." In Jo Freeman, ed., *Women: A Feminist Perspective*, Third Edition, pp. 568-681. Palo Alto: Mayfield Publishing.

May, Martha, 1987. "The Historical Problem of the Family Wage: The Ford Motor Company and the Five Dollar Day." In Naomi Gerstel and Harriet Gross, eds., *Families and Work*, pp. 111-131. Philadelphia: Temple University Press.

Mayfield, Margie, 1990. *Work Related Child Care in Canada*. Ottawa: Women's Bureau, Labour Canada.

McConnell-Ginet, S., 1978. "Intonation in a Man's World." *Signs*, 3: 451-459.

McCormack, Thelma, 1975. "Toward a Nonsexist Perspective on Social and Political Change." In Marcia Millman and Rosabeth Kanter, eds., *Another Voice*, pp. 1-33. New York: Anchor Books.

McDaniel, Susan, 1988. "Women's Roles, Reproduction and the New Reproductive Technologies: A New Stork Rising." In Nancy Mandel and Ann Duffy, eds., *Reconstructing the Canadian Family: Feminist Perspectives*, pp. 175-206. Toronto: Butterworths.

McDaniel, Susan, 1986. *Canada's Aging Population*. Toronto: Butterworths.

McLaren, Angus and Arlene McLaren, 1990. "Discoveries and Dissimulations: The Impact of Abortion Deaths on Maternal Mortality in British Columbia." In Katherine Arnup, Andree Levesque and Ruth Pierson, eds., *Delivering Motherhood: Maternal Ideologies and Practices in the 19th and 20th Centuries*, pp. 126-149. London: Routledge.

McLaren, Angus, 1985. "Birth Control and Abortion in Canada, 1870-1920." In Alison Prentice and Susan Trofimenkoff, eds., *The Neglected Majority Volume II*, pp. 84-101. Toronto: McClelland and Stewart.

McRobbie, A., 1978. "Working Class Girls and the Culture of Femininity." In Women's Studies, University of Birmingham, *Women Take Issue*, pp. 96-108. London: Hutchison of London.

Meissner, M., 1975. "No Exit for Wives: Sexual Division of Labour and the Cumulation of Household Demands." *Canadian Review of Sociology and Anthropology*, 12: 424-439.

Michelson, William, 1985. *From Sun to Sun: Daily Obligations and Community Structure in the Lives of Employed Women and Their Families*. New Jersey: Rowman and Allenheld.

Miles, Angela, 1984. "Integrative Feminism." *Fireweed*, 19: 54-81.

Millman, Marcia, 1980. *Such a Pretty Face*. New York: Berkeley Books.

Millman, Marcia, and Rosabeth Kanter, eds., 1975. *Another Voice*. New York: Anchor Books.

Mitchell, Juliet, 1973. *Women's Estate*. Toronto: Random House.

Moore, Maureen, 1987. "Women Parenting Alone." *Canadian Social Trends*, Winter: 31-36.

Morgan, David, 1981. "Men, Masculinity and the Process of Sociological Enquiry." In H. Roberts, ed., *Doing Feminist Research*, pp. 83-113. London: Routledge and Kegan Paul.

Morris, Cerise, 1980. "Determination and Thoroughness: The Movement for a Royal Commission of the Status of Women." *Atlantis*, 5, 2: 1-21.

Nagnur, Dhruva, and Owen Adams, 1987. "Tying the Knot: An Overview of Marriage Rates in Canada." *Canadian Social Trends*, Autumn: 1- 6.

National Council of Welfare, 1990. *Women and Poverty Revisited*. Ottawa: Minister of Supply and Services.

National Council of Welfare, 1988a. *Poverty Profile 1988*. Ottawa: Minister of Supply and Services.

National Council of Welfare, 1988b. *Child Care: A Better Alternative*. Ottawa: Minister of Supply and Services.

National Council of Welfare, 1984a. *Better Pensions for Homemakers*. Ottawa: Minister of Supply and Services.

National Council of Welfare, 1984b. *Sixty-Five and Older*. Ottawa: Minister of Supply and Services.

National Council of Welfare, 1979. *Women and Poverty*. Ottawa: Minister of Supply and Services.

Neill, Shirley, 1988. "Unionization in Canada." *Canadian Social Trends*, Spring: 12-15.

Ng, Roxana, 1988. "Immigrant Women and Institutionalized Racism." In Sandra Burt, Lorraine Code and Lindsay Dorney, eds., *Changing Patterns: Women in Canada*, pp. 184-203. Toronto: McClelland and Stewart.

Niemann, Lindsay, 1984. *Wage Discrimination and Women Workers: The Move Towards Equal Pay for Work of Equal Value in Canada*. Ottawa: Labour Canada, Women's Bureau.

Noel, Jan, 1986. "New France: Les femmes favorisées." In Veronica Strong-Boag and Anita Clair Fellman, eds., *Rethinking Canada: The Promise of Women's History*, pp. 59-66. Toronto: Copp Clark Pitman.

Oakley, Ann, 1981. *Subject Women*. New York: Pantheon Books.

Oakley, Ann, 1974. *Women's Work: The Housewife, Past and Present*. New York: Pantheon Books.

Ornstein, Michael, 1983. *Accounting for Gender Differentials in Job Income in Canada: Results from a 1981 Survey*. Ottawa: Women's Bureau, Labour Canada.

Pappert, Ann. 1980. "Today's Women: Yesterday's Dreams." *Homemaker's Digest*, October: pp. 166-180.

Parr, Joy, 1982. *Childhood and Family in Canadian History*. Toronto: McClelland and Stewart.

Pearce, Diana, 1979. "Women, Work and Welfare: The Feminization of Poverty." In K.W. Feinstein, ed., *Working Women and Families*, pp. 103-124. Newbury Park: Sage.

Pearson, Judy, 1985. *Gender and Communications*. Dubuque, Iowa: Wm. C. Brown, Publishers.

Phillips, Paul, and Erin Phillips, 1983. *Women and Work*. Toronto: James Lorimer and Company.

Pierson, Ruth Roach, 1986. *"They're Still Women After All": The Second World War and Canadian Womanhood*. Toronto: McClelland and Stewart.

Pierson, Ruth Roach, 1983. *Canadian Women and the Second World War*. Ottawa: The Canadian Historical Association.

Pierson, Ruth Roach, 1977a. "Women's Emancipation and the Recruitment of Women into the Labour Force in World War I." In Susan Trofimenkoff and Alison Prentice, eds., *The Neglected Majority*, pp. 125-145. Toronto: McClelland and Stewart.

Pierson, Ruth Roach, 1977b. "Home-Aide: A Solution to Women's Unemployment After the Second World War." *Atlantis*, 2,2 Part I: 85-97.

Pifer, A., and L. Bronte, eds., 1986. *Our Aging Society*, pp. 111-140. New York: W.W. Norton and Company.

Pool, I., 1978. "Problems of Data Collection on Women and the Labour Force." In *Women and Work: An Inventory of Research*, pp. 3-4. Ottawa: Canadian Research Institute for the Advancement of Women.

Posner, Judith, 1980. "Old and Female: The Double Whammy." In Victor Marshall, ed., *Aging in Canada: Social Perspectives*, pp. 80-87. Don Mills: Fitzhenry and Whiteside.

Prentice, Alison, Paula Bourne, Gail Cuthbert Brandt, Beth Light, Wendy Mitchinson, Naomi Black, 1988. *Canadian Women: A History*. Toronto: Harcourt Brace Jovanovich.

Prentice, Alison, 1978. "Writing Women Into History." *Atlantis*, 3,2 Part II: 72-84.

Priest, Gordon, 1988. "Living Arrangements of Canada's 'Older Elderly' Population." *Canadian Social Trends*, Autumn: 26-30.

Propper, Alice, 1990. "Patterns of Family Violence." In Maureen Baker, ed., *Families: Changing Trends in Canada*, Second Edition, 272-305. Toronto: McGraw-Hill Ryerson.

Proulx, M., 1978. *Five Million Women: A Study of the Canadian Housewife*. Ottawa: Canadian Advisory Council on the Status of Women.

Pryor, Edward, 1984. "Canadian Husband-Wife Families: Labour Force Participation and Income Trends, 1971-1981." *The Labour Force*. (May) Statistics Canada, Catalogue 71-001.

Pupo, Norene, 1988. "Preserving Patriarchy: Women, The Family and The State." In Nancy Mandel and Ann Duffy, eds., *Reconstructing the Canadian Family: Feminist Perspectives*, pp. 207-237. Toronto: Butterworths.

Ramkhalawansingh, Ceta, 1974. "Women During the Great War." In Janice Acton, Penny Goldsmith and Bonnie Shepard, eds., *Women at Work: Ontario, 1850-1930*, pp. 261-307. Toronto: Canadian Women's Educational Press.

Rich, Adrienne, 1980. "Compulsory Heterosexuality and Lesbian Experience." *Signs*, 5: 631-660.

Rich, Adrienne, 1976. *Of Woman Born*. New York: W. W. Norton.

Risman, Barbara, 1987. "Intimate Relationships from an Microsocial Perspective: Men Who Mother." *Gender and Society*, 1: 6-32.

Roberts, Wayne, 1979. "'Rocking the Cradle for the World': The New Woman and Maternal Feminism, Toronto 1877-1914." In Linda Kealey, ed., *A Not Unreasonable Claim: Women and Reform in Canada, 1880-1920*, pp. 15-45. Toronto: The Women's Press.

Roberts, Wayne, 1976. *Honest Womanhood*. Toronto: New Hogtown Press.

Rong, Xue Lan, Linda Grant and Kathryn Ward, 1989. "Productivity of Women Scholars and Gender Researchers: Is Funding a Factor?" *The American Sociologist*, 20: 95-100.

Rosen, Marjorie, 1973. *Popcorn Venus*. New York: Coward, McCann and Geohegan.

Rosenberg, Harriet, 1987. "Motherwork, Stress, and Depression: The Costs of Privatized Social Reproduction." In Heather Maroney and Meg Luxton, eds., *Feminism and Political Economy: Women's Work, Women's Struggles*, pp. 181-196. Toronto: Methuen.

Rosenberg, Harriet, 1986a. "The Home is the Workplace: Hazards, Stress and Pollutants in the Household." In Meg Luxton and Harriet Rosenberg, eds., *Through the Kitchen Window: The Politics of Home and Family*, pp. 37-62. Toronto: Garamond Press.

Rosenberg, Harriet, 1986b. "The Kitchen and the Multinational Corporation: An Analysis of the Links Between the Household and Global Corporations." In Meg Luxton and Harriet Rosenberg, eds., *Through the Kitchen Window: The Politics of Home and Family*, pp. 83-107. Toronto: Garamond Press.

Rossi, Alice, 1986. "Sex and Gender in an Aging Population." In A. Pifer and L. Bronte, eds., *Our Aging Society*, pp. 111-140. New York: W. W. Norton and Company.

Rossi, Alice, 1984. "Gender and Parenthood." *American Sociological Review*, 49: 1-18.

Rossiter, Amy, 1988. *From Private to Public*. Toronto: The Women's Press.

Rothman, Barbara, 1987. "Reproduction." In Beth Hess and Myra Marx Ferree, eds., *Analyzing Gender: A Handbook of Social Science Research*, pp. 154-170. Newbury Park: Sage.

Royal Commission on the Status of Women in Canada, Report, 1970. Ottawa: Information Canada.

Rubin, Lillian, 1976. *Worlds of Pain: Life in the Working Class Family.* New York: Basic Books.

Sangster, Joan, 1986. "The 1907 Bell Telephone Strike: Organizing Women Workers." In V. Strong-Boag and A. Fellman, eds., *Rethinking Canada: The Promise of Women's History,* pp. 137-156. Toronto: Copp Clark Pitman Ltd.

Savage, Candace, 1979. *Our Nell: A Scrapbook Biography of Nellie L McClung.* Saskatoon: Western Producer Prairie Books.

Schur, Edwin, 1983. *Labeling Women Deviant: Gender Stigma and Social Control.* Philadelphia: Temple University Press.

Schur, Edwin, 1982. "Making Sexism Deviant: Persistent Obstacles to Change." New York University: Center for Applied Social Science Research.

Schwartz, Felice, 1989. "Management Women and the New Facts of Life." *Harvard Business Review,* January-February: 65-76.

Scott, Ann C., 1984. "The Value of Housework." In Alison Jaggar and Paula Rothenberg, eds., *Feminist Frameworks.* Second edition, pp. 315-319. New York: McGraw-Hill.

Scott, Jean, 1892. *The Conditions of Female Labour in Ontario.* University of Toronto Studies in Political Science.

Segal, Lynne, 1987. *Is the Future Female?* New York: Peter Bedrick Books.

Sheffield, Carole, 1989. "The Invisible Intruder: Women's Experience of Obscene Phone Calls." *Gender and Society,* 3: 483-488.

Shostak, Arthur B., 1987. "Singlehood." In M.B. Sussman and S. K. Steinmetz, eds., *Handbook of Marriage and the Family,* pp.355-367. New York: Plenum Press.

Silvera, Makeda, 1983. *Silenced.* Toronto: Williams-Wallace Publishers, Inc.

Skolnick, M., 1982. "Toward Some New Emphasis in Empirical Research on Women in the Canadian Labour Force." In N. Herson and D.E. Smith, eds., *Women and the Canadian Labour Force.* Catalogue CR22-9/1981E. Ottawa: Minister of Supply and Services.

Smart, C., and B. Smart, eds., 1978. *Women, Sexuality and Social Control.* London: Routledge and Kegan Paul.

Smith, Dorothy, 1985. "Women, Class and Family." In V. Burstyn and D. Smith, eds., *Women, Class, Family and The State,* pp. 1- 44. Toronto: Garamond.

Smith, Dorothy, 1979 "A Sociology for Women." In J. Sherman and T. Beck, eds., *The Prism of Sex: Essays in the Sociology of Knowledge,* pp. 135-187. Madison: University of Wisconsin Press.

Smith, Dorothy, 1977. *Feminism and Marxism.* Vancouver: New Star Books.

Smith, Vivian, 1990. "Living in Fear." *Globe and Mail,* April 28, pp. D1, D8.

Stacey, Judith, and Barrie Thorne, 1985. "The Missing Feminist Revolution in Sociology." *Social Problems,* 32: 301-316.

Stanley, L., and S. Wise, 1983. *Breaking Out: Feminist Consciousness and Feminist Research.* London: Routledge and Kegan Paul.

Statistics Canada, 1990. *Women in Canada: A Statistical Report.* Second edition. Ottawa: Minister of Supply and Services.

Statistics Canada, 1985. *Women in Canada: A Statistical Report.* Ottawa: Minister of Supply and Services.

Statistics Canada, 1982. *Historical Statistics of Canada.* Second Edition. Ottawa: Minister of Supply and Services.

Stewart, Walter, 1984. "Election '84: Women Win Big!" *Chatelaine,* November: 73, 226-228.

Stoddard, J., and V. Strong-Boag, 1975. "... And Things Were Going Wrong at Home." *Atlantis,* 1,1: 38-44.

Stolk, Y., and P. Brotherton, 1981. "Attitudes Toward Single Women." *Sex Roles* 7: 73-78.

Strong-Boag, Veronica, 1988. *The New Day Recalled: the Lives of Girls and Women in English Canada, 1919-1939.* Toronto: Copp Clark Pitman.

Strong-Boag, Veronica, 1982. "Intruders in the Nursery: Childcare Professionals Reshape the Years One to Five, 1920-1940." In Joy Parr, ed., *Childhood and Family in Canadian History,* pp. 160-178. Toronto: McClelland and Stewart.

Strong-Boag, Veronica, and Anita Clair Fellman, eds., 1986. *Rethinking Canada: The Promise of Women's History.* Toronto: Copp Clark Pitman.

Swainamer, J. L., 1986. "The Value of Household Work in Canada." *Canadian Social Trends,* Autumn: 42.

Szekely, Eva, 1988. *Never Too Thin.* Toronto: The Women's Press.

Tavris, Carol and Carole Wade, 1984. *The Longest War: Sex Differences in Perspective,* Second Edition. New York: Harcourt Brace Jovanovich.

Taylor, C., 1980. "The New Masculinization of the Teaching Profession." *Canadian Women's Studies,* 2, 2: 56-57.

Trofimenkoff, Susan, 1977a. "One Hundred and Two Muffled Voices: Canada's Industrial Women in the 1880s." *Atlantis,* 3, 1: 66-82.

Trofimenkoff, Susan, 1977b. "Henri Bourassa and the Woman Question." In Susan Trofimenkoff and Alison Prentice, eds., *The Neglected Majority,* pp. 104-115. Toronto: McClelland and Stewart.

Tuchman, Gaye, 1978. "The Newspaper as a Social Movements Resource." In G. Tuchman and A. K. Daniels, eds., *Hearth and Home,* pp. 186-215. New York: Oxford University Press.

Vanek, J., 1974. "Time Spent in Housework." *Scientific American,* November, 116-120.

Van Kirk, Sylvia, 1986. "The Role of Native Women in the Fur Trade Society of Western Canada, 1670-1830." In Veronica Strong-Boag and Anita Clair Fellman, eds., *Rethinking Canada: The Promise of Women's History,* pp. 59-66. Toronto: Copp Clark Pitman.

Vickers, Jill, ed., 1988. *Getting Things Done: Women's Views of the Involvement in Political Life*. Ottawa: CRIAW/ICREF.

Vickers, Jill, 1986. *Women's Involvement in Political Life*. Ottawa: CRIAW/ICREF.

Vickers, Jill, ed., 1984. *Taking Sex Into Account*. Don Mills: Oxford University Press.

Vickers, Jill, 1978. "Where are the Women in Canadian Politics?" *Atlantis*, 3, 2, Part II: 40-51.

Vipond, Mary, 1977. "The Image of Women in Mass Circulating Magazines in the 1920s." In Susan Trofimenkoff and Alison Prentice, eds., *The Neglected Majority*, pp. 116-124. Toronto: McClelland and Stewart.

Wade, Susan, 1980. "Helena Gutteridge, Votes for Women and Trade Unions." In Barbara Latham and Cathy Kess, eds., *In Her Own Right: Essays on Women's History in British Columbia*, pp. 187-204. Victoria, B.C.: Camousun College.

Wall, Naomi, 1982. "The Last Ten Years." In Maureen Fitzgerald, Connie Guberman and Margie Wolfe, eds., *Still Ain't Satisfied: Canadian Feminism Today*, pp. 15-27. Toronto: The Women's Press.

Ward, K. B., and L. Grant, 1985. "The Feminist Critique and a Decade of Published Research in Sociological Journals." *The Sociological Quarterly*, 26: 139-157

Weir, Lorna, 1987. "Socialist Feminism and the Politics of Sexuality." In Heather Maroney and Meg Luxton, eds., *Feminism and Political Economy: Women's Work, Women's Struggles*, pp. 69-83. Toronto: Methuen.

Weitzman, Lenore, 1985. *The Divorce Revolution: The Unexpected Social and Economic Consequences for Women and Children in America*. New York: The Free Press.

Welter, Barbara, 1966. "The Cult of True Womanhood." *American Quarterly*, 18: 150-174.

West, Candace, and Don Zimmerman, 1987. "Doing Gender." *Gender and Society*, 1: 125-151.

White, Julie, 1980. *Women and Unions*. Ottawa: The Canadian Advisory Council on the Status of Women.

Wilson, E. O., 1975. *Sociobiology: A New Synthesis*. Cambridge, Mass.: Harvard University Press.

Wilson, S. J., "Women, Aging and Poverty in Canada." Paper presented at Gender and Aging Conference, St. Jerome's College, Waterloo, Ontario, Canada, 1989.

Woolacott, A. P., 1936. "Is the School Marm a Menace?" *Macleans*, December 1, pp. 19, 32, 46.

Zaborszky, Dorothy, 1987. "Feminist Politics: The Feminist Party of Canada." *Women's Studies International Forum*, 10: 613-621.

Zaretsky, Eli, 1976. *Capitalism, The Family and Personal Life*. New York: Harper and Row.

NAME INDEX

Abella, R., 37
Achilles, R., 33n
Acker, J., 7
Adams, O., 31n
Adamson, N., 2, 8, 10, 11, 12, 118, 119, 120, 121, 123
Akyeampong, E., 93
Alcoff, L., 10
Anderson, B., 110
Anisef, P., 98
Archibald, K., 96
Armstrong, H., 60
Armstrong, P., 53, 60

Baker, M., 27
Barber, M., 74
Barron, R. D., 101
Bart, P., 7
Bashevkin, S., 112, 113, 116, 117
Becker, G., 97, 100
Benston, M., 44
Berger, P., 126
Bergmann, B., 43, 45, 95
Bernard, J., 7
Black, N., 15, 16, 19, 51, 67, 77, 118
Blumstein, P., 56
Bose, C., 18, 58, 61, 67
Bourne, P., 15, 16, 19, 51, 67, 77
Boyd, M., 26, 27, 43
Brandt, G., 15, 16, 19, 51, 67, 77
Breines, W., 23
Briskin, L., 2, 8, 10, 11, 12, 118, 119, 120, 121, 123, 135
Brodie, J., 115, 117
Bronte, L., 38
Brown, S., 31
Bruce, M., 100
Burke, M., 92, 93
Burnet, J., 63

Chafetz, J., 32
Cheyne, J., 3
Chodorow, N., 5
Clemenson, H., 94
Cleverdon, C., 111
Coburn, J., 71, 78
Cochrane, J., 114
Cohen, M., 106

Connelly, P., 72, 79, 85, 88, 89, 96
Copp, T., 76, 83
Cowan, R., 15, 48, 52
Cronan, S., 10
Cross, S., 68, 73

Daly, M., 10
Daniels, A., 47
Danylewycz, M., 16, 68, 69, 79
Davey, I., 16, 68, 73
Davis, K., 25
Davitt, P., 69, 79, 80
DeVault, M., 59
Devereaux, M., 25, 41
DeVoss, D., 136
Doerr, A., 115
Dubinsky, K., 123, 125
Duffy, A., 35, 36, 37, 54
Dworkin, A., 32

Egan, C., 121, 135
Ehrich, C., 24
Eichler, M., 3, 5, 31n, 32, 33n, 39, 40, 58, 60, 124, 130
Eisenstein, H., 7, 125
Eisenstein, Z., 12
Ellis, D., 4, 27, 99
Epstein, C., 4, 35, 130, 131
Errington, J., 15
Erwin, L., 32, 33, 124

Feldberg, R., 80
Ferree, M., 34, 54
Field, D., 132, 133
Firestone, S., 9, 10, 11, 31
Fischer, L., 3
Fishman, P., 128, 129
Fox, B., 11, 51, 89
Fox, G., 126, 127
Fox, J., 89
Frager, R., 83
Freeman, J., 124, 128
Friedan, B., 23, 32, 34, 119, 125
Fuchs, V., 38

Galbraith, J. K., 52
Gannage, C., 75
Gaskell, J., 105n

Gerbner, G., 127
Gerson, K., 28, 35
Gibbons, P., 26
Gilman, C., 49
Glazer, N., 52, 54, 96
Glenn, E., 45, 80
Glick, P., 39
Goffman, E., 127, 135
Gower, D., 92,
Grant, L., 6
Gray, C., 115, 117
Gunderson, M., 87, 100, 103

Hamilton, R., 29
Harevan, T., 16
Hartmann, H., 43, 55
Hawrylshyn, O., 59n
Hayden, D., 49
Henley, N., 128
Hewlett, S., 32
Hickl-Szabo, R., 94
Hochschild, A., 34, 55, 56
Hollands, J., 6
Hooyman, N., 5
Hunt, L., 33, 56
Hunt, J., 33, 56

Jacklin, C., 3
Jaggar, A., 8, 9
Johnson, L. 75, 76
Johnson, S., 5

Kadar, M., 132
Kahn, A., 107
Kamerman, S., 107
Kanter, R., 5, 80, 101
Katz, M., 16, 68, 73
Kealey, G., 66n
Kealey, L., 112n
Kelly, J., 10, 16
Kessler-Harris, A., 103, 107
Kirschner, B., 5
Klein, E., 19
Kollock, P., 129
Kome, P., 54, 55, 56, 59, 119, 120
Kostash, M., 2, 8, 118

Lakoff, R., 129
Langevin, L., 115
Laslett, P., 17
Lavigne, M., 72, 75
Lenskyj, H., 9
Leslie, G., 73, 83
Levine, H., 30

Light, B., 15, 16, 18, 19, 51, 67, 77
Lindstrom-Best, V., 73
Lopate, C., 60
Lowe, G., 80
Luxton, M., 9, 53, 55, 56, 102

Maccoby, E., 3
MacDonald, M., 88, 89
Mackie, M., 6
MacLellan, M., 78, 112
Maclead, C., 76, 83
MacLeod, L., 44, 132, 133, 134
Mandel, N., 35, 36, 37, 54
Margolis, M., 18, 22, 23, 24, 48, 49
Maroney, H., 101, 102
Marshall, K., 31, 90, 91
Marshall, S., 124
May, M., 17
Mayfield, M., 37
McConnell-Ginet, S., 129
McCormack, T., 115, 116
McDaniel, S., 31, 32
McLaren, Angus, 20
McLaren, Arlene, 20
McPhail, M., 2, 8, 10, 11, 12, 118, 119, 120, 121, 123
McRobbie, A., 127
Meissner, M., 55
Michelson, W., 55
Miles, A., 10n
Millman, M., 5, 128
Mitchell, J., 8, 10, 11, 45
Mitchinson, W., 15, 16, 19, 51, 67, 77,
Moore, M., 40,
Morgan, D., 6
Morris, C., 119

Nagnur, D., 31n
Neill, S., 102
Ng, R., 43
Niemann, L., 103
Noel, J., 14
Norris, G. M., 101

Oakley, A., 5, 47, 108
Ornstein, M., 97

Pappert, A., 127
Pearce, D., 40
Pearson, J., 130
Phillips, P., 67, 68, 73, 80, 102
Phillips, E., 67, 68, 73, 80, 102
Pierson, R., 81, 82
Pifer, A., 38

Ponting, J., 26
Pool, I., 65
Posner, J., 41
Prentice, A., 15, 16, 18, 19, 51, 67, 77, 82
Priest, G., 41
Propper, A., 133
Proulx, M., 59
Pryor, E., 89
Pupo, N., 21, 35, 36, 37, 54

Ramkhalawansingh, C., 22
Rich, A., 10, 34
Risman, B., 36
Roberts, W., 21, 79, 80
Rong, X., 6
Rosen, M., 23
Rosenberg, H., 50, 51, 52, 54
Rossi, A., 36, 136
Rossiter, A., 34
Rothenberg, P., 8

Sangster, J., 83
Savage, C., 112
Sayer, L., 4, 27, 99
Schur, E., 128
Schwartz, F., 107
Schwartz, P., 56
Scott, A., 58
Scott, J., 68, 73
Segal, L., 10, 33
Sheffield, C., 131
Shostak, A., 23
Silvera, M., 74
Skolnick, M., 100
Smart, B., 134
Smart, C., 134
Smith, D., 7, 35, 44, 52
Smith, V., 131

Stacey, J., 5, 7
Stanley, L., 8n
Stoddart, J., 72, 73, 75
Strong-Boag, V., 19, 73
Swainamer, J., 58
Symons, G., 26
Szekely, E., 128

Tavris, C., 3
Taylor, C., 79
Thorne, B., 5, 7
Trofimenkoff, S., 66, 76, 77, 112
Tuchman, G., 121n

Van den Oever, P., 25
Vanek, J., 52
Van Kirk, S., 14
Vickers, J., 115, 116, 117, 122
Vipond, M., 71

Wade, C., 113
Wade, S., 3
Wall, N., 121
Ward, K., 6
Ware, N. C., 130
Weitzman, L., 40, 53
Welter, B., 18
White, J., 82, 83, 102
Wilson, E., 3
Wilson, S., 136
Wise, S., 8n
Woolacott, A., 78

Yanz, L., 135

Zaborszky, D., 117
Zaretsky, E., 44
Zinsser, J., 110

SUBJECT INDEX

Abortion, 10, 20, 31, 32, 33
Affirmative Action, 106
Aging of population, 41, 136
Anti-abortion movement, 32
Antifeminism, 32–33, 123–125

Baby boom, 23–24
Battered wives. *See* Violence against women
Birth control, 10, 20
Births to unmarried women, 39
Biological differences. *See* Sex differences
Biological determinism, 3

Canada/Quebec Pension Plans, 41–43, 57, 93
Canadian Census, 64, 65
Canadian Labour Force Survey, 64, 65, 86n
Child labour, 16, 68, 76
Childcare. *See* Day care
Childlessness, 31
Choice, myth of, 34–35
Clerical work, 79–80, 90, 94
Comparable worth, 105
Consciousness raising, 6–7, 120
Convents, 69–70
Cult of domesticity, 17–18, 49
  See also Separate spheres

Day care, 37, 41, 55, 68, 80
Discrimination (in employment), 100
Displaced homemakers, 43, 53
Divorce, 24–25, 39, 40–41
Domestic labour. *See* Housewives; Housework
Domestic Science movement, 50–51
Domestic service, 18, 72–74
Double day. *See* Housewives, employed
Dual labour market theory, 101
Dual spheres. *See* Separate spheres

Earning differentials. *See* Pay differentials
Economic dependence, 17, 39, 43, 96
  and emotional dependence, 43
Education
  convent, 69–70
  educational streaming, 99

  in domestic science, 18
  restricted access to, 77, 111
  See also Teaching
Employer attitudes. *See* Discrimination
Employment. *See* Labour-force participation
Employment equity, 106
Equal pay legislation, 103–106
Equal pay for work of equal value, 104–106
Equal Rights Amendment, 119, 123–124

Factory work
  conditions, 74–77
  legislation governing, 76
Families
  census definition, 13n
  pre-industrial, 13–14
  sociology of, 24
Family Allowance, 59n
Family wage, 17, 67, 82, 103
Fathering, 36
Feminism, 2, 8
  Institutional, 118, 119–120
  Grass-roots, 118, 120–123
  See Women's movement
Feminist critique
  of social science, 3, 5–6
  See Motherhood, feminist critique
Feminist Party of Canada, 117
Feminist theory, 6–8, 45
  See Liberal feminism; Radical feminism; Socialist feminism
Feminization of poverty, 40
Fertility, rates, 19, 22, 24

Gender, reproduction of. *See* Reproduction of gender
Gender differences. *See* Sex differences
Gross National Product. *See* Housework, and the GNP

Heterosexism, 9, 30, 32, 123, 127
Historical analysis, sources of data, 63–66
Home production, 14–15
  decline of, 15–16, 17, 18, 48–49, 67
Housewives
  and economic dependence, 39, 43, 53

as consumers, 51, 52
employed, 54–57, 62
changing responsibilities of, 48–51
double day, 54–57
status of, 58
Housework
and the GNP, 47, 58, 60
feminism and, 47–48
husband's resistance, 55–56
monetary value of, 59
payment for housework debate, 59–60
time spent on the job, 52, 55, 59
Human capital theory, 97

Immigrant women, 43, 67
and domestic service, 73–74, 76
Income differences. *See* Pay differentials
Interpersonal interaction, 128

Labour-force participation
and age, 69, 81, 84
and changing attitudes, 25–27
and children, 25, 87, 88
and economic need, 33, 88–89
and education, 84, 97, 98
and family status, 16, 22, 24, 31, 68, 69, 87–88
for industrialized countries, 86
Labour force survey. *See* Canadian Labour Force Survey
Liberal feminism, 8, 11–12, 30, 108, 109, 111, 119–120, 122, 132
Lone parents, 39–40

Marriage
anticipation of, 27, 127
idealization of, 127
rates, 16, 28
sociology of, 24
Marital breakdown. *See* divorce
Marxism, 8, 9, 10, 60
Mass media, 23, 30, 34, 50, 71, 121, 127–128
Material feminists, 49–50
Maternal feminism, 20–21
Members of Parliament, women
federal, 113–115
provincial, 114–115
Microtechnology, 94
Mommy track, 107
Motherhood
and paid employment, 22, 30, 34–36
challenges to, 24, 25

changing responsibilities of, 18–19, 21–22
contradictions in, 22, 23, 29, 45, 118
education for, 18
feminist critique of, 11, 29–32, 34, 45
ideology of, 13, 18, 21–22, 30
popular advice regarding, 19
Motherwork, 34, 51–52
Municipal politics, women and, 117

National Action Committee on the Status of Women, 33n, 118, 120
National Council of Women of Canada, 20, 21, 73, 76
National Organization of Women, 119, 121
New Left, 2, 8, 9, 30, 31
New Right, 32, 123, 124
See also Antifeminism
Nursing, 78

Occupational segregation, measurement of, 89–90
Office work. *See* Clerical work
Old Age Security, 41–43, 57

Part-time employment, 92–93
Patriarchy, 9
Pay differentials, 71, 94–95
among teachers, 79
among university faculty, 6
and education, 97–98
Pensions, private, 42
and part-time work, 93
for housewives, 57
See also Canada/Quebec Pension Plans
Person's Case, 113
Political participation of women
barriers to, 116
party affiliation, 115
women's auxiliaries, 116–117
See also Members of Parliament
Poverty
and age, 41–43
and children, 38
and lone parenthood, 17, 40
Pronatalism, 20

Radical feminism, 8, 9–10, 11–12, 31, 121, 122, 132
REAL Women, 124
Reproduction of gender, 4, 37, 99, 126–128
Reproductive choice, 10, 31, 32
Reproductive technologies, 10, 31

Reserve army, 96
Retirement income, 41
Royal Commission on Equality in Employment, 37, 106
Royal Commission on the Relations of Labour and Capital, 66, 76, 77, 80
Royal Commission on the Status of Women, 8, 30, 104, 116, 119–120
Royal Commission on the Sweating System, 75, 76
Royal Commission on the Textile Industry, 75

Senate appointments, 113
Senior citizens, activism among, 136
Separate spheres, ideology of, 1, 2, 17–18, 49, 50, 61
Sex differences
 inherent, 3–4, 123, 124
 in longevity, 41
 in verbal interaction, 129–130
Sexism
 in language, 130–131
 in social science, 3, 5–6, 24
Sexual assault. *See* Violence against women
Sexual harassment, 131, 132–133
Single parents. *See* Lone parents
Singlehood, 16, 23, 31, 88

Socialist feminism, 8, 9, 10–12, 102, 109, 121, 122, 132
Socialization. *See* Reproduction of gender
Sociobiology, 3
Suffrage, suffragettes, 21, 110, 112
Sweating system, 68, 74–76

Teaching
 in nineteenth century, 70, 78–79

Unemployment, 71, 84, 93–94
Unions, 37, 82–83, 101–102, 133, 135–136

Voting rights, 21, 111–113
Violence against women, 10, 44, 131–134

Wage differentials. *See* Pay differentials
Wage discrimination, 97–98, 103
Wages for housework campaign, 60
Widowhood, 41
Wife abuse. *See* Violence against women
Women, objectification of, 128
Women's movement, 2, 5–8, 30–31, 110, 118–123
 in the United States, 110–111
 media portrayal of, 121
 resistance to. *See* Antifeminism
 See also feminism
Women's studies, 2, 3, 5, 6, 7
World War II, 22, 80–82

── CUT HERE ──

STUDENT REPLY CARD

In order to improve future editions, we are seeking your comments on *Women, Families, and Work, Third Edition,* by S. J. Wilson.

After you have read this text, please answer the following questions and return this form via Business Reply Mail. *Thanks in advance for your feedback!*

1. Name of your college or university: _____

2. Major program of study: _____

3. Your instructor for this course: _____

4. Are there any sections of this text which were not assigned as course reading? _____
   If so, please specify those chapters or portions:

5. How would you rate the overall accessibility of the content? Please feel free to comment on reading level, writing style, terminology, layout and design features, and such learning aids as chapter objectives, summaries, and appendices.

── FOLD HERE ──

6. What did you like *best* about this book?

7. What did you like *least?*

If you would like to say more, we'd love to hear from you. Please write to us at the address shown on the reverse of this card.

— — — — — — — — — — — — CUT HERE — — — — — — — — — —

— — — — — — — — — — — FOLD HERE — — — — — — — — —

BUSINESS
REPLY MAIL

No Postage Stamp
Necessary If Mailed
in Canada

Postage will be paid by

7115

Attn: Sponsoring Editor, Social Sciences
The College Division
McGraw-Hill Ryerson Limited
300 Water Street
Whitby, Ontario
L1N 9Z9

CUT HERE

TAPE SHUT